What Do I Know?

Richard Eyre

WHAT DO I KNOW?

People, Politics and the Arts

NICK HERN BOOKS
London
www.nickhernbooks.co.uk

A Nick Hern Book

WHAT DO I KNOW?

First published in Great Britain in 2014
by Nick Hern Books Limited
The Glasshouse, 49a Goldhawk Road, London W12 8QP

Copyright © 2014 Chestermead Ltd

Richard Eyre has asserted his right
to be identified as the author of this work

Cover photograph by John Haynes

Designed and typeset by Nick Hern Books, London
Printed and bound in Great Britain by
CPI Group (UK) Ltd

A CIP catalogue record for this book
is available from the British Library

ISBN 978 1 84842 418 0

To
my granddaughters
Eva and Beatrix

We are, I know not how, double in ourselves,
so that what we believe we disbelieve,
and cannot rid ourselves of what we condemn.

Montaigne

Contents

CONTENTS

Epilogue

Introduction

'What do I know?'—'*Que sais-je?*'—is the question that Montaigne asks himself in one of his essays. It's a sound reminder of sceptical faith—if that isn't an almost-oxymoron. It's written in Latin, along with many other aphorisms and epigrams from Greek and Roman philosophers, on one of the roof beams in his library at the top of his famous tower.

I visited Montaigne's tower with my sister, who lived nearby in the Dordogne, a few weeks before her death last year. She had little in common with her neighbour: where Montaigne would think out loud in his writing and equivocate in his politics, she preferred the headbutt. She was a contrarian who loved an argument even though she would never concede defeat. My father (a difficult man himself) used to say that she went through life like a flame-thrower. She burned with a bright flame, and the flame could sometimes scorch you, but the flame illuminated the lives of everyone she came in contact with.

Montaigne had been provoked into starting to write his essays by the death of a great friend and it was his words that came to mind when my sister died: 'If you press me to say why I loved him, I can say no more than because it was he, because it was I.' So it was with my sister.

If I have anything in common with Montaigne it is that I write to discover what I think. Unlike Montaigne, who wrote obsessively—like a blogger before the event—I wrote because I was asked to do so. Those who asked me to write most of these pieces were Annalena McAfee, Claire Armistead and Lisa Allardice of the *Guardian*, Sarah Sands of the *Telegraph* and later the *Evening Standard*, Emma

Gosnell of the *Sunday Telegraph*, James Inverne of *Gramophone*, and Richard Lambert of the *Financial Times*.

The remainder of the pieces in this book were talks or lectures or eulogies. I would never have become a writer of any sort if it had not been for the publisher, Liz Calder; I would never have continued to write had it not been for my wife, Sue Birtwistle.

People

John Mortimer

John died in 2009. I was asked by his family to give the eulogy at his funeral in the parish church in Turville Heath, where he'd been born and lived for eighty-five years.

It was said by another national treasure, Alan Bennett, that Philip Larkin's waking nightmare was of thousands of schoolchildren massed in the Albert Hall chanting in unison: 'They fuck you up your mum and dad.' Alan's gloss on this was that, if your parents didn't fuck you up and you wanted to become a writer, then they'd have fucked you up good and proper.

The formula worked in John's case: his father diverted him from being a writer to becoming a barrister and unintentionally left him a great legacy: the law became his subject. The other indispensable legacy—a paradoxical one—was that while his father passed on a love of poetry, he withheld his own love. John didn't mimic this deficiency: in all his memoirs he showed an undiminished love of his father—and of his own children—and it's a remarkable homage to his father that John went out of the world in the same house that he was brought up in.

As a lawyer—as in life—John was unjudgemental: his sympathies were instinctively with the defendant. The only case he turned down was an assistant hangman who had committed murder—the idea of defending a man who was licensed by the state to kill criminals was beyond the limit of his tolerance. But his reputation for defending the indefensible—whether they were murderers or alleged pornographers—added to his allure as a buccaneering renaissance man who wrote plays and novels in his time away from the Bar. For John the law was

1

an English pageant full of tales of people who had been undone by greed, or poverty, or passion, or folly, and it was always for him underscored by a belief in justice and in liberty.

I never tired of hearing John's anecdotes and he never tired of telling them: the woman who was giving evidence in a case in which she'd been sexually harassed but was too shy to say out loud what had been said to her, so a note was passed round the court ending up with a dozing woman jury member, who was jolted awake by her male neighbour. The note read: 'I would like to fuck you.' The judge asked the woman to hand the note to the clerk. 'Merely personal, my lord,' said the woman and pocketed it. Then there was the camp judge who kept a Paddington Bear that sat beside him in his official car and on the bench when he was in court; and the woman who fell downstairs and sued her sons because she saw her husband in the hallway having his genitals devoured by the dogs—the sons having discovered him drunk and asleep in the hallway, had opened his flies and put a piece of liver there; and the prie-dieu in Norman St John-Stevas's bathroom; and much, much more. These stories had the status of folk myths, which John would tell and retell in his melodious, feline, light-tenor voice—quiet so that you had to attend carefully—performed with an actor's flair for spontaneity and timing.

When John finished a story he'd laugh—his laugh was more of a chortle than a chuckle—then he'd segue seamlessly into an observation about something like the decline of liberty and the Labour Party: 'They're awful,' he'd say, 'awful.' The laugh became increasingly husky and wheezy over the years but laughter remained John's default mode—a way both of putting troubles at a distance and of celebrating the fact that, as he said, 'Death's finality makes life seem absurd.'

I first got to know John as a more than casual acquaintance when, as an adoring father, he stood outside St Paul's School for Girls dropping off Emily at the gates as I did the same with my daughter, Lucy. I don't imagine that either teenage girl was particularly pleased at the time to be seen with their fathers, but I was hugely grateful to be able to chat to John and discover the man behind the public persona.

If you only knew John as a raffishly dapper wit in a three-piece suit with a silk handkerchief in his top pocket entertaining an array of admiring women aged from eight to eighty, you might have believed that he was a dilettante, an irresistible flaneur with a private income. The truth is, of course, that he worked enormously hard—every day of every year. On holiday with John you could never get up early enough to be up before he was at work. From sunrise he would be sitting outside under a tree with a pen and a pad of lined A4 on his lap. The house would wake hours later and John would write on until a late breakfast and an early glass of champagne, happy to hear the voices of women in the house; happier still if they were talking about him.

As a journalist he was a dogged and industrious pro. Like a barrister dutifully following the cab-rank principle, he never knowingly refused a commission. When Princess Diana died he was asked by the *Daily Mail*—not his natural constituency—to do a piece for them. He went to Kensington Palace and approached a mourner: 'Go away,' she said, 'I don't want to talk to the paparazzi.'

As a writer he didn't become adjectival—one doesn't speak of Mortimer-esque events—but one does speak of a Rumpole moment, and the character of Rumpole—John's alter ego who embodied the apparent oxymoron of a loveable lawyer—is an enduring monument to his talent. All his work—his plays and novels as much as his journalism—were in his own distinctive voice: witty, lucid, louche and sometimes ruefully acerbic—never less than when writing about those politicians he grew to despise.

John was very sensitive to criticism, doubtful always of his reputation. He needed attention and approbation—a legacy of his parents' failure to give him either, perhaps—and he always received praise as if the sun had just come out from behind a cloud, beaming owlishly with unaffected joy. He thrived on an audience, and their applause was no less essential than the champagne that followed it.

He was often called a 'champagne socialist'—it's one of those resentfully dismissive slurs, like 'chattering classes' and 'luvvies', that seek to make you believe that holding serious ideas about politics is incompatible with having a good time. It's true that John loved champagne more than socialism, and true too that he wasn't powerfully influenced by socialist principle or Marxist ideology. I never heard him urge state ownership or the retention of Clause Four or wholesale redistribution of wealth, but I did hear him talk admiringly of Bevan and Attlee. And Barbara Castle was a heroine of his, whom I met once at lunch in Turville Heath. She asked me if I was a right-wing spy. Then she went on to tell me that she didn't trust Tony Blair an inch.

John was unafraid to take on politicians with whom he disagreed either in public or in private, but he was always ready to be disabused of his prejudices by finding an unexpected humanity in an opponent. 'How *could* you like that man?' Penny would challenge; 'I speak as I find,' John would shrug in his defence, unjudgemental to the last.

John believed in social justice, human rights, freedom of speech and civil liberties, untrammelled by political correctness and doctrinaire purity, and if there were any 'ist' that could be attached to him it would be 'anarchist'. Having been an enthusiastic supporter of New Labour with the New Dawn in 1997, it didn't take long for his enthusiasm to curdle. He abhorred the threat to do away with juries in fraud cases, the introduction of ID cards, the lies over Iraq, the collusion in rendition and torture, the attempt to introduce forty-two-day pre-charge detention, the lethargy in improving the prison system.

In this matter he was an active advocate for penal reform as President of the Howard League. I was more aware of his work as the Chairman of the Royal Court Theatre and a board member of the National Theatre, where he tipped me off at my first meeting that there was an extremely pompous board member who had a habit of saying at board meetings: 'If I may… through the Chair…' John said he thought the man was eager to penetrate the Chairman.

As Chairman of the Royal Court, John was diffident but effective, giving the impression of a lack of strategy while being quite sure that he knew what to do. He once asked me casually in the back of a taxi if I thought Stephen Daldry would be a good idea to run the Royal Court. 'It'd be fun, wouldn't it?' John said, fun being his highest criterion for any activity. Some years later, when we were on holiday in Spain rather than Tuscany, John told us all that he was uncertain about who they should appoint as Stephen's successor; so we bought John a plant from a gypsy in the market that had to be soaked in water and could then answer your questions about the future. 'Ah,' said John, 'Why didn't I think of that before?'

John loved women. He loved women as he loved champagne and smoked salmon, Shakespeare and Byron, going to the opera and walking in his garden: women were part of the good things of life. But he loved women for themselves as much as for what they gave him—which was mostly adoration qualified by exasperation. He loved women not so much for his self-regard or self-satisfaction but because he was genuinely curious about how fifty per cent of the world thought and felt—a fifty per cent who were often ignored, abused and exploited.

He claimed to be a lazy man driven by guilt, but I think it was more that, as a lonely only child, he needed constant acknowledgement of his existence. So performance was at the centre of his life as an author, as a lawyer, and as an actor in *Mortimer's Miscellany*. He could recite continents of the canon of English poetry and had perfect recall of the lyrics of Cole Porter, the Gershwins, Rodgers and Hart and Noël Coward, which he'd sing with a slightly uncertain grasp of pitch. But the role he most enjoyed performing was as paterfamilias: to see John at the head of the table glowing with good humour surrounded by Penny and children and grandchildren and friends was to see a man who lived a life to the full and more.

You could say John was larger than life, you could also say that life was smaller than John. His legacy will be some hugely entertaining plays and novels, some dazzling epigrams and, in Rumpole, a character who can stand beside those of Shakespeare and Dickens. Above all, though, what will survive of John will be the affection of hundreds who are grateful for having had the luck to spend time with a man who was touched by greatness—who was humane, generous, liberal, loving, charming, funny, flirtatious, seductive, sexy, raffish, kind, sometimes bashful, never boastful, often vulnerable and full of self-doubt, fastidious, proud, just, indignant on behalf of victims and passionate on the part of the dispossessed, extravagant, wise, decent, tolerant—and unique. He multiplied the gaiety of nations.

John once told me that he'd met the great French actor, Jean Marais. Marais told John that he'd said to Cocteau: 'I want to do three things in a play—I want to be silent in the first act, I want to cry with joy in the second, and I want to come down a long staircase in the third.' Cocteau wrote a play for him that fitted the prescription.

John's prescription might have been this:

> I want to do three things in my life: In the first act I want to be very gifted and earn the admiration of many.
>
> In the second act I want to enjoy the company of my family and friends and of beautiful and intelligent women.
>
> In the third act I want to ascend a long staircase to Heaven through clouds of glory accompanied by choirs of angels.

Or as John Bunyan put it:

> When the day that he must go hence was come, many accompanied him to the river-side, into which, as he went, he said: 'Death, where is thy sting?' And, as he went down deeper, he said: 'Grave, where is thy victory?' So he passed over, and all the trumpets sounded for him on the other side.

Arthur Miller

I first met Arthur a year or two before I became Director of the National Theatre and presented several of his plays there. I wrote this for the Guardian *shortly after his death.*

A large part of my luck over the past twenty years was getting to know Arthur Miller, so when I heard in interviews—or was asked myself—the question 'Will Arthur Miller be remembered as the man who married Marilyn Monroe?' I felt a mixture of despair and indignation. The motives of the questioners—a mixture of prurience and envy—were, curiously enough, the same as the House Un-American Activities Committee when they summoned Arthur Miller to appear in front of their committee. I asked Arthur about it some years ago. 'I knew perfectly well why they had subpoenaed me,' he said, 'it was because I was engaged to Marilyn Monroe. Had I not been, they'd never have thought of me. They'd been through the writers long before and they'd never touched me. Once I became famous as her possible husband, this was a great possibility for publicity. When I got to Washington, preparing to appear before that committee, my lawyer received a message from the chairman saying that if it could be arranged that he could have a picture, a photograph taken with Marilyn, he would cancel the whole hearing. I mean, the cynicism of this thing was so total, it was asphyxiating.'

The question that lurked then—and lurks now—is this: why would the world's most attractive woman want to go out with a *writer*? There are at least four good reasons I can think of:

By 1956, when he married Marilyn Monroe, Arthur Miller had written four of the best plays in the English language, two of them indelible classics that will be performed in a hundred years' time.

He was a figure of great moral and intellectual stature, who was unafraid of taking a stand on political issues and enduring obloquy for doing so.

He was wonderful company—a great, a glorious, raconteur. I asked him once what happened on the first night of *Death of a Salesman* when it opened on the road in Philadelphia. He must have told the story a thousand times but he repeated it, pausing, seeming to search for half-buried details, as if it was the first time: 'The play ended and there was a dead silence and I remember being in the back of the house with Kazan and nothing happened. The people didn't get up either. Then one or two got up and picked up their coats. Some of them sat down again. It was chaos. Then somebody clapped and then the house fell apart and they kept applauding for God knows how long and... I remember an old man being helped up the aisle, who turned out to be Bernard Gimbel, who ran one of the biggest department-store chains in the United States who was literally unable really to navigate, they were helping him up the aisle. And it turned out that he had been swept away by the play and the next day he issued an order that no one in his stores—I don't know, eight or ten stores all over the United States—was to be fired for being overage!' And with this he laughed, a deep husky bass chortle, shaking his head as if the memory were as fresh as last week.

He was a deeply attractive man: tall, almost hulking, broad-shouldered, square-jawed, with the most beautiful large, strong but tender hands. There was nothing evasive or small-minded about him.

As he aged he became both more monumental but more approachable, his great body not so much bent as folded over. And if you were lucky enough to spend time with him and Inge Morath (the Magnum photographer to whom he was married for forty years after his divorce from Marilyn Monroe), you would be capsized by the warmth, wit and humanity of the pair of them.

It's been surprising for me—and sometimes shocking—to discover that my high opinion of Arthur Miller was often not held by those who consider themselves the curators of American theatre. I read a discussion in the *New York Times* a few years ago between three theatre critics about the differences between British and American theatre:

FIRST CRITIC. Arthur Miller is celebrated there.

SECOND CRITIC. It's *Death of a Salesman*, for crying out loud. He's so cynical about American culture and American politics. The English love that.

FIRST CRITIC. Though *Death of a Salesman* was not a smash when it first opened in London.

THIRD CRITIC. It's also his earnestness.

If we continue to admire Arthur Miller, it's because we have the virtuous habit of treating his plays as contemporaneous and find that they speak to us today not because of their 'earnestness' but because they are serious—that's to say they're *about* something. They have energy and poetry and wit and an ambition to make theatre matter. What's more, they use sinewy and passionate language with unembarrassed enthusiasm, which is always attractive to British actors and audiences weaned on Shakespeare.

In 1950, at a time when British theatre was toying with a phoney poetic drama—the plays of T.S. Eliot and Christopher Fry—there was real poetry on the American stage in the plays of Arthur Miller (and Tennessee Williams), or, to be exact, the poetry of reality: plays about life lived on the streets of Brooklyn and New Orleans by working-class people foundering on the edges of gentility and resonating with metaphors of the American Dream and the American Nightmare.

The Depression of the late twenties provided Arthur's sentimental education: the family business was destroyed, and the family was reduced to relative poverty. I talked to him once about it as we walked in the shadow of the pillars of the Brooklyn Bridge looking out over the East River. 'America,' he said, 'was promises, and the Crash was a broken promise in the deepest sense. I think the Americans in general live on the edge of a cliff, they're waiting for the other shoe to drop. I don't care who they are. It's part of the vitality of the country, maybe. That they're always working against this disaster that's about to happen.'

He wrote with heat and heart and his work was felt in Britain like a distant and disturbing forest fire—a fire that did much to ignite British writers who followed, like John Osborne, Harold Pinter and Arnold Wesker; and later Edward Bond, David Storey and Trevor Griffiths; and later still David Edgar, Mike Leigh, David Hare. What they found in Miller was a visceral power, an appeal to the senses beyond and below rational thought and an ambition to deal with big subjects.

His plays are about the difficulty and the possibility of people—usually men—taking control of their own lives, 'that moment when, in my eyes, a man differentiates himself from every other man, that moment when out of a sky full of stars he fixes on one star.' His heroes—salesmen, dockers, policemen, farmers—all seek a sort of salvation in asserting their singularity, their self, their 'name'. They redeem their dignity, even if it's by suicide. Willy Loman cries out 'I am not a dime a dozen, I am Willy Loman…!', Eddie Carbone in *A View from the Bridge*, broken and destroyed by sexual guilt and public shame, bellows: 'I want my name', and John Proctor in *The Crucible*, in refusing the calumny of condemning his fellow citizens, declaims 'How may I live without my name? I have given you my soul; leave me my name!' In nothing does Miller show his Americanism more than in the assertion of the right and necessity of the individual to own his own life—and, beyond that, how you reconcile the individual with society. In short, how you live your life.

If there was a touch of the evangelist in his writing, his message was this: there *is* such a thing as society, and art ought to be used to change it. Though it's hard to argue that art saves lives, feeds the hungry or sways votes, *Death of a Salesman* comes as close as any writer can get to art as a balm for social concern. When I saw the New York revival five or six years ago, I came out of the theatre behind a young girl and her dad, and she said to him 'It was like looking at the Grand Canyon.'

A few years ago I directed the first production of *The Crucible* on Broadway since its opening nearly fifty years previously. He loved our production and was closely involved with rehearsals. I never got over the joy and pride of sitting beside Arthur as this great play unfolded in front of us while he beamed and muttered: 'It's damned good stuff, this.' We performed it shortly after the Patriot Act had been introduced. Everyone who saw it said it was 'timely'. What did they mean exactly? That it was time*less*.

'There are things which he stretched, but mainly he told the truth,' is what Huckleberry Finn said of the author of *Tom Sawyer*. And the same could be said of Arthur Miller, which is perhaps why it's not a coincidence that my enthusiasm for his writing came at the same time as my discovery of the genius of Mark Twain. And it's not a surprise that what Arthur Miller said of Mark Twain could just has well have been said about him:

> He somehow managed—despite a steady underlying seriousness which few writers have matched—to step round the pit of self-importance and to keep his membership of the ordinary human race in the front of his mind and his writing.

Tennessee Williams

I wrote this for the programme of a production of The Rose Tattoo *at the National Theatre in 2007.*

Tennessee Williams was born in Mississippi in 1911. His father was a travelling shoe salesman who was an alcoholic and a bully. His mother was a minister's daughter, a Southern belle 'Miss Edwina' who lived on the verge of hysteria and later became a patient in a psychiatric hospital. His (adored) sister, Rose, was diagnosed in her teens as a schizophrenic and was given a pre-frontal lobotomy.

'At the age of fourteen,' he said, 'I discovered writing as an escape from a world of reality in which I felt acutely uncomfortable. It immediately became my place of retreat, my cave, my refuge. From what? From being called a sissy by neighbourhood kids, and "Miss Nancy" by my father, because I would rather read books in my grandfather's large and classical library than play marbles and baseball and other normal-kid games, a result of a severe childhood illness and of excessive attachment to the female members of my family, who had coaxed me back into life.'

His family provided the nourishment for all his writing, the overbearing patriarchs, the fading belles, the beautiful but frail young men foundering on the edges of gentility. The South was his garden, planted with overheated romantic relationships, saturated with sex and death, blooming briefly and decaying rapidly. In describing this garden he drew his syntax from the religion he'd acquired in Grandfather's rectories while his father was on the road selling shoes: Paradise, Purgatory and Hell.

Williams wrote, as he lived, compulsively. But for someone with such an apparently tenuous hold on life, he was extraordinarily tenacious and productive. During his lifetime at least sixty-three of his plays and playlets (thirty-two short plays, twenty-four full-length and seven mid-length) were published or given a major production or both. In a period of twelve years between 1945 and 1957 he wrote with a wild energy *The Glass Menagerie*, *A Streetcar Named Desire*, *Summer and Smoke*, *Camino Real*, *Cat on a Hot Tin Roof*, *Orpheus Descending* and *The Rose Tattoo*: plays that rang with the aspiration of the American Dream and the desperation of the American Nightmare.

During the 1960s (what he called his 'Stoned Age'), his work started to decline under the assault of depression—his 'blue devil' which he fought off with one-night stands, alcohol, barbiturates, uppers and downers. He became paranoid, accusing his partner, Frank Merlo, of conspiring to encourage his dog to bite him. They parted after fourteen years, and Merlo died two years later of lung cancer leaving Williams tormented by guilt. His subsequent depression led to a period in a mental hospital from which he emerged to write *The Night of the Iguana*, his last great play, in which these lines occur:

'How'd you beat your blue devil?'

'I showed him that I could endure him and made him respect my endurance.'

'How?'

'Just by, just by… enduring.'

Williams endured for over twenty years more until his death in 1983, sustained by an apparently indestructible blend of stoicism and drollery. When once asked for his definition of happiness, he answered: 'Insensitivity, I guess.'

In Williams' work time destroys, never heals. Only art survives. The point of his plays, he said, was 'just somehow to capture the constantly evanescent quality of existence'. Looking for lost perfection, his characters find themselves redundant: old, bereft, forgotten, tormented. He's the mouthpiece for those on the margins, women, gays, blacks, the mad, the wayward, the lonely. He offers up the irreconcilable versuses of life—masculine v. feminine, desire for love v. desire for freedom, animal lust v. genteel courtship, flesh v. spirit, rich v. poor, present v. past—but he never judges his characters or evangelises for a life less ordinary: between the polarity of Stanley Kowalski's lust and Blanche's cowed nymphomania there's Stella's wholly un-neurotic sexual fulfilment. 'Life,' says Maggie in *Cat on a Hot Tin Roof*, 'has got to be allowed to continue even after the *dream* of life is all over…'

Williams was defiantly out of the closet. His plays are not coded allegories larded with covert gay references. Nor does he write women as surrogate men in

11

drag—even if in the first draft of *Sweet Bird of Youth* the ageing Hollywood film star Alexandra Del Lago was a man called Artemis Pazmezoglu. He grew up in the South of the Depression Years, where to be gay and white was barely better than being black, and he observed the sober, heterosexual, clubbable, gullible subscribers to the American Dream with the eye of the outcast. When he chose to put homosexuality in his plays in *Streetcar*, in *Cat on a Hot Tin Roof* and in *Suddenly Last Summer* it was as explicit as the times would allow.

Nor was he any less daring in form. He challenged his directors and designers to rise to his extraordinarily expressive stage directions. This is the opening of *The Rose Tattoo*:

It is the hour that the Italians call 'prima sera', the beginning of dusk. Between the house and the palm tree burns the female star with an almost emerald lustre.

The mothers of the neighbourhood are beginning to call their children home to supper, in voices near and distant, urgent and tender, like the variable notes of wind and water.

He was a formal visionary, with a theatrical imagination barely understood in his times. He wrote theatre-poetry with a grammar that asked for gauzes to spill the action seamlessly from interior to exterior, complex lighting, slashes of iridescent colour, projections, and a vocabulary that included cries in the night, distant marimbas, the tinkling of a music box, the thrashing tail of an iguana.

Williams was ferociously hard-headed about the meaning of language and the music of it. Ignore the punctuation, you change the rhythm, the sound and the sense. A sentence like this (from *Cat on a Hot Tin Roof*) 'We drank together that night all night in the bar of the Blackstone and when cold day was comin' up over the Lake an' we were comin' out drunk to take a dizzy look at it, I said, "SKIPPER! STOP LOVIN' MY HUSBAND OR TELL HIM HE'S GOT TO LET YOU ADMIT IT TO HIM!"—one way or another!' has to be played on a single breath at least up to the first comma. The dialogue often seems overheated on the page, dipped in purple rhetoric and exuding oversweet, overscented vapours, but that's to ignore the sharpness of the ideas that animate it and the mordant wit that underscores it.

During the sixties, seventies and eighties, Williams' plays were out of fashion. Now there is rarely a week when the London stage is without the opening of a new production of a Williams play. Why? In the face of war, terrorism, social unrest, inequality, injustice and global warming, Williams offers the consoling hope that the only way to be human is to love one's neighbour as oneself. We must always rely on the kindness of strangers.

Harold Pinter

I knew Harold quite well for many years both in his sunny and his curmudgeonly disposition. I wrote this for the Guardian *on his death in 2008.*

———•—•———

Harold Pinter entered our cultural bloodstream years ago. People who have never seen a play of his will describe unsettling domestic events or silences laden with threat as 'Pinteresque'. He's become part of our language, of who and what we are.

What I am is a child of the late 1950s who grew up in West Dorset knowing as much about theatre as I did about insect life in Samoa. There were no theatres within reasonable distance—at least not ones which presented plays—so by the age of eighteen I had seen only two professional productions: *Hamlet* at the Bristol Old Vic and *Much Ado About Nothing* at Stratford. Then I saw *The Caretaker* and it struck me like a thunderbolt.

I hadn't been corrupted by reading about the 'theatre of the absurd' or by the critics' passion for kennelling a writer in a category, and I was innocent of the writer's supposed concerns with 'status' and 'territory'. The play seemed to me a natural way of looking at the world, unpredictable but as inevitable as the weather.

I loved the way that it didn't glut you with exposition, that things just happened in the play without their significance being spelled out. What it was about seemed irrelevant, what was important was what it was: a world like ours where the meaning of things was at best opaque and the most normal condition of life was uncertainty.

Above all it distilled normal speech—the kind you'd hear on a bus or in a pub—into a singular language syncopated with hard wit and percussive poetry. And it used silence as a dramatic tool. It woke me up to the fact that theatre was as much about the spaces between the words as the words themselves, that what was left off the stage was as important as what was put on it, and that feelings—particularly of men—are articulated obliquely or mutely, mostly remaining trapped like water under an icecap.

The 'voice' of the play was recognisable and yet alien, like a familiar object viewed from an unusual angle. The author of *The Caretaker* had a way of looking at the world that was as original as Francis Bacon, who I once saw standing at a bus stop, the strong wind pasting back his hair and flattening his face: he looked like a Francis Bacon. It wasn't unusual to have that experience with Harold. I once overheard this exchange with a friend of his:

FRIEND. How are you feeling, Harold?

HAROLD. What sort of question is that?

Which is the sort of question asked by a man who was sometimes pugnacious and occasionally splenetic, but was just as often droll and generous—particularly to actors, directors and (a rare quality this) other writers. Sometimes grandiose and occasionally intolerant, he could be disarmingly modest, unostentatious and comradely. And he was never, ever, afraid to speak his mind, particularly on political matters.

It shouldn't therefore be a surprise that the most powerful piece of political theatre I've ever seen was in Prague at the Činoherní Theatre in 1969 shortly after the Russian invasion. The play was *The Birthday Party*, and it seemed then that this play, set in an English seaside boarding house, had as much to say about totalitarianism and freedom as it did of fear and kindness. Years later Harold told me that, at the start of rehearsals for the first production of the play, he was persuaded by the director, Peter Wood, to say something to the actors about the meaning of the play. 'Just put it on the table,' he said, 'that Goldberg and McCann are the socio-politico-religious monsters with whom we are faced, and the pressures on any given individual.' He saw it, he told me, 'very, very strongly and very, very clearly at the time. I knew it was political, but I wouldn't just stand on a soapbox and say so.'

By the age of fifteen he had become passionately engaged by the Labour victory of 1945, which was a powerful ingredient in his considerable contempt for New Labour. He never had the luxury of choice about being political: growing up in a Jewish community during the war, aware of how close he could have been to the fate of many of his relatives, made him aware of the precariousness of democracy and the need to safeguard it. The Bomb and the Cold War turned him into a conscientious objector against National Service, a courageous position which led to two tribunals, two trials and the threat of prison. 'I took my toothbrush along to the trial,' he said, 'and it was my first, if you like, overt political act.'

If he didn't go to prison for his beliefs, he might well have done for the theft of a copy of Beckett's *Murphy* from Bermondsey Public Reserve Library (a tributary of the Westminster Library) in 1952, the crime amply justified by the fact that it had last been borrowed in 1939. This dogged persistence to hunt down the work of a writer who he had previously only encountered in an Irish literary magazine would seem to support the biblical genealogy of theatre history: Samuel Beckett begat Harold Pinter. But the truth is that Harold's work, while having things in common with Beckett and Joyce (and Kafka for that matter), was entirely *sui generis*: he always spoke with his own voice. He enchanted and ensnared us in the theatre; he provoked us to action outside it. He was a constant defender of human rights, a passionate polemicist, a fair cricketer, a good actor, and a playwright of rare power and profound originality. He said to me once of Arthur Miller that he was 'a hell of a fellow'. So was Harold.

Michael Bryant

I gave the eulogy at Michael's funeral at Mortlake Crematorium in 2002. He had a cardboard coffin. As it went offstage, the Pythons' anthem 'Always Look on the Bright Side of Life' played in the chapel.

———•—•———

Like most actors, Michael hated to talk about his work. He liked doing not talking, and he had as much interest in 'experiment' and 'research' as a cow has in veterinary science. The story about Michael being invited to study the habits of badgers for *Wind in the Willows* now has the status of myth, but I can vouch for its truth. 'I have made a discovery about the habits of badgers,' he said to me. 'Their movement and their posture bears an extraordinary resemblance to Michael Bryant.' As indeed they do.

Actually, in his approach to any part he was like a badger-watcher: he was silent, strategic, patient, and unobtrusive. He stalked a part. He didn't like discussion in rehearsal and he teased any actor who did. During rehearsals of *Racing Demon* he christened David Bamber 'Marlon' for his—in my view blameless—habit of enquiring what his character was feeling. It was not that Michael thought the question was irrelevant, simply that he thought that one should keep that sort of thing to oneself. He wanted only the most basic information: where to stand, what the furniture would be, should he be louder, softer, quicker, slower. He regarded the text as the only hard evidence at his disposal, and he would build his character like a detective assembling a case until one day—sometimes alarmingly late in rehearsal—the character was there, complete. It was as if he'd been marinating the part in secret until it was ready, and if you were to enquire about the recipe you'd be bluntly rebuffed. Yet for all his blimpish, witty, portly, matter-of-fact-plain-man-no-bullshit persona, there was no one more sensitive, more generous or more subtle than Michael.

He took a real interest in young actors, a kind of gruff paternalism that masked affectionate concern. He'd dispense pragmatic wisdom: don't drop your voice at the end of a line, let the audience in to your secret, be honest, don't try so hard. 'I'm going to learn everything from Michael Bryant,' said Keith Allen when he came to work at the NT. A sensible decision, even if I had to discourage him from following Michael's example in listening to the Test Match on his Walkman during the first readthrough of one of the plays in David Hare's trilogy—never, of course, missing a cue.

For me—as Director of the National Theatre—Michael was always there: 'Give me one good part a year and I'll throw in the rest—whatever you want.' And 'throwing in the rest' meant that in some small but crucial role, you could depend on a performance that would be perfectly crafted, beautifully observed and unimpeachably truthful. Michael believed passionately that a national theatre should be a community united by common aims, something that was worth more than the sum of its parts: he thought it was an ideal worth devoting your life to. And for twenty-five years he did. He was the conscience and heart of the National Theatre.

If there had been more than one Michael Bryant, running the National Theatre would have been a prolonged holiday. But, of course, there was only ever one Michael, and for once the cliché is true: we shall never see his like again. He was a great actor and at the same time a selfless member of a company. To see him on stage was to understand the adage that genius is in the detail, and to know him was to love him for his talent, his intelligence, his humanity, his loyalty, his constancy, his modesty and his wit. To all of which I can hear Michael's voice even now: 'Oh, bollocks!'

Kate Winslet

I wrote this profile for Vogue *in 2004. Kate was to be featured on the cover and, when asked who she'd like to be interviewed by, she named me.*

I'm staring at Kate Winslet's toe, the long toe next to the big toe on a long, narrow foot, a toe now red and swollen with a mysterious infection. Kate can't walk, and I'm cheated out of a lunch with her at The River Café. Nevertheless, it's not exactly a hardship to be sitting in the garden of the handsome, wide, white stucco, mid-Victorian house in Belsize Park that she's just moved into with the director, Sam Mendes: 'We're like teenagers rattling about in it.' If her toe is infected, the rest of Kate looks lovely, which is the word that always comes to mind when people say to me 'What's she like?' and I always say 'Lovely.' And I mean it.

She has, for a start, a lovely face: large cat's eyes, a mouth that's generous in all senses of the word, an unfashionably real nose, fine Slavic cheekbones and skin like a white peach. As she talks, lit by mottled sunlight through a copper beech, her face changes: voluptuous, tragic, jolly, childlike, exotic, ordinary. It's the same on screen as off.

Stupefied by boredom and vodka on a plane, I once watched *Titanic* twice through—the first time because I didn't recognise the actress playing Rose DeWitt Bukater, the young heiress with the intractable name (even though I'd seen *Sense and Sensibility*), and the second because I did recognise her and wanted to marvel at an actress who, almost within each shot, could move with such effortless agility from joy to pain, from the girl-next-door to a princess. She performed alchemy on this leaden film, giving the lumbering sets, the callow performances and the unconvincing special effects, the thing that they so conspicuously lacked: a heart.

When I directed Kate in *Iris* I sat for months in the editing room, detached like a surgeon, observing her expressive physicality, the skill with which she conscripted each part of her body—eyes, mouth, nose, hands, back, breasts, bottom, even her et cetera—to serve the part she was playing, the young Iris Murdoch. Always conscious of herself, she was never self-conscious. The film was based on the preposterously risky premise that the audience would accept that Kate Winslet (Young Iris) was the same person as Judi Dench (Old Iris). There was little physical resemblance between them but it worked. They matched: talent for talent, wit for wit, heart for heart.

Kate is the youngest actress ever to receive three Academy nominations; according to magazine polls she is one of the fifty most beautiful women in the world and the seventeenth sexiest woman in Britain; she is barely twenty-seven and she described herself to me as being, only a few years ago, 'a fat girl with dodgy hair and tree-trunk thighs'. How has she achieved her current state of grace?

Most actors start to act because they're shy or they stammer, or they want to attract attention, or they're searching for requited love. Kate, however, seems to have been born with an almost preternatural self-confidence, bordering on predestination, knowing, like the Dalai Lama, that she had been marked out as a special person. Musical prodigies often come from musical families. It's easy to spot them: musical skill is quantifiable. Acting is more subjective and elusive, but since Kate's father was an actor as well as her mother's parents and her uncle, her talent was recognised and encouraged, albeit impartially. Her two sisters, Anna, the oldest and 'the more obvious actress', and the youngest, Beth, have also become actors.

At the age of five Kate cried when she heard she'd landed the part of the Virgin Mary in the school nativity play, 'it was so important to me'. She graduated to a 'loud Cornish Fairy Godmother', 'an extremely demonstrative and frightening Dragon' and the Bonnie Langford part in *Bugsy Malone*. She'd always learn her lines quietly on her own (as she still does) and she'd always behave professionally. She was teased for it at school. 'I was amazed: what could be more important than the thing I really loved doing?'

When she was ten her father had a terrible accident. He caught his foot in a coil of rope when taking a large canal boat through a lock in France. The rope tightened and, had it not been for the speed of the helicopter ambulance and the skill of the French microsurgeons, he would have lost his foot. A woman said shortly afterwards: 'In a year's time it'll be as though it never happened.' And Kate thought: I'll wait a year, his foot will be normal and he'll be running around the beach with me. 'And of course that never happened. That was a great lesson for me, what a lie that was... A year later I felt I'd been betrayed.'

The 'great lesson', and she still applies it now, is this: never dissemble. I can't tell if that is true of her private life—certainly it's my experience of her—but it's true of her acting. She's invariably truthful—a paradox, of course, because all acting is faking, but acting becomes 'truthful' when the audience believes in the thoughts and feelings of the character, rather than being distracted by the actor's personality like a drunken bore at a party.

At the age of eleven, Kate won an audition to a stage school but her father was anxious about her becoming a stage-school clone. To convince him that she should go, she pinned her father to the sand as he lay on a beach in Norfolk. 'Dad, Mum and I can't bear it, I've got to get a uniform and tap shoes, can I go to the school, yes or no?' Her father gave in. To understand the full force of her argument as she sat on her father's stomach you have to understand that she was, as she says, a 'fat person'. She was nicknamed 'Blubber' at school and bullied, locked in the art cupboard: 'Blubber's in the cupboard. Are you crying, Blubber?' She wasn't, incidentally. By the age of fifteen, at stage school and doing small parts on TV, she weighed almost as many stones as her age: thirteen stone at fifteen. And at fifteen coming on sixteen she fell in love with a twenty-seven-year-old man.

In most narratives at this point you would expect two developments: protest from the parents and a vertiginous loss of weight to please her man—anorexia at the point of a pistol. But what happened is this: her parents and siblings approved of the boyfriend ('they adored him and welcomed him into the family') and her boyfriend loved her as she was.

It was professional vanity that changed her shape. 'I was cast in two episodes of *Anglo-Saxon Attitudes* and I was playing the daughter of a sculptress. I was introduced to the woman who was playing my mother and she was *enormous* and I realised why I'd been cast as the daughter. And I thought: shit, if I want a shot at playing *Alice in Wonderland* or Wendy in *Peter Pan*, I can't do it this size. I've got to do something about it.' So she did, and with the help of her Mum, a veteran of WeightWatchers (5'11" and 'strapping'), she dieted for a year and lost three stone. Then she was cast by Peter Jackson in *Heavenly Creatures*, by Ang Lee in *Sense and Sensibility*, by James Cameron in *Titanic* and within three years she'd become an international star and, perhaps as remarkable, remained uncorrupted by her success.

Talent without character is nothing. For all the luck of her natural gifts, Kate has behaved—at least in her professional life—with uncanny maturity. 'I've got an old head on a young body,' she says. The relationship with the boyfriend,

Stephen Tredre, lasted three and a half years and the age difference never mattered. 'I never felt intimidated by him… At the theatre school, I understood the teachers so much better than the pupils… I always had patience with older people, I didn't have patience with people of my own age.' Like a musical prodigy, she occupied a world where she was the equal of adults, as capable and talented as they were.

When she was shooting *Hideous Kinky* in Morocco, she was phoned by a mutual friend to be told that Stephen had died. Even though his cancer had been diagnosed a year before and they'd drifted apart earlier, it was a colossal shock. Added to that a new boyfriend, her 'karmic equal', turned out to be a cosmic shit. Doubly broken-hearted, she fell into the arms of the film's third assistant director, Jim Threapleton. He was twenty-four, she was twenty-three. 'He was real and normal and lovely and I fancied the arse off him.'

Two months later *Titanic* opened, the press embraced the couple—TITANIC ROMANCE!—and Kate was swept up by a tidal wave of commercial and romantic hype. 'This is for life,' she responded, satisfying the insufferable sentimental appetite of the media to make romantic fiction out of stuff of real life, and also grasping for a spot of constancy in a world which seemed to be changing for her with each new day. Four years later her marriage is over, she has a daughter, Mia, whom she dotes on, and a new partner Sam Mendes, whom (ditto). She is rueful, more guarded, less impulsive, and bruised by her discovery that nothing is more satisfying to the British press than the spectacle of glamorous discomfort: 'Sometimes I wish my life wasn't so interesting because of my success.'

Media ill-wishers were reporting that Kate and Sam were to split up within days of announcing they were together and, in addition, suggesting that their affair pre-dated Kate's all-too-public estrangement from her husband. As the hacks say: I can verify that it didn't. On the day it was announced (KATE-ASTRO-PHE screamed the tabloid front pages), I was working with Kate and she asked me, with an achingly contrived casualness, what I thought of the director she had recently met for the first time, 'your friend Sam Mendes'. The same friend, incidentally, who asked me what I thought of Kate Winslet…

I'm happy to think that in some faintly tenuous way I played Cupid by endorsing their evident mutual admiration, and I hope that these two manifestly decent and well-intentioned people are able to find enough time, peace and seclusion together. They have to learn to live a domestic life with a very lively two-year-old girl, with very demanding professional schedules, and with the ever-insistent scrutiny of a press keenly (and obscenely) interested in spotting and charting the fault lines in their relationship. This is stardom's law of gravity: privacy is exchanged for fame.

There may be those who think that this is only just, but it seems a savage transaction for a very good actress who never flirts with the press in that shameless stay-away-but-don't-stay-too-far tease of the endemically insecure. There is actually something quite genuinely diffident about Kate: 'My skin still crawls if you call me a movie star; I get embarrassed, I think: don't be ridiculous. Maybe it's because I'm British. To me Julia Roberts, that's a movie star. But if people say I'm an authentic movie star, that I think is an enormous compliment, but my God is that a responsibility.'

Her responsibility is this: 'Two things: I think it's my duty to wave a certain flag about being a normal woman with breasts and bottom the right shape and not emaciated… And men love a shape.' True. And the second thing? 'I don't think you should throw weight around… I do what I think is right but I'm always ready to pay the consequences. I'm a confident woman. I know what I want. You don't want to get into an argument with me.'

For all her maturity and her natural grace, you can still see something of the child in her, something that she probably denied herself in becoming a premature adult—the wilful tomboy who wears biker boots, says 'bum' and 'shit' and 'piss', rolls thin cigarettes from her Golden Virginia tobacco pouch and when asked about her Ben de Lisi dress at the Oscars said it was lovely 'but I wouldn't want to go for a pee in it.'

But she's careful, canny even, about how she dresses on public occasions, which seems to me professional common sense, given that almost everything that she wears outside her front door is judged by a jury of magazine readers who often demonstrate all the benevolence of a lynch mob. With the pick of the world's designers at her door she 'panics', but her embarrassment of choice is eased by the advice of her friend and style adviser, Cheryl Konteh. The choice, in the end, is always Kate's.

She loves dressing up, but most of the time dresses down in jeans, shirt or T-shirt (today she's wearing Levis and a pale striped muslin shirt), and even though she enjoys transforming herself, she isn't obsessed by her body and face. 'I don't mind looking like a pig.' Which, of course, she doesn't. Ever. She rarely visits a gym, has only ever had two manicures and one pedicure and, unless it's a public event, rarely wears more than a touch of blusher and a dab of lipstick. 'By rights I should have shrivelled skin, because I smoke,' she says, rolling another, 'but I don't. My skin is thanks to my mother.'

Perhaps it seems unfair that Kate has so much good fortune and so many gifts, but they have not been bought without pain and received without gratitude. And for those who feel that all glory should be paid for by pain, well, she has an infected toe. Satisfied?

Oh, and she can sing well.

Ian Charleson

Ian died in 1990 when he was playing Hamlet in my production at the National Theatre. I wrote this for the Guardian, *tears dropping on the keyboard.*

I didn't know Ian well until I worked with him on *Guys and Dolls* in 1982. I knew him then as an actor of charm, of wit, of skill, with a kind of engaging melancholy of the Mastroianni variety, which he could dispel with a sardonic and self-mocking wit. He often looked truly beautiful, even angelic; then a mischievous smile would appear and all thought of angels would fly away like frightened starlings.

I'd offered him the part in *Guys and Dolls* on the basis of his acting and of hearing him sing at parties. It was typical of him that he insisted on singing the score for me before he accepted the part, and equally typical that when he'd finished singing he said to me: 'You enjoyed that, didn't you, Richard?' He knew he could make an audience (and a director) cry with a romantic ballad, and he loved to do just that as much as he loved to torment me with his relentless mockery of my attempts to learn to tap-dance alongside the cast.

He was a fine, light, unfailingly truthful, romantic actor, something that the French value more than we do. Like Cary Grant, he had the gift of making the difficult look effortlessly simple. But with Brick in *Cat on a Hot Tin Roof* and with his Hamlet, he discovered a new gravity in his work, a weight and depth. He became, in my view, a real heavyweight.

We had talked some time before about the parts that he desperately wanted to play—Richard II, Angelo, Benedick and Hamlet, and—as he said to me recently—'Lear, God willing'. He had a real passion for Shakespeare, rather rare in his generation. He really loved the density of thought, the great Shakespearean paradoxes, the lyricism, the energy of the verse. He didn't want to paraphrase it; the meaning was for him in the poetry and the poetry in the meaning.

When I asked him to play Hamlet I knew he'd been ill, had even had pneumonia, and that he still had a chronic sinus complaint which gave him large, swollen bags under his eyes. On bad days it was barely possible to glimpse the face beneath the swelling, a malicious parody of his beauty. He was without vanity, but not without hope. He told me that he was HIV-positive and that he thought that the eyes would respond to treatment. When we embarked on rehearsals he was having regular, and immensely painful, acupuncture treatment, and later on, chemotherapy which exhausted and debilitated him. Later in his illness he defiantly rejected all treatment; he wanted to be himself, however painful that was.

About halfway through the rehearsal period we discussed the future—an unspecified projection. 'Do you think I can go on as Hamlet looking like this?' he said. 'You'll get better,' I said. 'We have to be positive,' he said. And we were. Our text was, of course, from *Hamlet*:

There's nothing either good or bad but thinking makes it so.

Hamlet is a poem of death. It charts one of the great human rites of passage— from immaturity to accomodation with death. Hamlet grows up, in effect, to grow dead. Until he leaves for England ('From this time forth/My thoughts be bloody or be nothing worth.') he is on a reckless helter-skelter swerving between reason and chaos. When he returns from England he is changed, aged, matured, reconciled somehow to his end. We see Hamlet in a graveyard obsessed with the physical consequences of death, and then in a scene with Horatio prior to the duel he talks to him about his premonition of death:

...thou wouldst not think how ill all's here about my heart. But it is no matter... it is but foolery... We defy augury. There's a special providence in the fall of a sparrow. If it be now, 'tis not to come; if it be not to come, it will be now; if it be not now, yet it will come. The readiness is all. Since no man of aught he leaves knows aught, what is't to leave betimes? Let be.

We talked a great deal about Hamlet's accomodation with death, always as a philosophical proposition, his own state lurking just below the surface, hidden subtext. Ian was very fastidious about the 'Let be.' It wasn't, for him, a chiding of Horatio, or a shrug of stoic indifference, it was an assertion, a proposed epitaph perhaps: don't fuss, don't panic, don't be afraid.

The definition of courage as 'grace under pressure' was perfectly suited to Ian. It was something more than stoicism. He defied his illness with a spirit that was dazzling, quite without self-pity, self-dramatisation, and at least openly, without despair. During rehearsals he was utterly without reserve. Where there had been a kind of detachment or caution, a 'Scottishness' perhaps, there was a deep well of generosity, of affection—a largeness of heart, and the only 'Scottish' characteristics that he showed were his doggedness and his persistence.

In his last performance of *Hamlet* he acted as if he knew that it was the last time he'd be on stage. He'd had flu and hadn't played the previous two nights; he was feeling guilt about what he saw as his lack of professionalism. 'If they pay you, you should turn up,' he said. His performance on that Monday night was like watching a man who had been rehearsing for playing Hamlet all his life. He wasn't playing the part, he became it. By the end of the performance he was visibly exhausted, each line of his final scene painfully wrung from him, his farewell and the character's agonisingly merged. He stood at the curtain call like a tired boxer, battered by applause.

When he became unable to perform, it was a real deprivation to him. Without that there was nothing to hang on to. 'You know me, Richard, if there are two people out there who I can impress, I'd be there if I could.' And he would, if he'd had the strength. We're often accused of sentimentality in the theatre, but it can't be sentimental to miss terribly someone whose company gave so much joy, whose talent really did add to the sum of human happiness, and whose courage was beyond admiration.

I had a letter from him a few weeks before he died, just before Christmas. He said:

> One day when I'm better I'd love to attempt Hamlet again, and all the rest; and together we can revitalise Shakespeare. Anyway I hope this is not a dream and I can't tell you how much of a kick I got out of doing the part, if only for the short time I could…

Let be…

Judi Dench

I've written and spoken many times about Judi and this piece appeared in 2004 in a collection called, rather winsomely, Darling Judi.

———·•·———

I'm looking at a photograph of four adults and two children—young boys—lined up on one side of a large kitchen table. They are watching six clockwork chicks (it's Easter) racing across the table. Bets have been laid; the form of the chicks is unpredictable. One charges forward then falls on its beak, one stutters in circles, one mounts the rear of another, one never moves. The faces of the players are infused with sporting passion, but one face is contorted, no, not contorted, illuminated by demented glee. It's Judi Dench, in an ecstasy of fun, combining three of her favourite things: love of company, love of games and love of betting. It's not perhaps the image that most people have of someone who, as the Japanese say, is a Living National Treasure, but it's closer than the weird caricature of gentility that is sometimes touted in the press—what Billy Connolly describes as 'those English twittering fucking women—they think she's one of them, and she isn't.'

Alan Bennett is also a Living National Treasure. We were once speculating about what the world's worst-taste T-shirt would be. Alan said he'd recently seen a young man wearing a heavy-metal T-shirt that read 'HITLER: THE EUROPEAN TOUR'. That's bad, I said, that's awful, but what about one that I saw shortly after thirty-nine Turin football fans had been killed in an accident at a soccer match against Liverpool that read: 'LIVERPOOL 39 TURIN 0'. Yes, that's ghastly, said Alan, but the worst-taste T-shirt, the very worst, he said,

would be one that read: 'I HATE JUDI DENCH'. Most of us have been wearing our 'I LOVE JUDI DENCH' T-shirts for years. Mine's a bit grey by now;
I've been wearing it since 1966.

That was the year I first saw Judi act. It wasn't on stage, it was on TV—a four-
part drama by John Hopkins called *Talking to a Stranger*, directed by
Christopher Morahan. I still think it's one of the few authentic television
masterpieces. It was about a suburban family disintegrating over a weekend,
seen through the eyes of each of its members: father, mother, daughter, son.
The performances of the actors—Maurice Denham, Margery Mason, Michael
Bryant—are vivid still in my mind, but the image of Judi is something more
than vivid: it has an aura, a corona like the glow around a high-voltage
element. In a room in Dorset, watching on a small black-and-white TV set, I
was dazzled by her passionate energy, her abandon, her vulnerability and her
sharp wit. She was a star.

It says everything about Judi and as much about the era that she didn't immediately gravitate to films. But this was the age of 'dolly birds' and 'Swinging
London'—and all the tatty crap that make it difficult to be nostalgic about the
sixties unless you were stoned all the time, living in Ibiza, or both—and film
producers (with Samantha Eggar as their role model) recoiled from this mercurial, round-faced young actress who could move from laughter to tears in the
blink of an eye.

And the theatre presented her with a world in which she was, if not entirely in
control of her destiny in the choice of parts, wholly in control of it when she
was acting. The theatre is a world where you can learn from night to night,
where you don't have to conform to a physical type, where you have the power
to convince an audience that you are whoever you choose to be. The theatre
thrives on metaphor—a room becomes a world, a group of characters becomes
a whole society—and, in enlisting the imagination of the audience, an actor performs an act of poetry. A passion for poetry—intensity of beauty in language and
gesture—is in Judi's genes.

Later that year I saw her on the stage for the first time. It was in a production of
Richard II; John Neville was playing the King. Judi was not actually supposed to
be in the show, but had appeared—it was a midweek matinee—as a conspicuously small soldier guarding the imprisoned monarch. She was dressed from top
to toe in chain mail with a helmet on her head that looked like a metal mixing
bowl. One by one the actors realised that they were sharing the stage with her
and a contagious frenzy gripped the whole company. They shuddered in unison, legless with laughter. Only John Neville—to Judi's fury—defiantly resisted
the bait and, in spite of the distraction, I still remember his performance as one
of the best I've ever seen in a Shakespeare play.

This happened at Nottingham Playhouse where John Neville was Director and Judi was playing Amanda in *Private Lives*, which alternated in the repertoire with the Shakespeare. I was working at the theatre, directing a schools' tour of Goldoni's *Mirandolina*. It was my first real job as a director and I owed it, in part, to Judi. I had been working in the nearby city of Leicester the previous Christmas at the Phoenix Theatre. I was a disaffected member of the chorus in an uncomfortable production of a musical for which I had no great affection: *The Boy Friend*. In order to deflect my growing despair (and that of some of my cast members) I directed a production of *The Knack*—a play by Ann Jellicoe—to be played for one Sunday night. By some special providence John Neville came to see the production with Judi, liked what he saw and offered me the job in Nottingham.

Which is how I came to meet Judi and began a friendship which will last until I fail to come round to her dressing room and be generous after a show—something I did once and for which she's never forgiven me. My crime—and it was a crime—was a failure of good manners, which for Judi is much more than obeying common courtesies, writing thank-you letters, sending cards of condolence and remembering birthdays (though it's all those as well). Her notion of good behaviour—of 'acting well', if you like—is tied up with what makes her such a good actor: her ability to empathise with other people, to imagine what a person—real or fictional—is feeling. She has the gift of compassion.

Judi's philosophy is a sort of Christian one but it's less a set of beliefs—she's a practising Quaker—than an instinct. Judi acts well in life and in her work but, while acting well on stage is difficult and demanding, it's an admirable but far from unique gift. What is rare—very rare—is for an actor to square the circle of work and life.

What are the things I remember most clearly of Judi when I first met her? Alone among my friends she always called me Rich (and still does), and I asked her to be in a play that I had written which she turned down without breaking my heart, even when hers was so busy being broken. She was always in love or falling in love, and sometimes both at the same time and usually with the wrong man, unsuitable but irresistible. She was like Ranyevskaya in *The Cherry Orchard*: 'What do I do? I fall in love with his double.' When we did the play for BBC TV years later she said to me, 'I've decided who this man in Paris is, this man who's made her so unhappy. You know who, don't you, Rich?' I did.

She was always a romantic and she still is, by which I mean she believes in the redeeming power of love. Being a romantic doesn't mean she's sentimental, even if there's a side of her that to a mean-spirited observer—the sort who calls actors 'luvvies'—might seem soppy: the first-night cards, soft toys, soft hearts and easy endearments that make up the stew of backstage life which, for all its superficiality, is threaded with genuine affection and appreciation of the value of real comradeship.

And with Judi laughter, a sound somewhere between a chuckle and a gurgle—sexy and subversive—is always bubbling up. She has an impish sense of humour. When we were rehearsing *The Cherry Orchard* she sent me a Christmas card in the shape of a man in a gorilla suit. And on the last night of *A Little Night Music* she faced Larry Guittard (whom we'd brought over from New York for the show), opened her dressing gown and revealed the words 'Go home, Yank' written on a bodystocking. And she thinks nothing of conscripting several dozen people to send mocking postcards to an actor friend to whom she'd given a £20 note to pay for a short taxi ride and whom she'd overheard say: 'You can keep the change.' 'Thank *you*, guv,' said the justly astonished taxi driver.

She revels in banter, bonhomie, and practical jokes, yet behind that wholly accessible, almost excessively generous façade there's an intensely private, even unreachable person; what Franco Zeffirelli called 'a secret garden'. It's one of the many paradoxes of her character: she's hard-headed but big-hearted, subversive but respectful of tradition, insecure but defiant in the face of fear, wildly passionate but almost always temperate. I've only once seen her very angry. A journalist in the *Daily Telegraph* had suggested that she was scene-stealing, systematically upstaging the other actors by ostentatiously moving props. You'd need to be very stupid and have a wilful ignorance of Judi's character to believe that she would behave so ungenerously to her fellow actors. She was volcanically angry, so angry that she became white-faced and the tips of her ears glowed red. If she had confronted the journalist at that moment, murder would have been too good for her.

Paradoxes are the oxygen of good actors: you have to seek attention for yourself but you can't be narcissistic, you have to perform but not show off, you have to communicate but in someone else's voice and, if you don't find the balance between these opposites, acting is just showing off. But to play one thought while thinking three or four others and moving dexterously around a stage or film set is the essential professional requirement. No less essential requirements for life as an actor are resilience and fortitude. They breed stoicism or guts: 'grace under pressure', Hemingway called it.

'The peculiarity of this profession,' said the actor Macready, 'obliges the man of sorrows to affect a buoyancy of spirits, whilst perhaps his heart is breaking.' No one could have followed his dictum more earnestly than Judi when we filmed *Iris* not many weeks after her husband Michael Williams's death. Mike had been her north, south, east and west, more so than I had realised, and her grief was a terrible thing to witness. Grief can make you cruel; with Judi it made her determined, producing a ferocious energy that translated into an unusual immersion in preparing for the part. This involved a previously untried approach: reading the script before she started to work on it.

In the past she has recklessly courted disaster by insisting on starting with a blank page so that the whole of the process—from the acceptance of the part until the end of the readthrough on the first day of the rehearsals—has been a blindfold journey, where she's innocent of what's around each corner. She wouldn't even use Denholm Elliott's test for accepting a role: 'I open a script in the middle,' he said to me once, 'and if I think there's anybody in it that I'd like to have a drink with, I turn back to the beginning and read it.' Not Judi: she'd ask someone to paraphrase the script for her or just rely on her sense of smell—and I'm not sure I'm being metaphorical.

With *Iris*, because the period leading up to it was a period of forced unemployment while she was caring for Michael, she departed from her normal preparation for a part, which is to rely almost entirely on her instincts and, through a process of osmosis, soak up the details and absorb the character's life without allowing anything of herself to encroach on the character. To prepare for playing Iris Murdoch she read the script (two drafts even) and watched a documentary. She was fascinated by Iris Murdoch's accent—particularly the way she sounded the 'h' in words like 'which' or 'whist' as she does herself. Discovering that their mothers were from the same background, genteel Dublin Protestants, was another point of access to the character.

More typical of her approach to studying a part was to sit in the car when we were filming in Oxford outside the house that John Bayley had shared with Iris Murdoch. What she gleaned from this was their diffidence to possessions: the windows of the house were open and his dusty little car was in the driveway, unlocked, while he was away. She accumulates small details like a detective, asks you questions that seem barely relevant to the character she's playing, then leaves you as soon as you answer, as if she'd disturbed you while you're reading a book, afraid that talking about it more will muddy her instinct. It was through intuition rather than study that she achieved that alchemical physical transformation at the end of *Iris*, when her eyes became vacant but her soul still seemed at home. She didn't go to old people's homes to observe patients suffering from Alzheimer's Disease; she asked little about my mother, who had had a cruelly long decay into the terminal stage, and she talked for a short time to an old friend of hers who was in the very early stages of the illness. The rest—the progressive descent into oblivion—she guessed.

Judi works through doubt, scepticism and guesswork and, like a prospector panning for gold in a stream, is never content until she's found something solid. The way she works is entirely idiosyncratic; it's like Churchill's description of Russia: a riddle wrapped in a mystery inside an enigma. Like all good actors she doesn't really have a method, still less *The* Method. One of the things I dislike about *The* Method is that with its catechism of 'impro', 'emotional memory', 'private moments' and 'relaxation exercises', it's become a credo rather than a process. Actors become more concerned with finding themselves than the author's character. All acting 'methods' have to be empirical, they're just means to an end; if they're codified—like Stanislavsy's and Lee Strasberg's—the means become the end.

The aim, whether it's in theatre, film or television, Shakespeare, Scorsese or *EastEnders*, is to be—or more importantly to *appear* to be—spontaneous: you have to look as though the thoughts and words and feelings and actions are occurring for the first time. However it's achieved, all actors have to keep a corner of their brain actively deployed as a monitor, cold, detached, critical and unengaged. It's their third eye, that facility for being utterly aware of what they're doing and yet appearing utterly unselfconscious and innocently spontaneous. That's what the job is, Judi would say. Nobody does it better.

She has technique to burn—she can turn a line on a fragment of a syllable, a scene on the twist of a finger—but her technique never shows. She has the ear of a musician and the eye of a painter. With her voice—that bluesy alto—she can bend a note from joy to a sob, and she has a dancer's dexterity, always using her body expressively. In film they say you should hold everything in, in theatre the opposite. But Judi breaks the rules, in any medium she seems mercurial and yet constant, she's entirely open yet never lets you feel—as in life—that you've glimpsed the whole person. David Hare wrote a speech for a character in *Amy's View* that describes this phenomenon. With astonishing prescience it was written before Judi had been cast: '…it may be presumptuous but I feel I'm beginning to understand your technique… You never play anything outwards. I've noticed you keep it all in. So you draw in the audience. So it's up to them. And somehow they make the effort… They have to go and get it themselves. What I don't know is, how do you do it?'

The answer is: I really don't know. In rehearsal the elements of her performance seem disparate but gradually—and invisibly—the elements come together: head, heart, voice and body into a marvellous harmony—never a wasted gesture, never a superfluous move. She always reminds me of what a famous English play-agent called Peggy Ramsay told me once about recognising whether an actor is in character: 'Look at the feet, dear.'

When I was editing *Iris*, the editor was reluctant to cut the beginning of one take. He'd say 'Look at this!' and show me a shot of Judi in which you could see her laughing—she'd been telling a joke—then you could hear my voice saying 'action' and within four frames—that's 1/6th of a second—there was a woman in the latter stages of decay from Alzheimer's Disease, or more to the point there *wasn't* a woman, there was an absence of a woman, totally vanished behind the eyes. It was like watching a musician rehearse. 'Bar 34,' says the conductor, gives the downbeat, and the soloist and orchestra pick up on the first note of the bar, no shuffling, no prevarication: pitch and tempo perfect.

I think Judi is a genius and I know exactly how she would react if I said so to her face. 'Oh, Rich,' she'd say and shrug like a cat arching its back. And then she'd laugh. That word 'genius' is rather debased currency—we tend to sprinkle it about like Italian waiters with peppermills—but I think it's accurate to call Judi a genius, because she's one of those people, like Oscar Peterson or Yehudi Menuhin or Cary Grant, who appear to do what they do brilliantly as if it cost them nothing, as if it was effortless. Judi acts like Matisse draws, never taking his hand from the page.

Once, at the end of a day's rehearsal after the actors had left the room, the stage manager held up a script and called out to me in horror: 'Judi's left her script.' At the time I think I was shocked too that Judi could be so cavalier, but now I understand that it's her way: she harvests the part in rehearsals, lets it ferment outside. Only when we were doing *Amy's View*, for the first time in her life she found that her way was failing her. Tired from promoting a film and from every other call on her seemingly inexhaustible well of energy, she wasn't picking up the lines in rehearsals. She found she had to take her script home and learn her lines in the bath. She was sufficiently worried to tell me that she thought she'd have to withdraw from the play. She wasn't using her pessimism as a charm to ward off ill spirits; the insecurity was genuine and she overcame it. Only then I realised that a controlled sense of panic underlies all her work: the way she chooses her parts, the way she rehearses, the way she performs.

Why does she act? Maybe there's no more sufficient answer than the existential proposition: because that's what she does because she was born to do it. All actors act because they want their existence to be corroborated: they want to be seen, they want approval, but however fine the actor's performance and however distant the characterisation from the actor's personality, the audience doesn't draw a fine line between approving the performance and approving the actor. So in seeking approval the actor is seeking love. If this implies a childhood devoid of affection, it's hard to square with Judi, who was loved and encouraged by her parents and has a way of overturning everyone she meets with affection.

All of us ask ourselves: am I loved? Judi's acting is an attempt to answer this question of others and of herself. Every part she takes on has to test her; it has to be something that she thinks she might not be able to do. Every time she acts she has to feel just enough fear to keep self-love at bay and need to find affirmation from the audience. The lure of acting—of doing something really well—is that when she's finished a performance there's a sense of triumph over the fear: danger is overcome and love is requited. She'd be frightened if she wasn't frightened. While there's danger and insecurity there can never be boredom, which could be why she's still at the peak she's been at since she played Juliet in 1957.

Iris was a film about enduring love. It wouldn't and couldn't have been made without Judi as an actor and as a person. It was her character, as much as that of

Iris Murdoch (or at least the Iris Murdoch mediated through John Bayley's accounts of her), that was at the heart of the film. When I was writing the screenplay with Charles Wood, we decided to end the film with Iris redux—a lecture given in her prime cross-cut with her dying on a hospital bed, both watched lovingly by her husband. Her lecture was a paraphrase of a lecture Iris Murdoch had given, but it could just as easily have been improvised by Judi:

> Human beings love each other, in sex, in friendship, and when they are in love, and they cherish other beings—humans, animals, plants, even stones. The quest for happiness and the promotion of happiness is in all of this, and the power of our imagination. We need to believe in something divine without the need for God, something which we might call Love or Goodness. Indeed as the psalm says: Whither shall I go from thy spirit, wither shall I flee from thy presence? If I ascend unto Heaven thou art there, if I make my bed in Hell behold thou art there. If I take the wings of the morning and dwell in the uttermost parts of the sea, even there shall thy hand lead me, and thy right hand shall hold me.

Stuart Burge

I read this at a memorial gathering at the Royal Court Theatre in 2009 to mourn the death and celebrate the life of Stuart, who had been its Artistic Director.

I met Stuart first when he came to Edinburgh, where I was living and working, to ask me if I would succeed him as Director of Nottingham Playhouse. With admirable economy he had also come to Edinburgh to ask my then girlfriend—who was called Sue Birtwistle—to start a Theatre-in-Education company.

It turned out that her employment at Nottingham had a smoother ride than mine. While she got on with starting her company, my appointment was delayed because the board of the theatre, under a bullying Chairman who looked like a giant pink baby, weren't so sure about me. 'Complete maniac, awful man,' said Stuart of the Chairman. He was more or less right, but Stuart did manage to persuade the board to allow me to succeed him, and apart from the Chairman pulling my hair and telling me to get it cut, thanks to Stuart I survived in Nottingham long enough to get married, have a daughter and spend five of the happiest years of my working life. When I told Stuart we were getting married, he was appalled. 'You're not doing it for the board's sake, are you?'

For some months Sue and I lived in the flat beneath Stuart. When I was away, Stuart would act as her alarm clock—tap-dancing on the ceiling to wake her, then cooking her a hard-boiled egg, which she carried to the Playhouse as she walked with him to the offices. When I was there we'd often eat with Stuart in the evening, when Stuart would tell us stories of his life as a dancer, which Sue at least had evidence of; or he'd talk about his time as an actor at the Old Vic; or his experiences as an improbable intelligence officer in Italy; or tell us limitless anecdotes of productions that he'd worked on. One evening Stuart was telling us a story while he was cooking what he called Chinese vegetables—that was essentially vegetables of all descriptions thrown at random into a wok. He was telling us about a film he'd made—'that... er... um... one about the... er... dictator, it's... er... Shakespeare... you know... um...' '*Julius Caesar*?' 'Yes, that's the one. I was working with that American actor? Er... You know the tall one with the hairpiece.' 'Oh, you mean Charlton Heston.' 'Oh, yes, Chuckles!' The story involved Stuart trying to discuss a difficult aspect of interpretation with Chuckles while he was on his horse and Stuart was at ground level, and then the wind came and blew the hairpiece away. At which point in the story Stuart exploded into volcanic laughter, tipped back on his heels, kicked a leg high in the air and his shoe performed a perfect parabola, landing—without Stuart being aware of it—in the Chinese vegetables. Sue picked it out discreetly, Stuart continued the story, and only later did he discover that he was only wearing one shoe.

One of the things I loved about Stuart's stories was that he always relived them—the joy and the anger were always in the present tense. I loved the fact that he was never nostalgic. The great days were never in the past. He was an optimist: I once walked into his office in Nottingham and he was sitting at his desk with a list of all the leading actors in the world. He was on the phone. 'Er... Marlon,' he said, 'I suppose there's no chance of you coming to Nottingham to play in this wonderful play by Gorki. No one's ever heard of it but you'd love it... Oh, well, thanks, just thought I'd ask.'

It was typical of Stuart that he'd be championing a play that no one else had done or had thought of doing. His productions of Peter Barnes' *The Ruling Class*, *The Devil is an Ass*, *Lulu*, *King John*, *Another Country* and *The London Cuckolds*—and a number of TV productions of work by D.H. Lawrence, Trevor Griffiths and Troy Kennedy Martin—completely belied the diffidence with which he talked of his own talent. When I told him I was going to do *Hamlet* at the Royal Court he laughed. 'Terribly difficult play, much too difficult for me.' He downplayed his talent out of a genuine modesty but also a real dislike of hype and self-advertisement. He was gifted and lucid as a director. He cast well, he cared a lot about narrative—and cared in the right way about what the audience understood and what they felt.

And he loved actors, even if he was rarely able to remember their names. 'I cast that singer in a TV play—you know he's incredibly famous now—played the harmonica'. 'Bob Dylan?' 'Er... Is that the one?' Or on another occasion: 'I saw that play with—what was his name? That one that became a lord. Oh, yes, Olivier. Made a film of *Othello* with him. Terrible.' But then Stuart occasionally had trouble remembering his own name. He once rang Gillian Diamond when she was casting director at the Royal Court. 'Hello, Stuart? This is Gillian.' 'No, you're Stuart, I'm Gillian.' And when he first introduced my wife to his wife Jo in Nottingham, he said: 'This is my wife… er … er …' 'Jo,' said Jo.

Some of this amnesia was selective or tactical—a form of persuasive charm married to strategic evasion. I wish I'd learnt Stuart's knack of disappearing whenever you had a knotty problem to confront him with, but perhaps that too was part of his elvish self—the ability, as Peter Barnes said in his obituary, to make 'vagueness into an art form'. But you underestimated Stuart at your peril: he was very shrewd—canny, really—and sometimes quite calculating. He could be very tough but he was also tender and generous and quite without envy. He gave me a lesson when I once dismissed a production that I didn't like with gratuitous ferocity. 'You don't have to be so severe,' he said, 'it doesn't make your work any better if say that you dislike someone else's.' In fact, Stuart taught me the first and most important rule about running a theatre: that you have to take joy in other people's work.

It often strikes me as odd that on first nights we all rely on that form of sympathetic magic—wishing each other good luck—as if the hard work of rehearsals and dedication and expertise and even talent weren't enough. But they aren't, of course. We all need luck—not so much the luck of the wind of fashion blowing our way—but the luck of working with the right people at the right time of our lives. Or—and this is just as important—the luck of having people take an interest in you at the right time in your life.

For me, Stuart was part of my luck. He approached me when I didn't know what to do with my life, and he became a friend and a mentor for the next thirty years. He never changed during those years. He always had that air of being both amused and bemused by life. And he looked the same as long as I knew him—the knotted silk scarf round his neck beneath the boyish face, a pair of glasses straying distractedly somewhere or other, and a chuckle at some new absurdity that had come his way. What survives for me of Stuart is my memory of a droll, humane and gifted man who was forever young.

Peter Hall

Peter was eighty in 2010. The Independent *commissioned this piece to celebrate his birth-day. He rang me after he'd read it, surprised—it seemed to me—that anyone had written kindly about him.*

I was a latecomer to the theatre, fifteen when I saw a play called *Hamlet* of which I knew almost nothing (I was a science nerd). I knew even less of the actor who played Hamlet—Peter O'Toole in his unreconstructed state—dark-haired, wild, violent, mercurial and thrilling, before stardom and Lawrence of Arabia turned him blonde and small-nosed. I was hooked on Shakespeare.

It was some years before I had the opportunity to follow up my new passion but then, within a shortish period, I saw two productions at Stratford-on-Avon which changed my life. The first, in 1962, was Peter Brook's production of *King Lear* with Paul Scofield, in which the play was revealed in all its elemental force in a production which refused the audience the comfort of making judgements on the characters. As it did for many of my generation, it made me think I wanted to be spend my life working in the theatre. The second production was Peter Hall's *The Wars of the Roses* (his and John Barton's conflation of Shakespeare's history plays), which was swift, graphic, unsentimental, brilliantly acted and brought Shakespeare into the world of contemporary power-politics. It made me think I wanted to be a director. Both productions were part of the work of the newly created Royal Shakespeare Company.

The RSC was Peter Hall's creation. Like Harold Wilson standing outside the door of Number 10 as a child aspiring to become Prime Minister, Peter Hall had always harboured the dream of running the Stratford theatre. And when his dream was realised by being invited to Stratford at the age of twenty-seven to be Director of the Shakespeare Memorial Theatre—young, ambitious, talented and iconoclastic—he managed to persuade the Chairman of the Trustees that the part-time summer Shakespeare festival could and should evolve into a major European theatre company. It was a remarkable vision and remarkably achieved in the face of considerable opposition from the theatre's board, from the commercial theatre and from the newly emergent National Theatre under Laurence Olivier.

Peter Hall recruited an ensemble of actors on three-year contracts and a team of directors and designers. John Barton, then a university don, joined him as one of the associate directors, along with Peter Brook (then, as now, the most celebrated British director), while the designer John Bury, who had worked for years with Joan Littlewood, developed an ascetic house style, using natural materials—iron, wood and stone—and clothes that were rough and lived-in.

Over the seven years that Peter Hall ran the company, the RSC opened a London home at the Aldwych, continued to produce a succession of fine Shakespeare productions, put some outstanding new plays at the centre of the repertoire—without precedent for a classical company—and acquired an international reputation. It's not hard to see why the reputation and influence of this period has endured, and has acted as a benchmark and provocative inspiration to succeeding generations of actors and directors.

It's not hard too, when you talk to Peter now, to realise that nothing could match or did match the frenzied thrill of reinventing the British theatre in the early sixties. Apart from forming an astonishingly successful theatre company, he created the template of the modern director—part-magus, part-impresario, part-politician, part-celebrity. He was—and is—the godfather (in both senses) of British theatre, and like many directors, writers and actors of several generations I have much to be grateful to him for.

I've known him well since 1974 when he came to Nottingham Playhouse to see my production of Trevor Griffiths' play, *Comedians*. The night he came was memorable as much for his presence as for the fact that at the conclusion of Jonathan Pryce's monologue, the line 'Still, I made the buggers laugh…' provoked a sensational response. A woman shouted out: 'You didn't! You didn't!' and the lights came up on a chilled and shaken audience. When I met Peter after the show he told me that it was one of the most remarkable moments he'd ever had in a theatre, and congratulated me on my direction of the moment. It was years before I confessed to him that I was as shocked as everybody else, that the woman wasn't planted, that it had never happened before and that it had nothing to do with me or my direction. It was years later still that I discovered the identity of the woman who cried out—a charming, forthright gardening expert and mother of a now successful actor.

Peter Hall brought *Comedians* to the National Theatre (then housed at the Old Vic) and then brought me to the National Theatre (by then moved to the South Bank) as an associate director. My first production there was *Guys and Dolls*, and I discovered that Peter was a patient, generous and astute producer. For a theatre company that was teetering on the edge of a deficit it was an extraordinarily courageous thing to have agreed to let a novice at staging musicals direct the NT's first musical. If Peter was nervous he never showed it, and I learned from him the indispensable maxim of producing: that no advice is worth giving to a director (or actor, writer or designer) that they are not able to act on; the rest is self-indulgence.

Peter has a protean energy and an apparently insatiable appetite for work that, were he not so apparently self-assured, would denote a deep-set insecurity. No one that could twice contemplate suicide, as he confesses in his autobiography, could claim to be without self-doubt, but it's a mark of his strength that he invariably radiates confidence and, if he receives a critical drubbing, emerges like a large shaggy dog coming out of the river, shaking the abuse from him and pounding enthusiastically towards his next production. Restlessness is Peter's natural condition. He has a sort of existential itch: he lives to direct and directs to live. A few years ago I told him that I wouldn't be directing anything new for nearly two years. 'I'd go mad,' he said.

Of his countless productions, four stand out for me both as entirely exemplary productions and as wholly characteristic of the work and the man: *The Wars of the Roses* and *The Homecoming* at the RSC, *Antony and Cleopatra* at the NT and Britten's *Midsummer Night's Dream* at Glyndebourne. They were great productions, all marked by a highly focused energy, by lucidity, by musicality and by humanity.

At the age of eighty the energy is still apparent not only in his voracious appetite for work, but in his persistent evangelism for theatre and for public funding of the arts. His lucidity remains a characteristic of any conversation with him. He takes a delight in excoriating politicians for their philistinism, in arguing for Beckett over Brecht, in promoting the primacy of Shakespeare, in advocating the importance of verse-speaking. His musicality is inherent—he's been a gifted and knowledgeable musician since childhood—and it's apparent in his fervent concern for verse-speaking, his insistence that playing Shakespeare is like playing jazz—play the line, listen to the beat, it's how you nearly break the rhythm that enables you to express the emotion and allows you to express what the character feels.

Peter is not clubbable nor is he gregarious, but no one who has seen him, like a Tolstoyan patriarch, in the company of his six children could deny his warm love for them and theirs for him. There's a sweet circularity in the fact that he's returning to *Twelfth Night* and to the National Theatre to coincide with his eightieth birthday. It's his fourth production of a play that he first directed as a student at Cambridge in 1954. With his brilliant daughter, Rebecca, as Viola, I can't imagine a more perfectly appropriate birthday present or a happier way of celebrating his extraordinary career.

Tony Harrison

After my film of V *was shown on Channel 4 in 1987, a new edition was published. This was its preface.*

I was driving through France discussing the French for roof rack (*'le roofrack'*, recently dehyphenated). In addition to *le roofrack* we would need, I said, some *corde* and possibly (showing off now) *une amarre.* 'What's that?' said a sceptical wife. 'A hawser,' I replied. 'Hawser? Hawser?' she ruminated. 'That's a Tony Harrison word.' And together, like infants learning 'Hiawatha', we chanted from *V*:

> When the hawser of the blood-tie's hacked, or frays

It's as characteristic a Harrison line as one could find: rhythmic, memorable, muscled, alliterative, dramatic and impenitently English.

It's one of the many paradoxes, the v's if you like, of Tony's work that it is such a recognisably English voice; not a metaphorical 'voice', but a sound that, once you have met its author, unforgettably animates the poetry on the page and dramatises it when he reads it aloud. It's not Received Pronunciation (against which he rails evangelically), nor the fluting sound of college common rooms or cathedral cloisters. It's not dry, muted or ascetic. It's musical, sensual, work-ing-class and Yorkshire. It's not a professional Yorkshire voice that speaks from an ersatz tradition of thee-thou-beery-blokey defiant little Englanders, but a voice with a sense of place and class. A heartland from which the speaker has been separated.

The baker's son from Leeds is probably the most cosmopolitan man I know. Multilingual (Greek, ancient and modern, Latin, Italian, French, Czech and Hausa), much travelled—a citizen, as they say, of the world, living, often rather precariously, between London, Florida, New York and Newcastle. An expert in many cultures, with a curiosity about many others. Fastidiously knowledgeable about food, wine, music and the theatre. Tender, witty, wry, volatile, living up (or down) to the Yorkshire stereotype only in his rare but formidable stubbornness and intransigence.

The man is the work. It is not so much that it is autobiographical (though much of it is) but that the content invariably dramatises the ambivalence at the heart of his character and attempts to reconcile them. Tony does not deal in the familiar English mode of ellipsis and reticence, but in an unremittingly direct address that is at times almost unnerving. Those opposite valencies that he invokes in *V* are not a poet's conceits but are the syntax of his daily life—heart/brain, soul/body, male/female, family, freedom, class, culture; this is the divided territory in which he searches for harmony and despairs at its elusiveness.

I don't know if despair is his constant companion; melancholy certainly is. More than once I've heard him say that if it weren't for his ability to write he would go mad, that writing is a way of expressing, of reducing, of controlling, thoughts and feelings that would otherwise spray into chaos. It was, appropriately, the author of *The Anatomy of Melancholy* who said that all poets are mad. Perhaps without their poetry they would be.

For all this, Tony is a cheerful companion and a highly organised and practical professional man. He is, after all, as well as a poet, a playwright and a director—both disciplines that give short shrift to the dilettante. As a writer he is as methodical as any writer I know. He collects and collates information about subjects that attract him in a series of quarto-sized notebooks with quotations, newspaper cuttings, photographs, ideas, fragments of lines, all laid out meticulously. The Japanese film director Ozu used to go to his country cottage for weeks to write his scripts. When he emerged he described the script by the number of cases of sake he'd had to consume to write it. With Tony it's notebooks.

The notebooks contain, among other things, a continent of information about Greek drama on which he is unquestionably an absolute authority and a zealot. He has little patience with the dabblers in the Greek repertoitre, or, indeed, for all forms of cultural tourism. It might be argued that as a theatrical practitioner he is himself merely an enthusiastic amateur. This is not so; for many years as a translator (*The Misanthrope, Phaedra Brittannica, The Oresteia*), and as a co-author (*The Mysteries*) he has not only closely observed the processes of theatre-making but has been at times a de facto co-director, and as a director and author (*Trackers* and *Square Rounds*) he has a real understanding of the singularity of the medium—an acute sense of space and of language.

He is impatient with the aspects of the job that often make you feel like a night-nurse, dispensing comfort, advice, treatment and solace to actors while wondering why they don't just do it. There are few directors, however, who are more conscientious in ensuring that the minds of the actors are concentrated with an almost religious rigour on their performance. He is the only director I know who (in *Trackers*) invites the cast to drink champagne from a three-thousand-year-old cup before going on stage.

In his poetry and his plays the sense of rhythm is as important as the meaning. Dramatic language without the sinew of rhythmic pulse is completely inert to him, and he can be violent and unforgiving about performances and productions of verse plays where the actors and directors have been deaf to the pulse of the poetry. You should be able to feel the language, to taste it, to conscript the whole body as well as the mind and the mouth to savour it.

In the same way Tony wants the whole body of society, not just its head, to be involved in art. He wants art and literature to be accessible to everyone, for the distinction between High and Low art to be annulled, and for art to be removed from the clutches of class distinction. However, his hatred for the pap of popular culture is almost boundless. He has a committed loathing for the propagators and purveyors of this pap and, in spite of his determined compassion, for the consumers as well. He's a populist in the same sense as Chekhov who, when told by a Narodnik actor that Gogol needed to be brought down to the level of the people, said that the problem was rather that the people needed to be brought up to the level of Gogol. If ever there was an anthem set to this theme it is *V*.

In Russia they used to kill their poets '*pour encourager les autres*'. The reward for the English poet is at best indifference and at worst becoming Poet Laureate. With *V*, Tony violated both ends of that spectrum. Whatever was invoked by that poem it was not indifference. Indignation, outrage, joy, sorrow, pity perhaps, and paradoxically, for a man who would violently shun any form of honour, he became the uncrowned poet laureate—a truly public poet.

Poets who read their work in public can often be maddeningly diffident and awkward. Tony is not of this school. He is a poet who performs rather than reads, without self-regard and without self-indulgence, and without the spurious 'performance' values that actors often bring to the reading of poetry. He does not, however, neglect the demands of volume and articulation, the sense of the event, and the awareness of his audience. He is metrically unnervingly constant. When we were filming *V*, you could have set a metronome at the beginning of the performance and forty minutes later the poet would still have been in sync with it. In addition, he could accomodate with an actor's instinct instructions about camera movements and eye-lines. He could, as we say, 'take direction'.

I first became aware of the rumbling storm provoked by Channel 4's intention to show the film of *V* when I was making another film which also provoked severe climatic disturbances, *Tumbledown*. There were similarities in the response to both films. In both cases, before the transmission, in fact before anyone even on the production team had seen the finished films, there was a chorus of outrage, misrepresentation, prejudice, insult, bullying and condescension from MPs, journalists, peers and pundits.

Popular newspapers, as ever, found rich resources of moral indignation. I was standing in a North London car park on a grey dawn, waiting for the day's filming to begin, when a cheery make-up assistant thrust a copy of the *Daily Mail* into my hand. 'You've made the front page,' she said. I read, and I hope to do full value to the pungent prose: 'FOUR LETTER TV POEM FURY!' Only with hindsight was I grateful to the *Mail* and their even more downmarket clones for having unwittingly brought to the poem an audience whose size could never have been imagined without their gift of free publicity. It was an audience who largely came to the poem out of curiosity and was surprised to find that not only could they understand it, but they were moved, amused, even educated by it.

The film's editor was a man who, like many victims of our educational system, had been turned off poetry at an early age. 'It was not for me,' he said. One of the greatest pleasures of making the film was watching Ray become drawn into the poem so that he felt each nuance, each rhyme, each rhythm, each shift of thought with an ever-increasing vividness. Indeed, all of us involved in making the film became evangelistic in support of the poem—it's way of yoking sophisticated and ambitious philosophical speculation to minute physical observations; its astonishing variety contained within an unvarying scheme of rhyme and scansion; its pessimism as much as its optimism; and above all, its endless celebration of what it wouldn't be too grand to call the human condition. We all thought, as Ray put it, that the poem was fucking amazing. I still do, and when Tony told me that a parents' action group had succeeded in persuading the Manchester Education Committee (via the office of that renowned figure of the new enlightenment, Chief Constable James Anderton) to withdraw his poetry from the school curriculum, I felt once again that, as in Russia, poetry was dangerous. The Russian poet Gumilev (who was shot) said that dead words smell badly. These are the words of the acknowledged legislators of our world, who proscribe, censor, inhibit and monitor what we should read and see, and, by implication, think and feel.

If I had the slightest influence over educational policy in this country, I'd see that *V* was a set text in every school, but of course if we lived in that sort of country, the poem wouldn't have needed to be written.

When I became Director of the National Theatre, I asked Tony what I should do there. 'Improve the wine,' he said. (As it turned out, rather more difficult than changing the repertoire.) We were having dinner a few days afterwards, several of us, in a smallish room in a restaurant. Tony had, of course, ordered the wine. Lots of it. On the wall behind my head was a small etching of Andrew Marvell, which Tony caught sight of. He started to recite *To His Coy Mistress*. One Yorkshire poet speaking through another, the intervening centuries becoming transparent. There was silence in the room; the air suspended. It was moving, funny, soulful, inspired by what Lorca called *duende*. 'The magical quality of a poem,' said Lorca, 'consists in its always being possessed by the *duende*, so that whoever beholds it is baptised with dark water.' It's that dark water that Tony is immersed in, and he wants to take us with him, sink or swim.

Rose Gray and Ruthie Rogers

Rose and Ruthie asked me in 2003 to interview them for Vogue, *who wanted to do a feature about them. It had to be done quickly, which meant on the phone as they were in London and I was in New York. Rose died in February 2010.*

———•———

Becoming indivisible is the test of a partnership: Rodgers and Hammerstein, Morecambe and Wise, Posh and Becks. To those members of the English middle class who love Italian food, Ruthie Rogers and Rose Gray have become indivisible and a part of speech. You can describe a meal as 'sort of River Café' without having been to the restaurant or read a River Café cookbook. It's cooking with a simple vocabulary but a rich syntax, an approach to food that's an approach to life: the best ingredients, simply treated, honestly presented.

Ruthie and Rose look like sisters. They both have blonde/grey hair, fine Nordic features and eyes the colour of seawater—Rose from the Baltic, Ruthie the Mediterranean. They both have an art-school training, a gift for friendship and a personality that makes them Tuesday's children: full of grace. 'We're so different,' they chorus, but the differences are only of background: Ruthie's from an intellectual Jewish family, Rose from a family of 'Church of England conservatives'. 'What binds us and makes us like sisters,' says Rose, 'is that we have an almost identical understanding of Italian food. When we go to Italy, we fall in love with the same things, and when it comes to the business of our creative cooking we are so parallel and so complementary to each other.'

Which is what a conversation is like with the two of them, as they overlap and interrupt, seamlessly continuing each other's thoughts. They visit Italy several times through the year as the seasons change. Rose: 'You want to see what they're doing in Tuscany with the fennel, say; you want to go to the north in Piemonte to see the polenta season starting. Italy is so diverse in its regionality, there are many parts of Italy that Ruthie and I haven't been to. There are always going to be dishes from these regions that will be our new dishes...' And Ruthie picks up: 'You can go to Tuscany and go from one restaurant to another a hundred yards apart and even a basic recipe like pappa pomodoro (thick soup made of bread and tomatoes) they'll be making in a different way.' 'But you keep it simple,' says Rose. 'And search for interesting ingredients,' says Ruthie; 'people come to us now with new brands of beef, pigs, salads, organic eggs...'

They came to a love of Italian food through diverse but converging routes. Ruthie grew up in New York so it was South Italian food she was used to: 'tomato saucy, meatbally'. Her real introduction to Italian food was through travelling: 'I was so impressed the first time I went to Florence that you would have a bruschetta with olive oil and garlic on it, and a fish would come with a few herbs and olive oil and no thick cream sauce. Italian food had purity and lightness.'

She came to London to study graphic design at the London College of Printing and met Rose. 'A friend of mine took me over to the house of this amazing woman who was dealing with all these kids and she was cooking some huge couscous and looking fabulous—the whole scene was amazing—and then I lost contact with her and then it turned out when I met Richard (Rogers) that Rose and Richard had known each other, well you can carry on...' And Rose does: 'When I was at Guildford Art School, Richard was at Guildford Tech doing his A levels.' Laughter from both: 'Poor Richard,' says Ruthie. 'And,' Rose again, 'I met Dada, Richard's mother, who played a large part in both of our ideas about Italian food.' 'So when I met Richard,' says Ruthie, 'there was all this connection between us. I went to live in Paris with Richard when he went to do the Pompidou Centre, and Rose went to live in Italy.' 'We actually had seven or eight years when we didn't see much of each other but when we went to each other's houses we both noticed that the other cooked well.'

Like most of her generation—growing up in the sixties—Rose was influenced by Elizabeth David, but whereas most of her contemporaries leant towards David's *French Provincial Cooking*, Rose was drawn to David's *Italian Food* when it was published in paperback in 1963. 'It was the first Italian cookbook I owned. If you were interested in what was going on in Europe, or were a cook, or were a greedy person, Elizabeth David played such a huge role in educating the educated English. And Italy was a place that everyone went to, at that time it seemed the most modern and wonderful place to go—the films, the design—it just felt that that's where your spirit belonged.'

Rose started to cook professionally when a London friend, the Australian actress and Rocky Horror diva Little Nell Campbell, opened a club—Nell's—in New York. Nell wanted to serve some Italian snacks in the club and 'I thought of my friend Rose who cooked for fun, so I lured her to New York.' Rose discovered the joy of being paid and realised 'what I loved more than anything else was deciding what to cook and cooking it and I loved seeing people eating it and adoring it and I loved being so highly praised for doing what I suddenly realised I loved doing.' When she returned to London, Tuscany was becoming fashionable and Rose had developed a taste for running a restaurant. So had her friend Ruthie.

'At that time, 1987,' says Ruthie, 'Italian restaurants used to be opened by waiters not cooks…' 'With spaghetti bolognese and a cold boiled artichoke sitting on a trolley,' adds Rose. 'We both thought: why can't you have in London not only the kind of food you have in restaurants in Italy but the home cooking? And we wanted the theatricality of it—a stage that you set every day, twice a day.' 'And when we first opened,' says Ruthie, 'you walked across the stage—the kitchen—to get to your seat. You could see the actors, the people cooking. Even though it's changed, there's still that connection between audience and actors.'

The similarities between theatres and restaurants are close: you live to please and you please to live. Praise or blame, it's immediate, it's all in the present tense. You work during other people's leisure time, and you have time off when everyone else is working. You belong to a separate caste from the customers, and you feel gloriously detached from their humdrum daily routine. But restaurants—and sometimes theatres—are notoriously autocratic places to work, where chefs tyrannise their staff for no better reason than to pass on the abuse they received during their apprenticeships. 'We never worked in an environment where people shouted and yelled and bullied… Once we had a kitchen that was open, well, you have to behave,' says Ruthie.

The best restaurants, like the best theatres, are model societies, more than the sum of their parts. 'It all relates together,' says Ruthie, 'how important the people are cooking next to you, the waiters, everything has to come together and everybody behaving well for the same aim: we want people to come, and to leave happier than when they arrived.' Which is why the stupidest thing that could be said (and was) to Rose or Ruthie of The River Café is this: 'We could franchise this, you know.' You can't franchise the ability to make people happy.

If there's a model for the way that they run The River Café it's an appropriately Italian one: the family. 'When we started to think how we would run it,' says Rose, 'we thought along domestic lines, the way we raised our children—treating people as individuals. And we thought: this is like an enlarged dinner party, we'll get the waiters to help do such and such, we'll talk to the chefs about who's going to do what… We just treated it in the same way. At that time there were only four or five of us—like a small family—and we decided what we were going to cook and the way we cooked it, and even today with seventy-five staff we still have exactly the same procedures. We look in the fridge, we talk to the waiters, we discuss with the chefs…'

For two people who occasionally eat two lunches when they're on their Italian research trips, they're extraordinarily thin and lithe but wildly, not neurotically, energetic. They look much younger than their years, fine advertisements for the green adage, 'You are what you eat.' They cackle together at the thought of retirement or that either of them might be sitting around in a chair counting the takings. 'We'll die at our stoves,' says Rose.

Jocelyn Herbert

Jocelyn died in 2003. Seven years later, to celebrate setting up her archive at the Wimbledon College of Arts, I gave the inaugural Jocelyn Herbert Lecture at the National Theatre.

If I say that Jocelyn was a vitally important figure in the theatre of the last fifty years, you might think I'm merely expressing a personal preference. After all, directors who make public statements about theatre have a way of inflating their personal preferences into public manifestos. So if I say that Jocelyn Herbert changed the way in which we look at design in the theatre and the way in which we create it, you might think that I'm simply acting as an advocate for a much missed friend. You would be wrong.

I first met Jocelyn in the late 1960s through a friend who worked for many years as her assistant. She lived then—and for the rest of her life—in a small terraced cottage on the less smart side of Holland Park. Her house embodied her persona—spare, ascetic, simple. Her sitting room was presided over by a Matisse cut-out—a copy of *The Snail*—and a beautiful photograph of George Devine, whose spirit and values never left her. She had a rather godmotherly attitude to my career, encouraging me to develop my own taste, chiding me over some of my choices, and referring to the Royal Court Theatre as the 'Court' as if it were some distant lost paradise or fallen regime.

Jocelyn had been born into the theatre—at least in the sense that her father was a successful comic playwright, as well as being a journalist and MP. Her mother was a good painter and pianist, and Jocelyn was sent at the age of fifteen to Paris to learn to speak French, play the piano, and to paint at the studio of André Lhote, a Fauvist—later cubist—whose work even at this distance has a striking vigour.

In the theatre in Paris she was impressed by the work of the director Michel Saint-Denis. It was her first encounter with a theatre that seemed to take the art form seriously. A few years later Saint-Denis lost the funding for his Paris company, and he left France to start the London Theatre Studio in Islington, with the intention of developing the skills of actors, directors, designers and technicians, teaching them to understand how each contributed to the whole. The Studio later became the Old Vic School, and both schools brought to the British theatre an understanding of the importance of the text and its context, of improvisation, of mask work, of the importance of physical and vocal agility. Above all they took theatre seriously.

Saint-Denis recruited George Devine as his assistant and the design team, Motley, to run the design course. Motley was a trio—Margaret (always known as 'Percy') Harris, her sister Sophie, and Elizabeth Montgomery. Their intention, shared by Saint-Denis, was to create an approach to design in which meaning took precedence over decoration. Their aim was to clear the stage of unnecessary clutter. As Percy Harris said to me shortly before she died: 'We were reacting against fuss. Fuss and rabbit fur. Everything was so complicated, and it looked so complicated, and I don't know where they did their research, I suppose from paintings, but you get different views of paintings according to what type of life you live.'

The 'fuss' she referred to was painted scenery and clothes that bore no relation to reality or to any guiding idea of the look or purpose of a production. At the Old Vic, Percy told me, the actors used to go to pick out their costumes in the wardrobe, and the wardrobe master—an old man called Orlando—used to say: 'Would you like to have a nice clean pair of tights? Well, you can't have them.' The actors used to fight to get to the wardrobe first for the few good costumes on the rails.

And Motley thought the West End theatre was nonsense—lacking in any kind of belief in anything. 'Just froth,' said Percy, 'That's what we thought, but whether it was I don't know, but that was what we felt. There were no plays which really taxed one's intellect at all.' For Percy and her partners the modern theatre began with Edward Gordon Craig. This is from Craig's book *The Art of the Theatre*, a catechism for the rebirth of the theatre:

> The Art of the Theatre is neither acting nor the play, it is not scene nor dance, but it consists of all the elements of which these things are composed: action, which is the very spirit of acting; words, which are the body of the play; line and colour, which are the very heart of the scene; rhythm, which is the very essence of the dance.

George Devine used to go to see Craig often in France. For him, Craig's lesson was that everything on stage had to emerge from the play, that you didn't need to put everything on the stage, that you could select, that distillation was better than elaboration. In short, that less is more.

It was not until 1956, having spent a decade or so bringing up four children, that Jocelyn started her professional life, joining Devine's English Stage Company at the Royal Court Theatre with the Motley trio, painting the proscenium and the auditorium, 'hanging about on ladders', as Percy said. Jocelyn became a prop-maker and the following year Devine asked her to recreate the designs of Theo Otto for *The Good Woman of Szechwan*, which Brecht had given him permission to perform at the Royal Court with Peggy Ashcroft. For Jocelyn it was a collaboration with perfect synchronicity: she had fallen in love a few years earlier with the work of Bertolt Brecht, and now she fell in love with George Devine.

Jocelyn had first seen Brecht's work in Paris. When I asked her about it she said, 'I was in France and I heard that his company were playing in Paris, and I got a bus up to Paris and went to see *The Caucasian Chalk Circle*. I had to go without any shoes because I'd walked all round somewhere and got terrible blisters. And I thought I'd never seen anything as wonderful. It was partly the sheer beauty of it but also the play itself was so full of different meanings and saying so many different things… I think it was the sort of revolt against naturalism really that impressed me. What was wonderful with Brecht was, you know, everything was utterly real but utterly poetic as well.'

Brecht's company, the Berliner Ensemble, came to London in 1956 and had an enormous triumph with *Mother Courage*. I've talked to many people about that production in London. For most what it signified was that the theatre could be about something serious, that the theatre was being used for some kind of purpose unlike anything that they'd seen before, and whether that purpose was aesthetic or political didn't seem to be really definable. It was both, of course, because the two were indelibly linked together.

The importance of that production can't be exaggerated: the use of space, the sense of the power of the empty stage, the placing of a single chair, the grouping of the actors. Some British directors were so ravished by its perfection that they reproduced it with British actors, with the aid of the Berliner Ensemble Model Book in which productions were recorded in minute detail with photographs and copious notes. Coupled with the inert translation authorised by the autocratic Brecht Estate, the failure of these attempts to replicate the work of the Beliner Ensemble perfectly illustrated the fact that the aesthetic was inseparable from the politics. The film director Alan Parker once asked Ken Loach how he got such reality and honesty in his films. And Ken said: 'It's not to do with the How, it's to do with the Why.'

Jocelyn and George Devine took from Brecht both a philosophical basis—lucidity was all—and a cue for a visual style: white light, a simple stage, real objects, use of real materials in the costumes, the exposed lighting bars and the permanent surround. And Devine's policy of doing 'new plays as though they were classics and classics as though they were new plays' was a Brechtian tactic: it meant giving working-class characters the fully dimensional quality which the West End theatre had denied them while, at the same time, restoring a long-forgotten realism to Shakespeare and other classics.

At the Royal Court Jocelyn became a professional designer almost by accident. After recreating *The Good Woman*, she designed the British premiere of Ionesco's *The Chairs* and became a lifelong friend of Beckett after designing the first English-language production of *Endgame*, then the world premieres of *Krapp's Last Tape* and *Footfalls*, and the English premieres of *Happy Days* and *Not I*. Beckett said of her: 'She doesn't want to bang the nail on the head.'

She worked on Arnold Wesker's Trilogy, where she gave a lyricism to social observation, and gave a fluent and spare visual narrative to John Osborne's *Luther*. By the time of George Devine's death in 1965, a Royal Court ethos and aesthetic had been established. It was an amazing time, said Jocelyn. 'For a brief period our work, and our lives, had a centre.'

When I remember Jocelyn now, I remember her quiet, determined voice, her modesty, her frequent amusement at the stubbornness of those she most admired, and her face—which had the beauty of a gothic saint. For her, art was as much a way of looking at the world as of living your life. She was far from a puritan but everything she did was pure and it was beautiful. She was from a very English tradition, but her Englishness sat at ease with her cosmopolitanism. What do I mean by Englishness?—a quiet passion, a spare use of colour, an elegant line. Above all, clarity.

The last time I saw her in her studio she was surrounded by the silt of nearly sixty years' work in theatre—her designs and masks and photographs and memorabilia. She talked touchingly of Beckett, who taught her to play billiards. 'If I was rich,' she mused, 'I would have a huge room with a billiards table. I've always longed to have that...' And somehow she would have placed it perfectly—cues, balls, bright-green baize, with a grace and purpose that would have been planned but would have seemed spontaneous.

Jocelyn had a gift for organising space which made the commonplace seem mysterious and beautiful, and the mysterious and beautiful seem real. This is a poem that Brecht wrote in dedication to his friend Caspar Neher:

> The war separated
> Me, the writer of plays, from my friend the stage designer.
> The cities where we worked are no longer there.

When I walk through the cities that still are
At times I say: that blue piece of washing
My friend would have placed it better.

Patrick Marber

When Patrick's first collection of plays was published in 2004 he asked me to write the preface.

Patrick Marber has said that without me he wouldn't have become a playwright. This is a fiction. I no more made him a writer than the team of monks who left Lhasa to seek out the new Dalai Lama made a tiny baby into a spiritual leader. It was his destiny, just as it was Patrick's destiny to become a playwright.

When you run a theatre you depend on the luck of finding talented actors, directors, writers on your doorstep who are keen to have your support. It was part of my luck at the National Theatre to be on the spot when two remarkable plays by then unknown writers came into my hands.

The first was a play that I read when I should have been meeting President Havel in Prague at a performance of *King Lear* but was prevented by a snowfall that crippled London and paralysed Heathrow. I sat at home and read a vast play about the American Right, McCarthyism, Mormonism, Marxism, the Millennium, homosexuality, AIDS, God and angels: *Angels in America* by Tony Kushner. I knew halfway through the first page—a virtuoso monologue by the monstrous lawyer Roy Cohn—that I wanted to put the play on. It had wit, intellect, originality and the unmistakeable authority of a real writer's voice.

The second comet that flew in my direction was *Dealer's Choice*. I had been tipped off by the playwright, Nicholas Wright, who worked alongside me at the National Theatre as an adviser on repertoire and at the NT's Studio as a roving consultant and amanuensis. He has perfect pitch as a talent spotter so when he told me about a writer who was the 'real thing' I didn't have to be persuaded with a cattle prod to read the play.

I knew a little of Patrick Marber as a comic writer and performer on radio—*On the Hour* and *Knowing Me, Knowing You*—and on TV—*The Day Today* and *The Alan Partridge Show*. The shows satirised the earnest self-righteousness of populist current-affairs programmes and the nauseatingly vain, sycophantic, self-serving celebrity interviewers, spraying clichés over their interviewees like Grand Prix drivers with champagne. These days we've become inured to Alan Partridge; his satirical edge has been dulled by his real-life counterparts who have seamlessly merged with their satirical models.

There have been two occasions when I've had to stop driving because of a radio programme. On the first occasion I was listening to Joan Jara, the English wife of the Chilean folk singer, Victor Jara, who was tortured and killed by the Pinochet government, describing how she had identified his body—walking along the long corridors and dressing rooms of the football stadium in Santiago looking at the faces of corpses on floors, benches and tables. His broken hands—he was a guitarist—were what she recognised first. Her unemphatically factual delivery was unbearably moving and I was blinded by tears. The second occasion was the first time I heard *Knowing Me, Knowing You* and laughed so much that I was a danger to myself and a threat to other drivers. Alan Partridge was—and is—one of the great comic creations; that his co-creator should want to write a play for the National Theatre Studio I found vastly flattering.

As a first-time playwright, Patrick was hardly a stranger to dialogue and narrative. But sketch writing, whether it's for TV or stand-up comedy, is a different discipline to writing plays. The sketch writer has to start with an epigrammatic idea, sprint down a straight narrative track and cross the finish with a clinching punchline. The playwright, however, has to play a long game: be an expert at sleight of hand, juggle revelation against concealment, portray character through action rather than description, and keep an audience occupied in one place at one time.

You know with plays as you do with actors—and indeed directors and conductors—if the piece of work is in the hands of someone who knows what they're doing: the play or performance or production or concert has an assurance; someone is in charge. Orchestras can be inspired by some conductors and seem commonplace in the hands of others—'the masters of the brilliant wave' as James Galway calls them—just as some directors can animate a cast of actors while others, no matter how articulate and intelligent, seem unable to do more than direct the onstage traffic. So it is with plays. If you have to read a lot of plays you become an unforgiving judge: if the dialogue becomes flabby and generalised, the narrative meanders, the characters are unfocused and the meanings opaque; in short, if the author is unable to bring his orchestra in on the beat, then you become as impatient as Madame Defarge.

I knew from the opening page of *Dealer's Choice* that this was the work of a writer who knew what he was doing:

> STEPHEN *is sitting at a table in the restaurant, drawing.* SWEENEY *is in the kitchen preparing food.*
>
> *Kitchen.*
>
> *Enter* MUGSY.
>
> MUGSY. Evening, Sween.
>
> SWEENEY. All right, mate.
>
> MUGSY. Hey, Sween, this bloke I know won the lottery.
>
> SWEENEY. Oh yeah?
>
> MUGSY. Yeah, he lives on my street. Eight million quid.
>
> SWEENEY. Reckon he'll bung you a few?
>
> MUGSY. Nahh, he's a stingy bastard. He's bought a Ferrari. Takes his trouty old mum out for a spin. 'Cept it's up on bricks now, kids nicked the wheels.
>
> *Beat.*
>
> What I could do with eight million quid.
>
> SWEENEY. Lose it?
>
> MUGSY. Oh yeah? Call.
>
> MUGSY *tosses a coin.*
>
> SWEENEY. Heads.
>
> MUGSY *catches the coin and looks at it… heads.*
>
> MUGSY. Bollocks.
>
> *He hands the coin to* SWEENEY.
>
> SWEENEY. Business as usual.

It was terse, funny and revealing and, like all good plays and unlike fiction, was as much about the spaces in between the lines as the lines themselves. As they say of racehorses, you could see the breeding: Mamet out of Pinter, trainer and jockey Marber. And, like Mamet, Patrick wasn't making judgements about his characters; they occupied the grey zone, neither virtuous, nor malign, not noble but not terrible.

I read *Dealer's Choice* and saw it in a 'workshop' production at the NT Studio—the culmination of readings, improvisations and rehearsals directed by the author. Soon after seeing the play, I had a meeting with Patrick. I can't remember what I said to him. I probably pushed a row of adjectival barges out to sea: outstanding, funny, compelling, touching, skilful, mature. I may have been planning to suggest that we look for another director for the play, but I was—if not shrewd—opportunistic enough to recognise that if I had, Patrick would have politely withdrawn his play and taken it somewhere where they would let him direct it. He was, after all, a poker player.

I think at the time—1994—that Patrick was thirty, though as a friend says of him, 'He's always been thirty-nine', and there was something impressively grown-up about him. At a distance you might read into his stocky but slouchy build that he was an ex-footballer with a faint resemblance to one of the Portuguese team in the '66 World Cup, but close up his face was altogether too quizzical and thoughtful for a sportsman. That he was watchful, cautious, wary and tough might have been expected in a poker player (albeit one who had to be bailed out by his father in his early twenties), but the paradoxes were unexpected: he could be both diffident and determined, he would mumble discursively yet be wholly lucid, he would oscillate between trust and suspicion.

He had—and still has—a reputation for being a benign curmudgeon, earned by his Eeyorish habit of dolefully bemoaning his misfortunes, but it's a protective scepticism that conceals tenderness and a real capacity for love and friendship. What's more, it's an insulation against being hurt. No one who met Patrick with his then constant companion, his West Highland terrier, Riley, could have made the mistake of equating this droll if sometimes mournful man with the solitary and unfulfilled characters of his first play. Which is, of course, why he's a real writer.

And he had—rare among his generation—a love of the theatre. I had the wrong impression that he'd been an usher at the National Theatre (a profession with an illustrious heritage: from David Hare to Colin Firth to Matthew Bourne), but no, he'd been brought by his parents. 'I was a child when I saw your *Guys and Dolls*,' he said. (Well, eighteen.) His frequent visits to the theatre had given him an encyclopaedic knowledge of theatre and a sophisticated sense of technique in writing, acting, direction and design.

This is from my diary at the time:

> 4th February 1995. *Dealer's Choice* has started previewing. It's a
> marvellously enjoyable piece of work, not at all like a first play…
> Patrick's spent years looking at and thinking about theatre, but his TV
> training shows (virtuously) in his avoidance of long speeches. His mum

(who I encounter round every corner: 'Hello, I'm Mrs Marber') took him to the NT regularly as a child. He's exacting almost to a fault and is frustrated that the actors are never quite accurate enough for him. He finds it hard to trust them.

It's true about Patrick and actors—or was—but acting in a West End production of David Mamet's *Speed-the-Plow* may have made him more sympathetic to the sometimes almost alchemical process by which good actors arrive at a good performance. He can be exasperated when actors seem confused or obstinate, or wilfully head down a blind alley in their attempts to inhabit a character, demonstrating the truism that the only truth about 'The Method' is that there are as many methods as there are actors. To him it's so clear, it's all there in the text: meaning, intention, rhythm, nuance, pacing, pausing.

In this, as is other respects, he resembles David Mamet, who said: 'You can delineate the intention by correctly delineating the rhythm of the speech.' Patrick's writing, like Mamet's, asks of the actors that they follow the score and perform it without the intrusion of 'personality'. Mamet again: 'There is nothing we feel nothing about—ice cream, Yugoslavia, coffee, religion—and we do not have to add these feelings to a play. The author has already done that through the truth of the writing, and if he has not, it is too late.'

I commissioned another play from Patrick. It was to be for the National's 900-seat Lyttelton theatre—an auditorium that can swallow up productions like a Bermuda triangle. I believe that he got quite far with it: a yuppie reading group (reading *Middlemarch*) meet in a flat owned by one of them (something in the City); a car alarm goes off; they go outside to find a group of black youths trying to steal the car; they make a citizens' arrest, dragging the boys back into the flat. And then? It could have been a brilliant platform for a play about class, race, education, culture and crime. But I got *Closer* instead.

There are very few British plays (as opposed to plays in English) about sex: *Twelfth Night*, *Measure for Measure*, *A Midsummer Night's Dream*, *Private Lives*, *Look Back in Anger*, Rodney Ackland's *Absolute Hell*, David Hare's *The Blue Room*, Christopher Hampton's *Les Liaisons Dangereuses*, Tom Stoppard's *The Real Thing*. And... er? According to its author, *Closer* is about the 'shock of passion'. The shock of sexual passion is twofold: that you are able to feel any emotion so strongly and that pain is the inseparable partner of desire and jealousy.

It was said of *Closer* that it was about 'sexual politics', but it's a strength of the play that it's not. It's about sex. Politics is about generalities whereas sex, unless it's pornography, is, like art, all about specifics. *Closer* is extraordinarily specific about the minutiae of sex and the geometry of relationships. In the play sex is tender, romantic, loving, casual, intense, brutal, selfish, squalid, savage; a blessing and a curse. It's the underscoring of each life. 'Why is the sex so important?'

is the agonised cry of Anna to her partner when they're confessing their mutual infidelities. 'BECAUSE I'M A FUCKING CAVEMAN' screams Larry, the mild dermatologist.

The prurient would enquire what *Closer* had been 'based on', as if all art were disguised memoir. It's based on life, and I doubt if there was anyone who saw this play, young or old, gay or straight, man or woman, who didn't recognise its observations with painful and guilty recognition. The radical claim of its author—as far as the theatre is concerned—is that any play about a relationship is a lie if it doesn't encompass the sexual side.

Patrick told me of two women in their late sixties coming out of the auditorium in the interval of a preview of *Closer*, the last lines of the act still ringing in their ears:

LARRY. You like his cock.

ANNA. I love it.

LARRY. You like him coming in your face.

ANNA. Yes.

LARRY. What does it taste like?

ANNA. It tastes like you but sweeter.

LARRY. That's the spirit. Thank you. Thank you for your honesty. Now fuck off and die. You fucked-up slag.

Said the woman ruefully to her friend: 'I must have missed out on a lot in my youth.'

It was said of *Closer* that the play had echoes of Strindberg, but it's more that Strindberg had leaked into *Closer*, because with some prescience, shortly after *Dealer's Choice* had opened, Simon Curtis and Michael Hastings asked Patrick to do an adaptation for BBC TV of a nineteenth-century play about sex and class and the pain of living together, living apart and just plain living: *Miss Julie*. The third play in this collection is *After Miss Julie*: Marber after Strindberg.

In general, updating classics can be a minefield and a shift of period often seems to be no more than a meretricious fashion choice: is it to be Schiaparelli or Dior, Edwardian frocks or sixties miniskirts? Occasionally a shift of period enhances the original, clarifying status and occupation and removing a layer of thick varnish. Sometimes a really unexpected harmony occurs between past and present, and such is Patrick's version of *Miss Julie*.

The play is often revived in 'star' revivals—posh actress gets down and dirty with working-class actor—and almost invariably it lives down to expectations:

audiences go expecting fireworks and find candles on a birthday cake. Moving the action from Sweden of 1888 to England of 1945, as Patrick has done, solved several problems in this notoriously difficult play.

First, the action of the original is set on Midsummer Night, in Sweden the night in which darkness never falls, a night of carnival and sexual abandon when the world is turning upside down. Relocating the play to the July night of the Labour landslide victory (the setting of *Absolute Hell*) provided a brilliantly illuminating parallel which injected a sense of social and sexual liberation in a truthful and accessible context: Britain on the cusp of revolution. The signs of class distinction—speech and manners—become brilliantly clear, and the allure of the one class to another gathers a real sense of political as well as sexual momentum.

Second, the shift in period gives specific reference points for an English audience, enriched by our knowledge of the history of 1945 and the irony of living in another age ushered in with a Labour landslide. In addition there's the enjoyably familiar paradox of the owner of the house—a Labour peer—being an aristocrat whose class is threatened. And with the detail of the lonely girl being shuttled between her suicidal father and emancipated mother, Miss Julie's hysteria, which usually seems merely enervating, becomes engaging and plausible.

Thirdly, it eliminates another layer of distancing—that odd and unavoidable disjunction that comes of seeing foreign plays with foreign settings and names played with English dialogue, idiom and physical behaviour. And fourthly, Strindberg's electrifying but baggy play has been edited, shortened and reshaped to its advantage. What's more, another English dimension has been injected, one alien to the Swedish original: wit. It's a fine addition to the catalogue of plays written by the post-war generation of playwrights about the period before their birth. 'I have been unfaithful to the original,' says Patrick characteristically, 'but conscious that infidelity might be an act of love.'

To be a playwright as prodigiously successful—and young—as Patrick is enviable. What's hard is keeping going. A playwright has to endure the effect of living to please and pleasing to live, year after year after year, all the while avoiding the unenviable occupational hazards of putting the mind and the ego in jeopardy. I've no doubt that not only will Patrick survive, but that his best work lies ahead of him.

David Hare

This was written for the Cambridge Companion to David Hare *in 2007. It's the only thing I've ever written for an academic publication and a strange induction it was. No money changed hands and when it was published all the contributors sent each other messages congratulating themselves and each other on the fact that they'd been published. Notwithstanding the strangeness of the circumstances I was very happy to have an occasion to write about David and his work.*

Paul Scofield once wrote this to a friend of mine who'd been rash enough to ask him to give a lecture on the subject of acting. 'I have found that an actor's work has life and interest only in its execution,' he said. 'It seems to wither away in discussion, and become emptily theoretical and insubstantial…' If discussing acting is difficult—'writing on water', Garrick called it—imagine the folly of trying to describe directing, an activity of which audiences are largely unaware unless it's intrusively self-advertising, and which even its practitioners find hard to define and harder still to describe. It's something you do, like gardening and, like gardening, you only learn about it by doing it.

Directing is the process of understanding the meaning of a play and staging it in the light of that knowledge, underscored by a view of what the writer is trying to say and why. In the case of a play by David Hare the 'why' is as important as the 'what'—the politics and attitudes to class and gender are seamlessly woven into the writing. But even the most innocent of comedies reflects a view of the world that a director endorses or indicts by his choices in casting, design, costume, and performances: they demonstrate a view about how people live, how they behave, and how they are influenced. What do the characters earn? Where were they born? What do they believe in? Answering these questions is central to deciding how a director physicalises the world of a play and how the actors speak and move and dress.

Beyond that, as David Mamet has observed, 'choice of actions and adverbs constitute the craft of directing': get up from that chair and walk across the room. Slowly. Add to this the nouns 'detail' and 'patience' and the maxim 'Always remember tomorrow is not the first night', and you have said more or less all that can be said of the craft of directing.

In rehearsal the writer provides the actors with the territory to be explored and the director draws the map of the journey they are to take together. He or she encourages the actors to approach their project with the innocent optimism of new settlers, bound by the same social rules and sharing a common aim, and exhorts them to bury their egos for the good of the whole, however clamorous and individualistic they may be. The actors have to work to a common pulse, even if each chooses a different tempo. That pulse will always be derived from the play: water doesn't rise above its source. Hidden in the heart of every theatre director lies the desire to be an *auteur*. However, theatre directors cannot play God: they are negotiators, diplomats, mediators, suspended between the writer's need to impel the play forward and the actor's desire to stand still and create a character, obliged to interpret the blueprint, not to redraw it. They are the builders, not the architects.

Nevertheless the tension between the recognition of this truth and the desire to dispense with the architect remains, and it accounts for the fact that many directors are drawn to directing the classics exclusively, where the author is obligingly not present at rehearsals. With a new play there will always be a tension—more often than not a fruitful one—between the author and director. In spite of the obvious advantage of having the author present to ask for advice and refer to for meaning, and the obvious distinction between the roles of writer and director, there will always be an implicit (and sometimes explicit) competition for territory that has to be negotiated by both parties with a blend of self-effacement and self-assertion.

'The playwright has two alternatives,' said Tennessee Williams. 'Either he must stage the play himself or he must find one particular director who has the very unusual combination of actively creative imagination plus a true longing or even just a true willingness to devote his own gifts to the faithful projection of someone else's vision. This is a thing of rarity.'

Many playwrights direct their own work because they are fearful that their vision will be blurred or diluted when mediated through other hands. David is not one of these. He is a first-rate director, who became a writer when he ran his own theatre company because he wanted material to direct. His own productions of Trevor Griffiths' *The Party*, Christopher Hampton's *Total Eclipse* and Bernard Shaw's *Heartbreak House* possessed an exemplary and passionate lucidity. He directed his collaborations with Howard Brenton—*Brassneck* and *Pravda*—with a fearless bravura and, among the many productions of his own plays, *Plenty* stands out still as one of the most significant productions in the life of the National Theatre. Staged with a paradoxically lush austerity it provided theatrical images—and performances—that remain luminously vivid twenty-five years later.

David knows what the craft of directing is and what it demands of all parties, which begs the question of why, on most occasions in the last fifteen years, he has chosen not to direct his own work. The answer is probably a weariness with the business of bringing a play to life, the barter and the diplomacy involved, and perhaps a writerly desire to preserve his objectivity by avoiding the politics of the rehearsal room, watching the furnace but not putting his hand in it.

In his memoir *Acting Up*, he describes two kinds of director—the interventionist and the editor: 'Crudely, interventionists possess a vision of the work towards which they are, at all times working. The show is already conceived before they begin and they have an idea of the production which they need the actors to help them achieve. They have, in short, a Platonic show in their heads. Editors on the contrary work pragmatically, looking all the time at what they are offered, refining it constantly, and then exercising their taste to help the actor give their best.' The two directors who have directed the bulk of his work in recent years are Howard Davies and myself. Howard he categorises as an interventionist, me as an editor. The truth, in my experience, is somewhere in between.

The first play of David's that I directed was *The Great Exhibition* at Hampstead Theatre Club in 1972. After that—or was it because of that?—he directed his own work until he wrote *The Secret Rapture* in 1988 and offered it to me when I had just started to run the National Theatre. I was directing an ill-advised revival of a production of Ben Jonson's *Bartholomew Fair* which I had staged successfully at Nottingham Playhouse and I asked Howard Davies to direct *The Secret Rapture*. Was it an 'interventionist' production? Possibly, in that the stage was dominated by a large and very beautiful oak tree and haunted by the ghostly presence of one of the characters—neither of which gesture was indicated in the script.

But is this any more interventionist than the design that Bob Crowley and I evolved two years later for *Racing Demon*, when we presented the play in the Cottesloe theatre on a raised stage in the shape of a cross that ran the length of the auditorium? No walls, no decoration, just the actors and furniture and light. This was our response to a play which had a series of soliloquies in which the characters addressed God, and had twenty-three scenes set in streets, housing estates, a bedroom, a kitchen, a study, the garden of a bishop's palace, the lounge of the Savoy Hotel, a cathedral, the General Synod and more, and yet was an intimate and warm-hearted study of failed love—of God as well as man—as much as an exploration of an institution.

In all David's plays the sense of place is a prime ingredient. No playwright creates more evocative rooms: whether they're in echoing country houses or on factory floors, cheap two-room conversions or basements glowing dimly in the London blackout, they share a sharp density of atmosphere. The tattiest seaside boarding house or the emptiest provincial nightclub has a desolate magic about it, just as it would in a novel by Graham Greene or Patrick Hamilton.

The world of *Racing Demon* is one of dirty South London streets, bicycle clips, Goon Show jokes and Tony Hancock tapes, empty churches and clarinet lessons, devoid of metropolitan swagger and shot through with a sense of loss. 'Is everything loss?' says the defeated Lionel Espy in the last scene. An epilogue follows, a sort of optimistic epiphany, as Frances imagines herself flying off to the sun:

> I love that bit when the plane begins to climb, the ground smooths
> away behind you, the buildings, the hills. Then the white patches. The
> vision gets bleary. The cloud becomes a hard shelf. The land is still
> there. But all you see is white and the horizon.
>
> And then you turn and head towards the sun.

Bob Crowley and I matched the sense of hope with a glare of white light, an image that we thought of as both literal and transcendental. Others saw it as 'interventionist' direction.

Working with Bob begins slowly in casual discussion, aided by sketches, anecdotes, photographs, and reference books. The design always starts as a tone of voice and of colour, formless as a moving shadow, and through discussion and illustration, the play starts to come off the page and acquires a three-dimensional shape. It's at this stage that there's the danger of imposing specious order, of tidying everything up to conform with a design conceit. The director has to guard against this by continuing to ask the questions: 'What's this for?', 'What does this mean?'

In the five plays of David's that I've worked on with Bob we've always tried to find a staging that allows the physical world to breathe in the mind, that conjures up the required environment but dispenses with walls and ceilings and decorative elements. We weren't inventing a style, rather inheriting what Caspar Neher did with the Berliner Ensemble, and Harley Granville-Barker and, later, Jocelyn Herbert did at the Royal Court Theatre and John Bury at the Royal Shakespeare Company: making scenery expressive and metaphorical, rather than decorative and literal. We wanted everything we placed on stage to be specific and real, while being minimal. As Granville-Barker said: 'If the designer finds himself competing with the actors… then it is he that is the intruder and must retire.'

The second play of the Hare Trilogy, *Murmuring Judges*, required us to find a way of unifying the three universes of the judiciary, the police and the prison system. Bob devised a beautiful unifying device—a metal floor onto which a vast metal pillar descended that became the hub of the three worlds. With the help of giant projections on the back walls of the Olivier theatre, we sped from the lobby of the High Court to a police charge room to a prison hall to the auditorium of the Royal Opera House with vertiginous ease. We defined the space with furniture, light fittings and actors, sometimes combining the three worlds in a multiple image only achievable in the medium of theatre—simultaneous action in separate areas of the stage occurring in the same time continuum. Probably the weakest of the Trilogy from the author's point of view, from the director's and designer's it was the most exhilarating to stage.

With *Amy's View* we had the problem of staging a four-act play that for three of its acts was set in the spacious drawing room of a large house near the Thames owned by the widow—a successful actress—of a painter, and then it moved to a poky dressing room in a West End theatre. It set out to establish, and subvert, the upper-middle-class world of the four-act 'country house' play. The stage directions at the beginning of the play read as follows:

> *The living room of a house in rural Berkshire, not far from Pangbourne. The year is 1979. To one side there is a large summer-house-cum-verandah, full of plants. At the back, a door leading to a hall and staircase. The room has an air of exceptional taste, marked by the modern arts movement of the 1920s and '30s… This was once the home of an artist, Bernard Thomas, and all round the room is evidence of his work, which is rather Cézanne-like and domestic in scale.*

And more.

It's a very specific description and one that we decided to distil into its essentials rather than attempt to reproduce. For instance, we thought that if the paintings were put on the wall the audience would be distracted by considerations of what school of painting they belonged to and how good they were, and they would become dominant objects that upstaged the actors. Our solution was to have barely perceptible ghostly images on the walls of the room and to make those walls of gauze, relying on the audience to imagine the paintings. By making the walls diaphanous and semi-translucent, the room suggested the beauty and the resonance prescribed in the stage direction, and dispensed with the heavy baggage of stage 'reality'—cornices, ceilings, door frames, light fittings.

The end of *Amy's View*, again a sort of epiphany, provided a different sort of challenge. We had to change the set from the dressing room to the stage of the theatre and then suggest that we were backstage just before the opening of a play. In the rehearsal draft of the play there was an explicit stage direction of the setting of the play—a shipwreck had taken place, spars and tattered sails remained, and there was the suggestion of a desert island—and the first line of the play was spoken: 'Who's there, tell me who's there.' Bob and I argued for a simple and, we thought, more expressive theatrical gesture.

Of this moment David said to me, only half-facetiously, that he expected something brilliant of me, a *coup de théâtre*. We decided to reverse the image, so that the actors walked away from us upstage rather towards us. We wanted to create a gesture, innocent of technology, that would highlight the vulnerability of two actors walking on a bare stage towards an imagined audience. It had to be an image that would draw together the play's use of theatre as a metaphor for the endurability (and vulnerability) of human relationships and at the same time act as an assertion of the power of theatre itself. And it had to avoid being an attention-grabbing piece of bravura staging. We achieved it in the simplest possible way with the sound of breaking waves, two huge pieces of white silk, music and lighting. The magic—as with most things in the theatre—was in the timing.

In essence what Bob and I have tried to do consistently is to find a physical style for presenting the plays that exploits the 'theatreness of theatre', the poetic property of theatre in which everything is metaphorical, everything stands for other things—a room stands for a house, a group of people for a society—and the audience fills in the gaps with their imagination.

The end result—the *mise-en-scène*—is always the result of a dialogue, a dialectic even, between designer, author and director. There is generally a difference of emphasis rather than substance and only on one occasion—directing *Skylight*— have the differences become fundamental. The play was designed by John Gunter, with whom I've worked many times, and in our early discussions we decided that we would like to stage the play (in the Cottesloe theatre) in the round or as a traverse production with the audience on both sides of the action. I've done other productions like this—*The Voysey Inheritance*, *Vincent in Brixton*, for instance—and I was attracted to the potential intensity of the emotional debates happening within touching distance of the audience. David was opposed to this. He repeatedly stressed his desire for the set and the staging to be 'painterly'. He had written, as always, very specific physical details which he wanted translated into a stage reality. So we created this, every detail of Kyra's life, from the age of the frying pan to the choice of the books on the shelves, with scrupulous accuracy, making a painterly whole that fulfilled the author's description:

> *A first-floor flat in north-west London. There is a corniced plaster ceiling and underneath the evidence of a room well lived in: patterned carpets which have*

worn to a thread and a long wall of books. The kitchen area at the back of the
room looks cluttered and much used.

Apart from moving the kitchen area, where much of the action was set, downstage, nearer the audience, we conceded to David's views without regrets. This,
from Tennessee Williams, should be the director's credo: 'Just as it is important
for a playwright to forget certain vanities in the interest of the total creation of
the stage, so must the director.' And its corollary, from Howard Brenton: 'Knowing when to speak and when to shut up is nine-tenths of being a playwright in
the theatre.' It's an article of faith with David who, after the initial close examination of the text, invariably retires from the rehearsal room for a week or ten
days. It allows the actors and director an opportunity to take 'ownership' of the
play, and to stumble and shuffle around with scripts in their hands free of the
judgement of the author. The play gets staged during this period; in my case an
empirical process without too many explicit instructions. The choreography of
a scene should emerge from character and narrative rather than from precon-
ceived design.

For a man who is never uncertain of his opinions and never shy of expressing
them, David is a tactful collaborator. He acknowledges that there is an area of
choosing actors where judgement is subjective and occasionally, but only occasionally, our tastes differ. Actors in his plays need to be technically adept, be witty,
intelligent and respond to his rhythms. His dialogue is deceptively non-natu-
ralistic; it resists paraphrase and actors can sometimes find it surprisingly difficult
to learn. Like all good playwrights, while he simulates natural conversation, his
dialogue is highly structured and highly musical. There is nothing that pains him
more than an actor who is unable to 'hear' the rhythms.

No less painful to him are actors who are unable to get his jokes. They're sometimes elusive on the page. None of us in rehearsal for *Murmuring Judges* imagined
that this exchange—between a Home Secretary and a High Court Judge (Cuddeford)—would be a literal show-stopper at the top of the second act.

> CUDDEFORD.…(*He nods, suddenly incisive.*) Now it's *this*, it's this sort of
> thing, Home Secretary…
>
> HOME SECRETARY. Kevin…
>
> CUDDEFORD. What would you call it? This slow *silting* of tradition, this
> centuries-long building-up, this accumulation of strata, which makes
> the great rock on which we now do things. It's infinitely precious.
>
> *The* HOME SECRETARY *frowns.*
>
> HOME SECRETARY. Yes, but it must also be open to change.
>
> CUDDEFORD. *Open.*

He says it enthusiastically.

HOME SECRETARY. It must not become hidebound.

CUDDEFORD. Hidebound?

HOME SECRETARY. Yes.

CUDDEFORD. Small chance of that! (*He leans forward, sure of himself.*) Remember, all the time judging brings you in touch with ordinary people. In our courts. We see them every day. Ordinary, common-as-muck individuals. Some of them quite ghastly, I promise you that. (*He nods.*) This makes us alert to public opinion. We're closer to it, perhaps, than you think .

HOME SECRETARY. Are you?

CUDDEFORD. It's reflected in the way we sentence. Everyone claims it's our fault if we sentence too high. But the tariff for rape...

HOME SECRETARY. I know...

CUDDEFORD. ...has shot up from what?

HOME SECRETARY. I know this...

CUDDEFORD. ...Maybe eighteen months deferred to over five years. It's not at *our* wish. It's because we have listened to what the public, at least the female part of it, wants us to do. (*The* HOME SECRETARY *is smiling, familiar with this argument.*)

HOME SECRETARY. Yes, I admit. But it's a rare exception. There are figures from Germany. Did you read those? (CUDDEFORD *frowns.*)

CUDDEFORD. Germany? No.

HOME SECRETARY. I sent them over. I circulated all High Court judges.

CUDDEFORD. I read little from Germany.

He turns to SIR PETER, *diverting, but the* HOME SECRETARY *is not letting him off the hook.*

Like most judges, I have no time to read, off the case. Maybe, if I'm lucky, a thriller.

HOME SECRETARY. There they've reduced all prison sentences radically, by up to one-quarter, even one-third, without any effect on the criminal statistics.

CUDDEFORD *looks at him warily.*

CUDDEFORD. Really? Germany?

HOME SECRETARY. The same is true in Sweden.

CUDDEFORD. Sweden? (*He turns to* SIR PETER.) Peter, had you
heard this?

SIR PETER. No. No, actually. (*He looks down, feeling himself on thin ice.*)
Word hadn't reached me.

CUDDEFORD. It hadn't reached me either. (*He frowns.*) I think it's to do
with the mail.

The effectiveness of this exchange in performance illustrates a maxim of David's:
'If the audience are with you for the first half, you have ten minutes for free at
the beginning of the second.' The 'for free' passages in his plays contain some
of his most exhilarating and skilful comic writing: the Savoy Hotel scene in *Racing
Demon*, Tom's post-coital monologue in *Skylight*, Esme's story about her
fictional nursing career in *Amy's View*.

His jokes are almost invariably effective in performance; if they fail they are
honed, replaced or cut. He is never unaware that in writing for the theatre the
words on the page are only half the story. He places jokes judiciously at the
beginning of his plays—'bumsettlers', he calls them—which allow the audience
to feel that they're being let into the play, that they can be assured that they're
in the hands of a writer who is aware that the point of theatre is that the audience
and the actors occupy the same space and time.

At the core of every play of David's is a debate and in order to present a debate
it's necessary to present two sides to an argument. Without debate any form of
political play—and his plays are indelibly political—becomes frozen in polemic.
In all his plays Hare shows that he possesses the fiction-writer's Philosopher's
Stone: the ability to empathise with and to create characters wholly opposed to
his view of the world and to endow them with life and vibrancy: Lambert le
Roux in *Pravda*, Marion in *The Secret Rapture*, Tom in *Skylight*, Victor Mehta in *A
Map of the World*, the Bishop of Southwark in *Racing Demon*, Frank Oddie in
Amy's View.

In the plays of the Trilogy, the scenes in which there is a confrontation between
two opposing characters embodying two conflicting ideologies emerged late in
the writing process: they were written after readings of a rough draft of each play
in the National Theatre Studio. It was part of the process of directing the plays
to participate in the readings and the discussions that followed them. In each
case the reading was an essential step towards evolving a bringing together of the
themes of the play. In terms of the 'music' of the plays and their themes and
meanings, these scenes are essential: they are what David refers to as the '*scènes
à faire*'.

It's part of the joy of directing his work that there is a sense of inevitability about these substantial dialectical encounters which detonate with such satisfying eloquence and emotional force. And it's part of the joy too to collaborate with a writer who has the ability from time to time to surprise himself with his advocacy of a life far removed from his own. Take this wonderful defence of the ordinary by the young evangelist, Tony, in *Racing Demon*:

> Like everything else in England it turns out to be a matter of class. Educated clerics don't like evangelicals, because evangelicals drink sweet sherry and keep budgerigars and have ducks in formations on their walls. (*Nods, smiling.*) Yes, and they also have the distressing downmarket habit of trying to get people emotionally involved. (*Stares at them.*) You know I'm right. And—as it happens—I went to a grammar school, I was brought up—unlike you—among all those normal, decent people who shop at Allied Carpets and are into DIY. And I don't think they should always be looked down on. And tell me, please, what is wrong with ministering to them?

It's a voice not often heard in his plays, a voice that emerges from his childhood; pure Bexhill-on-Sea.

He has a very considerable knowledge of actors and of their processes (even more so since his adventure in performing his own solo show *Via Dolorosa*). Occasionally he becomes impatient with actors who appear to be treading water, exploring character at the expense of playing a scene, and on occasions we have argued about the need to intervene (his instinct) against the need to let an actor find their way (my instinct). Above all he's aware that the actors have to mine their emotions—a sometimes untidy and haphazard process—and that the director's most important job is to enable them to do this successfully. And he's aware that sometimes the absence of the playwright is as important as his presence.

David understands the ecology of theatre—how difficult ensembles are to maintain, how anxiety is actors' daily bread, how necessary it is for leading actors to assert their leadership. In the early stages of rehearsal when the play is anatomised and eviscerated by the actors and director scene by scene, line by line, word by word, he's an exemplary companion: curious to see how actors respond to what he's written, curious too to discover whether he has written the play he thought he had. At this stage he's generous, droll, entirely collaborative, collegiate even, swapping advice and taking suggestions: Do we need this line? Could this line be better? Is this speech too long? Do you mean to say this? Then as the performance draws closer the easy relaxation declines into tension, the body becomes taut as a wire, the skin becomes almost translucent, the knuckles become white and the notes hail down on the director by fax or email, voluminous, highly detailed, specific, remorseless, runthrough after runthrough, preview after preview, until the first night and then, as in silence after a storm, you can hear the dust falling between the walls.

At the first performance, with inspiring courage, David sits in the body of the audience listening to them as much as to the actors. Subsequently, after this bloom of boldness, the fear returns and he watches the show curled in a foetal position in the stage manager's box, or crouched behind the back-row seats. Nevertheless, however hermetic and paranoid he appears, he's always ready, if not eager, to know what the objections are to the play and production, whether it's the writer's job or the director's to fix the problem or, as he puts it, is it 'him' or is it 'me'?

When David asked me to direct *Racing Demon* I asked him what he thought I'd bring to it. 'Another point of view,' he said. What this point of view consists in is probably a stubborn persistence to examine fiction against reality. Is this truthful? How does this measure against my experience of the world? These are questions that I ask of a writer just as I ask of an actor, an invitation to examine the only model available to us: Is this what you would do in real life? 'He and I are well suited,' he writes in *Acting Up*, 'playing to each other's strengths. People usually said that it was because I was romantic and overreaching, whereas Richard was careful and classic.'

No director of his work can ignore Hare's romanticism: it runs like an artery through all his work. It's partly expressed in a belief in the possibility of fulfilled love and in its redeeming power. Partly too in the belief—a far from naive one— that things can be changed, that it's possible to create a better life, and that Britain—or more particularly England—in the post-war period has squandered the opportunity to do so by deceit, cowardice, complacency and greed. 'There will be days and days and days like this,' says Susan Traherne at the end of *Plenty*. Of course it's ironic, but then again it's not: the hope is real.

If a romantic view is always present in his work, so too is a political one. The belief in the possibility of radical change, of revolution, in his early work has not decayed with the death of socialism into a cynical belief in the immutability of man. His plays remain concerned with social justice, with the question: how should you live your life? In its public form, expressed in the Trilogy, the questions were asked of our public institutions: How does a good person change people's lives for the better? Can an institution established for the common good avoid being devoured by its own internal struggles and contradictions? Is man a social animal interested in justice, in equality, in love? It's a moral view but for all his mordant criticism, he's far too self-aware to become a Shavian moralist. He has the pen of a polemicist but the soul of a romantic.

If his appetite for moral debate and enquiry remains undiminished, so too does his love—unquestionably romantic—for the medium of theatre itself. In its communal aspect—its ability to tell stories to a live audience—and its indissoluble reliance on the human form and human voice, it acts a model of social possibilities.

The director Jonathan Kent, who knows David and me well, often says, particularly when we're bickering, that we're like an old married couple. It's not a bad image of the relationship between a director and author. Directors are ever hopeful of making a successful marriage of actor and character, of text and design, of play and audience. They have to be dogged yet pliable, demanding yet supportive. And if this sounds like a prescription for a perfect marriage partner, it's because it is.

Charles Wood

Charles asked me to write this preface when a new edition of his plays was published in 1999.

You could call Charles Wood a playwright, a poet and a painter. The playwright speaks for himself on the stage and on the screen; the poet is revealed in the text through the repeated rhythms, the hint of rhyme, the stylised translation of conversation, and in the emergence of an idiosyncratic and obsessional voice; the painter is latent in the stage directions: indelible images of a sandhill and a tank in the desert; a decorated Indian elephant; a small Eurasian girl holding the hand of a Malaysian rubber planter in a clearing in the jungle while a record of a British nightclub singer plays on a wind-up gramophone; a moonlit soldier stumbling through a perpetual night under the burden of his full kit, a rough beast slouching towards Bedlam.

The work is not easy to perform. It's hard for actors to find naturalness within dialogue that is so highly distilled and so insistently singular, and it takes time, imagination and confidence to allow his scenes to realise their full potential. There's a remarkable scene in *Jingo* (which I directed unsuccessfully in 1976) at the end of the play: the Brigadier responsible for the failure of the British to defend Singapore demands that an English woman gives him a spanking as punishment. Only after the play had been playing for some weeks was the full potency of this tragicomic scene realised—the dismal demise of the British Empire, embodied in the childlike demand of an upper-class Englishman to be smacked on his bare bottom with the back of a pearl-handled hairbrush, became eerily touching and uncomfortably resonant.

Charles's writing invariably describes closed societies—the army, the British Empire, the theatre—all having their private languages, their peculiar customs, and all steeped in an irreducible Englishness. But the consuming preoccupation of this humane and gentle man is the activity that devours humanity and gentility: war. As with Wilfred Owen, it is the pity of war that he is concerned with, but it is also the glamour—the weapons, orders, insignia, regalia, shoulder flashes, scarlet tunics, cap badges, ranks, battle honours, regimental history, and the private syntax of men amongst men. And the horror—the mud, the blood, the brains guts limbs and lives that get shed in foreign fields far from home. And before the confusion, folly and fear of battle, the strutting neatness, cleanness, pomp, order, hierarchy and absurdity of the soldier's life in peacetime.

Charles served for three years with the 17th/21st Lancers, which provided him with the seam to mine his raw material, but perhaps as importantly both his parents were actors. Like soldiers, actors are veterans of many ill-conceived campaigns, are ever-sceptical of the leaders who have dragged them there, and they develop a carapace of wit and covert disdain of their superiors to conceal their fear and their boredom.

Charles's seam is not so much warfare as the profession of soldiering, and the point of being a soldier is to break the ultimate taboo—the point is to destroy the enemy on our behalf, to kill people. This apparently self-evident truth is hidden from the recruit by the seductive panoply of uniforms, gold braid, pipes, drums, marching, medals, and the promise of adventure. Charles writes lovingly of all this, but his invariable conclusion is that, for all the chivalry and courage, no war, just or unjust, can be acquitted of bestiality: the means never justify the ends. His indictment of war is invoked like a litany: it isn't worth it, it isn't worth it, it isn't worth it.

He shows how war corrupts all relationships, between country and country, man and man, man and woman, but he also shows how irresistibly alluring it can be to young men and older politicians. There is no contemporary writer who has chronicled the experience of modern war with so much authority, knowledge, compassion, wit and despair, and there is no contemporary writer who has received so little of his deserved public acclaim.

John Osborne has always been credited with changing the course of British drama with *Look Back in Anger*, a play that now seems, for all its abrasive, self-pitying, iconoclastic rhetoric, to look back, not in anger, but with a fiercely desperate nostalgia. If John Osborne was always looking forward to the past, Charles Wood has always looked the present in the face through the prism of the decline of the British Empire, the legacy of the First World War, the vainglory of the Falklands War, or the immutable stalemate of Northern Ireland.

John Osborne and Charles were friends, both actors, both half in love with the tatty shabbiness of backstage life. If I had to make an unenviable choice between the two of them, I would say that it was Charles who has been responsible for the theatrical revolution, but one that has barely begun to take place. The best play to emerge in the nineties, in my view, is Tony Kushner's *Angels in America*. It is fearlessly ambitious in form and in content, in its determination to exploit the medium, and its refusal to accept the conventions of naturalism—in speech and in staging. In form it attempts everything that Charles attempted in his play about the Indian Empire, *H*, in the sixties, but Charles was unlucky: he was ahead of his time, and he never found the collaborators who could match the breadth of his epic vision.

I can't help feeling guilty that I haven't done more to argue the case for Charles's work in the theatre, which is the only court that means anything to a playwright. Why? Fashion and faint-heartedness, I suppose; his subject matter is so uncompromisingly painful and tells such uncomfortable truths about mankind—or at least about men. I did direct a film of a screenplay of his: *Tumbledown*, about the Falklands War. A friend of mine sent me a letter he'd received from a distinguished military historian complaining about the film. 'I am all for attacking the establishment,' said the letter, 'but I am choosy about who does it.' I'm choosy too, and I am grateful that Charles has been there to challenge and disturb the orthodoxies and theologies of those who sent soldiers to war, and to chronicle the suffering, the stoicism, the heroism and the folly, not only of those who have done the fighting, but also those who have had to pick up the pieces afterwards.

Alan Bennett

I was asked by Cameron Mackintosh to write about Alan—'a few hundred words, dear'—when I directed a musical based on Alan's film script for A Private Function.

———•———

The test of a writer's fame is the extent to which their work becomes part of the currency of everyday language. To say that something is 'very Alan Bennett' is as common a part of everyday speech as 'Dickensian' or 'Orwellian'. What we mean when we describe something as 'very Alan Bennett' is that it is droll, sharp, overheard and unexpected—like the woman who a friend of mine caught discussing a play she'd just seen: 'How did you like it?' asked her friend. 'Alright, if you like laughing.'

Alan Bennett's personality is on show everywhere: there is no playwright who is so liked by the public, so familiar and, like Noël Coward, so quintessentially English. And, like Coward, no other playwright has made his writing such a forceful, forthright channel for his own sensibility. What is that sensibility? Well, it's paradoxical. He's a diffident, even modest man, but bears out his axiom that there's no such thing as false modesty: all modesty is false. He has nothing to be modest about: he's prodigiously gifted and prolific. He's also an extraordinarily nice man, although he recoils from the description: 'I'm just as bad as the rest of them, only I don't like to show it.' He's not, of course.

Although he's shy, uncomfortable in large gatherings and allergic to self-promotion, no writer in this country is more easily recognised by his voice and his boyish features. He has been famous since the early 1960s when *Beyond the*

Fringe made a star of him as well as Peter Cook, Jonathan Miller and Dudley Moore. Even though he's a very private and reticent man it's hard to think of another writer who would have answered—even if true—to a question about his sexual orientation: 'I'm like a man dying of thirst in the Sahara being asked if he'd prefer Perrier to Malvern water.' He's publicly courageous too—turning down a doctorate at Oxford to protest the creation of a Rupert Murdoch Chair of Language and Communication. 'It's like creating a Saddam Hussein Chair in Peace Studies,' he said.

He's extraordinarily intelligent and learned—in some ways the epitome of book-ish high culture—and his work is intellectually ambitious. Even his most complicated ideas about art are unfailingly communicated in a language that is accessible without patronising and, what's more, full of jokes. He has an unfail-ing eye and ear for the minutiae of ordinary life—the scraps of speech overheard on the bus or in the supermarket. His literary voice is universally recognisable: it's the voice of the mildly oppressed or suppressed, the silent victims of petty domestic tyranny (mostly women), the murmurs of lives not quite realised.

His spoken voice is as recognisable as his literary one: indelibly Yorkshire, it pro-claims identification with his background. He was born in Leeds, his father a butcher, his mother the dearly loved, mildly exasperating figure whose compli-cated household routines, eye for class-giveaways, surrealistic leaps of logic and, later, her Alzheimer's, inform so much of his writing. When he went to Oxford and stayed on as a lecturer in Modern History, he chose (and it was an uncom-mon choice then) not to change his accent, a decision that speaks of an honesty, a desire not to break faith with his past.

It also speaks of his feeling of being an intruder in an unreal world: 'I somehow regarded the nightly experience of dining in hall as a kind of theatre, a theatre in which the undergraduates were the audience and the actors were the dons...' It's hard to be a writer in this country and not write about class and, for Alan, given that 'common' was his mother's deadliest insult, impossible. He writes like a spy observing the nuances of class distinction from outside—those grada-tions between working, upper-working, lower-middle, middle-middle and so on that inform all British society. He's as brilliant at mimicking old-buffer-speak, literary mandarin-speak, don-speak, Bloomsbury-speak—those who 'speak properly'—as he is with the speech of the people he grew up with.

His plays about spying are clearly an attempt to settle his ambiguous feelings about England—of affection and identification, but at the same time alienation. Just as his plays about royalty are attempts to reconcile his contempt for defer-ence with a fascination with authority and power. He's always been a political writer, not in an obvious ideological sense, but in his concern with the way peo-ple live and the way that politics shape people's lives. The effect of the creation of the Welfare State in the aftermath of the war and the subsequent decline of its values is a constantly recurring theme. *A Private Function* is an example of that. He's always argued that the state institutions of health and education are deficient not so much in funding or efficiency but in heart. Life exists in all the things that politics isn't: family, friendship, love, sex.

Alan has a painterly approach to writing: he returns to the same subjects frequently. I first met him when he was in the grip of an obsession with Kafka. He sent me a typescript marked with ink blots, crossings-out and corrections in an elegant calligraphic hand. 'I wonder if you can make anything of this,' he said. It was a film called *The Insurance Man*, the insurance man being Franz Kafka, played in our BBC film by a fledgling actor called Daniel Day-Lewis. The companion to the film was a farce called *Kafka's Dick* which ended in Heaven at a never-ending samba party presided over by God. 'I'll tell you something,' says Kafka in the last line of the play, 'Heaven is going to be hell.'

Marlon Brando

I wrote this for the Guardian *shortly after Brando died in 2004.*

A friend of mine had a framed black-and-white photograph of Marlon Brando hanging on the wall in her hallway for many years: Stanley Kowalski, body curved sinuously, arms folded across sweat-stained grey T-shirt, hands pushed defensively under biceps, eyes direct and challenging. A few weeks ago, on the day that Brando died, the picture fell from the wall, breaking the glass.

It wouldn't be much of an exaggeration to say that for my generation of would-be actors Brando was a saint—and I don't mean a secular one. We revered him, genuflected before his image, scavenged for anecdotes of his life, attempted to imitate him, attempted to be him. I even possessed a sacred relic—a few frames filched from a 16mm copy of *On the Waterfront*, which I kept in my wallet along with two unused condoms for many years.

Even though he gave very few performances in which he didn't seem to be taking his revenge on the studios or the director or the audience or whatever malign force he could find to blame, I still regard Brando as the best film actor ever. He was mercurial, feline, melancholy, witty and, like all great actors, androgynous. He had an almost mystical authority, the beauty and sexual promise of a Caravaggio youth, dangerous to men and women, gay and straight. For us, in the early sixties, he showed what Keats had meant: beauty was truth, truth beauty; that was all we knew and needed to know. That I am now disappointed by his waywardness, selfishness, laziness, greed, misogyny,

80

meanness of spirit and disdain for his genius, does nothing to diminish the fire of my passion.

Each age defies knowledge of evolution: it imagines that its revolutionary ways of seeing will endure perpetually. When Brunelleschi and Masaccio invented perspective in the early-fifteenth century they were as certain that an artistic limit had been reached as the passengers on the first railway trains were that their bodies would disintegrate if they went any faster than thirty miles an hour, or as modernists were that all other 'isms' in art would become redundant. But each generation comes to regard yesterday's novelty of vision as today's archaism. Acting is no less immune to such creationist theology.

Brando was my discovery of perspective. He showed me that people reveal their characters as much in the details of their gestures and posture as by what they say or—as importantly—don't say. If it seems odd now that people couldn't see perspective before Masaccio, that it had to be invented, it seems odder still that actors, engaged in a craft dedicated to imitating nature, should need to discover naturalism when it was all about them. Couldn't actors before Brando *see* that people didn't behave and move and talk like, well, actors?

Which is why I felt so exasperated by so many of the tributes of Brando, which referred to him as 'the Great Mumbler' or a 'devotee of The Method'. The first accusation made him seem like a fool, the second like a follower of a dubious religion.

To deal with his mumbling first: watch him in *Reflections in a Golden Eye*; or *The Chase*; or as Mark Antony in *Julius Caesar*. Or as Fletcher Christian in *Mutiny on the Bounty*—a haughty and handsome patrician with a perfect English accent that he'd culled from a young upper-class English actor called Tim Seeley, whom he befriended for the duration of the film and cruelly dropped as soon as his purpose was achieved. 'I played many roles in which I didn't mumble a single syllable,' he said in his autobiography, 'but in others I did it because it is the way people speak in ordinary life.' And, defying the image of the self-indulgent narcissist, he added that he was all too well aware of how restricting it was: 'It served the American theatre and movies well… but you cannot mumble in Shakespeare. You cannot improvise.'

If Brando was not a mumbler still less was he a Method actor. Temperamentally he could never be part of a group, still less a collective that resembled a cult. The Method emerged from a semi-permanent New York company of playwrights, directors and actors called The Group. In their programme for training actors lay the genesis of the Actors Studio, founded by one of The Group's directors, Lee Strasberg who, as Arthur Miller once told me, was 'so bad that they had to find something for him to do'.

With Stanislavsky as his model, Lee Strasberg encouraged his actors to systematise their work: the catechism of 'impro', 'emotional memory', 'private moments', and 'relaxation exercises' became their credo. What could only have meaning as empirical practice became a method—or worse still, '*The* Method'. Brando's teacher was not Strasberg but Stella Adler, an actress from The Group who had studied in the US with two Russian ex-pupils of Stanislavsky. 'In ordinary life,' said Brando, 'people seldom know exactly what they're going to say when they open their mouths… They pause for an instant to find the right word, search their minds to compose a sentence, then express it. Until Stella Adler came along few actors understood this…'

There are as many 'methods' of working as there are actors. Some lose themselves in research, like archaeologists or detectives, as if to elevate the business of acting into a pseudo-science. Others improvise and paraphrase. Others still literally become the character, on set and off. In the days when it mattered to him, Brando researched parts; he inhabited them. He ushered in an approach that is now widely followed by most professional actors, who are following Stanislavsky's pragmatic methods even if they never invoke his name.

Brando got bored by acting. He found the childlike part of it—the impersonation and dressing up—increasingly silly, not a proper activity for a grown-up, well, for a grown man: too feminine by half. Brando, for all his womanising, seems to have disliked women as much as he disliked the feminine in himself. Whatever the causes, he was cursed by hating the thing that had made him famous. When I made a series about twentieth-century theatre for the BBC, *Changing Stages*, I wanted him to talk about acting. The producer rang him in Los Angeles and he talked to her very amicably for about forty-five minutes, even sang:

> *Just a wee deoch an doris, just a wee drop, that's all.*
> *Just a wee deoch an doris afore ye gang awa.*
> *There's a wee wifie waitin' in a wee but an ben.*
> *If you can say, 'It's a braw bricht moonlicht nicht',*
> *Then yer a'richt, ye ken.*

He was enthusiastic to sing and discuss the work of Harry Lauder and the plight of the American Indian, but said that he would rather do anything in the world than talk about acting. I did speak to Kim Hunter, the Stella of the Broadway production of *Streetcar*, about his acting. 'He was just an absolutely marvellous actor to work with,' she said, 'His sense of truth about what he was doing just came to you like a fireball—it brought the best out of you. And he would tell you if you were missing a word out of a speech. He cared about the commas.'

Harley Granville-Barker

I've written several pieces about Granville-Barker—a preface to his Prefaces to Shakespeare *re-published in 1993, his entry in the* Dictionary of National Biography *in 2005, and this for the* Guardian *in 2011.*

All theatre has a tendency to decline to the condition of the superficial and silly. Every now and then someone comes along, shakes it up and demonstrates that it's an art to be fought for and to be taken seriously—not a respectable art, but an art to be respected. At the beginning of the twentieth century in Britain it was someone whose influence, if not his name, resonated throughout the entire century: Harley Granville-Barker. He possessed a passionate certainty about the importance of the theatre and the need to revise its form, its content, and the way that it was managed. He ushered in a style of production that still approximates to our ideas of the best in contemporary Shakespearean production and production of contemporary plays.

Granville-Barker was born without the hyphen in 1877. His mother was an entertainer who did bird imitations; his father a dilettante architect/property developer. He had little education. He started performing at the age of thirteen, and at the age of fourteen went to a stage school in Margate. He was a playwright by the age of seventeen, a successful actor (he originated several of Shaw's protagonists, notably Marchbanks in *Candida*) by the age of twenty-three, and he was running the Royal Court Theatre by the age of twenty-seven.

During his three years at the Royal Court—from 1904 to 1907—he produced over thirty-seven new plays by seventeen authors (several of them by Shaw), encouraged women playwrights, and inspired the regional repertory movement. The fiftieth anniversary of the birth of the English Stage Company at the Royal Court is currently being celebrated; Granville-Barker was its spiritual father.

He can also claim parenthood of the National Theatre. Before running the Royal Court, he wrote (with William Archer, a critic and the first translator of Ibsen's plays into English) *A Scheme and Estimates for a National Theatre*. The scheme covered everything from staff and choice of plays to wages, royalties and pension funds. A committee was formed to raise the necessary money, state aid being assumed to be out of the question.

He wrote six plays; the best, which he wrote while running the Royal Court and directing and acting in plays there, is *The Voysey Inheritance*. It's a complex web of family relationships, a fervent, but never unambiguous, indictment of a world dominated by the mutually dependent obsessions of greed, class, and self-deception. It's also a virtuoso display of stagecraft: the writer showing that as director he can handle twelve speaking characters on stage at one time, and that as actor he can deal with the most ambitious and unexpected modulations of thought and feeling. The 'inheritance' of the Voyseys is a legacy of debt, bad faith, and bitter family dissension. Edward's father has, shortly before his death, revealed that he has been cheating the family firm of solicitors for many years, as his father had for many years before that. Towards the end of the play Edward Voysey, the youngest son, confronts the woman he loves:

> EDWARD. Why wouldn't he own the truth to me about himself?
>
> BEATRICE. Perhaps he took care not to know it. Would you have understood?
>
> EDWARD. Perhaps not. But I loved him.
>
> BEATRICE. That would silence a bench of judges.

Shaw would have used the story to moralise and polemicise. He might have had the son hate the father; he might have had him forgive him; he might have had him indict him as a paradigm of capitalism; he would never have said he loved him. Shaw was a brilliant polemicist who dealt with certainties and sometimes (but not often enough) breathed life into his sermons, while Barker was a committed sceptic who started from the premise that the only thing certain about human behaviour is that nothing is certain.

By the time he was forty he retired. He fell wildly in love—'in the Italian manner' as Shaw said churlishly—with an American millionairess. He married her, acquired a hyphen in his surname, moved first to Devon to play the part of a country squire, and then to France to a life of seclusion. But he had decided to

withdraw from the theatre years before: 'I made up my mind... to give up acting when I was thirty and producing when I was forty.' Out of his exile emerged
his *Prefaces to Shakespeare*, a practical primer for directors and actors working on
the plays of Shakespeare, and two plays, both of them still awaiting a public performance.

In his Shakespeare productions he aimed at re-establishing the relationship
between actor and audience that had existed in the Elizabethan theatre—and this
at a time when the prevailing style of Shakespearean production involved not
stopping short of having live sheep on stage in *As You Like It*. To achieve this, he
abolished footlights and the proscenium arch and built an apron over the orchestra pit. 'It apparently trebled the spaciousness of the stage... To the imagination
it looks as if he had invented a new heaven and a new earth,' said Shaw.

Granville-Barker demanded that the text must come first, and that the director,
designer and actors must serve it with clarity, lucidity, realism, and grace. He
established the premise of modern theatre design by showing that scenery had to
be expressive and avoid being decorative or literal. It had to be real and specific
while at the same time being metaphorical and minimal—like the cart in *Mother
Courage*, the nursery in *The Cherry Orchard*, the dining table in *The Voysey Inheritance*. An actor said of him that 'he worked from the inside to the outside. He
had an exceptional interest in what was theatrically effective, but never got it by
theatrical means. It had to be won by mental clarity and emotional truth—in fact
the very opposite to the method of most producers.' He was not only the first
modern English theatre director; he's been the most influential.

In 1989, shortly after I had directed *The Voysey Inheritance* at the National Theatre, the theatre was presented with a wonderful bronze bust of Granville-Barker
by Kathleen Scott (widow of the Antarctic hero). For a while it sat on the win-
dowsill of my office like a benign household god. Then it was installed on a
bracket in the foyer opposite a bust of Olivier, the two men eyeing each other
in wary mutual regard. A few months later it was stolen. Perhaps it was an act of
homage.

Mary Soames

I wrote this piece for the Guardian *when Mary died in June 2014. She was Churchill's youngest child.*

———•———

Mary Soames was Chair of the National Theatre Board from 1988, during most of my time as Director. Her appointment was greeted by many people with surprise, and by some with alarm. I heard it said by a Labour MP that her mandate would be to privatise the National Theatre, and by a Tory that she was being put in to 'sort out the pinkoes'. My own response was one of curiosity: not so much as to why she had been chosen as to why she had accepted. She was not a regular theatregoer, and had no conspicuously advertised ambitions to hold public office. With hindsight I think Mary agreed to chair the Royal National Theatre Board because it was an adventure that she couldn't refuse, and, perhaps an unsurprising thing to say about a Churchill, because it was her destiny. The National Theatre never had cause to regret her appointment, and neither I think did she.

Whatever apprehensions I may have had about Mary were dispelled during our first lunch together. 'You'll have to help me out,' she said with unaffected candour, 'I know absolutely nothing about the theatre: Christopher didn't like going.' During the meal she revealed a sharp intelligence, marked with self-deprecating diffidence ('I know nothing about anything'), a remarkable memory for names and literary quotes, and a facility for telling anecdotes larded with perfectly recalled detail and dialogue. They often featured her father and boasted a supporting cast that included Stalin, Roosevelt, General de Gaulle, Noël

Coward, Robert Mugabe and all the Mitford sisters. She once asked me to dinner with Jessica Mitford ('Richard, dear, could you bear to come to dinner to break the ice'), whom Mary hadn't seen since Jessica had eloped to the Spanish Civil War with Mary's then sort-of-boyfriend, Esmond Romilly.

I was particularly taken by Mary's ability to keep several sentences bouncing in the air at once, even while she dropped her handbag on the floor, picked up the contents, draped an errant tape measure round her neck, and continued as if this were the most natural thing in the world. I remember reading a newspaper profile of Mary before I met her. 'She is a great giver,' it said. 'The heart comes pouring out and when it reaches you it is warm.' No one who met her could doubt that. I did help her out as she'd requested, and in return she gave herself without reserve and without condition to the life of the National Theatre.

Mary became an assiduous student of theatre politics, of plays, of styles of production, and of the sometimes bizarre and often self-indulgent behaviour of the people who made up the world she had joined. I found her taste in plays and in acting to be infallible, even if she was always tentative about asserting it, and she had an unerring ear, nose and eye, for the bogus. Her loyalty never wavered, and even when concerned by hostile criticism or bad box-office, or provoked by artistic controversy—the mud bath in *A Midsummer Night's Dream*, the simulated gay sexual intercourse in *Angels in America*, the depiction of the Queen in *A Question of Attribution*—she remained steadfast in her support of the artistic policy.

I once went with Mary to her parents' house, Chartwell. She gave the breath of life to it. I sat in her father's chair in his study, facing a photograph of her at the age of eighteen as she sat on the other side of the desk, still beautiful at the age of sixty-nine. You could almost hear her father pacing, dictating to a file of secretaries, exhausting one after another, irrepressible until the onslaught of depression, always the corollary of excessive appetite for work.

He dominated his family as Kafka said his father had dominated his: 'Often I picture a map of the world and you lying across it. And then it seems as if the only areas open to my life are those that are not covered by you or are out of your reach.' Yet Mary remained untouched by the fire of celebrity and expectation that consumed his other children.

She was not, in spite of her lineage, a natural politician or administrator, and she had to work extraordinarily hard to succeed as she did at the job. She had an irreducible sense of duty and endured without complaint a few financial crises, several bruising encounters with the architect, Denys Lasdun, many Olivier Award Ceremonies, countless sponsorship occasions, and an infinity of meetings of the board, the Finance and General Purposes Committee, the Masterplan Sub-Committee, the Catering Committee, the National Theatre Development Council, the National Theatre Foundation, and the South Bank Theatre Board.

After Mary left the NT Board I'd meet her from time to time and we always fell on each other as old friends, hungry for gossip and comradeship. I saw her last a few weeks ago. She was frail and her memory was intermittent but she was still beautiful and she still showed flashes of her old wit and great charm. Whenever I go through Parliament Square, I'll always remember passing the statue of her father as we drove back together from the theatre, often late at night, and Mary saying, 'Night, night, Papa.' She told me once that late in his life, when he was frail and incommunicative, she had asked him if there was anything in his life that he had wanted to do but hadn't, anything that he regretted, and he said: 'I'd like my father to have lived long enough to have seen me do something good.' He would have been inordinately proud of his daughter.

Politics

Margaret Thatcher

I wrote this piece at the request of Sarah Sands of the Evening Standard *when Margaret Thatcher was critically ill in 2008. When she died five years later there didn't seem any reason to revise it.*

———•————

> It was a strangely wondrous evening yesterday leaving so much to think about. I still find myself rather disturbed by it. But if they can do that *without* any ideals, then if we apply the same perfection and creativeness to *our* message, we should provide quite good historic material for an opera called *Margaret* in thirty years' time!

Over thirty years has passed since Margaret Thatcher wrote this to her speech-writer, the playwright Ronald Millar, after he had taken her to see *Evita*. If Andrew Lloyd-Webber and Tim Rice were to turn their hands to composing *Margaret*, despite the good historical material, they would be up against it. The central character would lack sympathy, the recitative would be repetitive and the libretto would be unrewarding. Essential songs would include 'I Just Owe Almost Everything to My Own Father', 'Where There is Discord, May We Bring Harmony', 'We Can Do Business Together', 'Rejoice! Rejoice!', 'The Bowling's Going to Get Hit All Round the Ground: That is My Style', 'No. No. No.', 'There is No Such Thing as Society', 'I Shall Let My Name Go Forward' and the tearful finale 'Thank You Very Much. Goodbye'. The arc of its action would rise to vainglorious cavalcade, then decline to tragic farce. Its epigraph could be supplied by Enoch Powell: 'All political lives, unless they are cut off in midstream at a happy juncture, end in failure.'

At a time when the reputation of politicians is lower than paparazzi, it may be hard to believe that thirty years ago a new Prime Minister stood in Downing Street and quoted St Francis of Assisi without being tarred and feathered. If Thatcher's remarks now seem only mildly hammy it's because our sensibilities have been dulled by seeing Tony Blair earnestly laying his sincerity on the line about non-existent weapons of mass destruction, Gordon Brown, with an equivalent measure of earnestness, promising change, change, change, and David Cameron failing to convince even himself of his policies. Thatcher's prayer was intended to advertise her aspiration to offer politics governed by a conviction, as she later said, of the need to 'change Britain from a dependent to a self-reliant society'. In an age when our banks have become dysfunctional as a consequence of their eager pursuit of her philosophy of rampant materialism, it's hard not to believe that her mission was a disaster.

Her flagship policies were privatisation of state industries and the reduction of state spending, of trade union power, of the government's role in the economy, of tax and of inflation. She set out to reverse what she saw as the decline of Britain and promote its position in the world. Luck plays a large part in any politician's life. It was luck that allowed her to stand as leader of the Tory party and it was luck that the Falklands crisis provided her with a platform which she worked to such magnificent self-advantage and which became the transforming event of her premiership.

Her economic policies were not new. She was not the first Tory politician to advocate tax cuts or slash spending or sell council houses or privatise state industries (she left the railways to her successor) or deregulate the press and TV. Nor was she the first Tory leader to criticise the unions, to stand up to Communism or to speak against the federalising instincts of the EU. She was, however, the catalyst who gave spin to the acceptance of the infallibility of the market as a guarantee of prosperity, to the triumph of capitalism. In the 1970s some of us had anticipated a political revolution in the opposite direction. It seems none of us was right.

Thatcher's major achievement was to implant her personality on the nation. She became personally dominant—and domineeringly personal and self-promoting. In mitigation it must be said that for all her corrosive attitudes, her belligerence, her grating voice, her lack of empathy and irony, she was up against the patronising and sexist grandees of the Tory party. That she had a battle to include Jews in her cabinet—five out of twenty ('More old Estonians than old Etonians,' said Harold Macmillan)—says much of the inclinations of the old guard that she overthrew.

It is hard to separate Thatcher from the 'ism' to which she gave her name. What was it apart from the cult of the leader? A philosophy? An ideology? Thatcherism was ideological only in that, like Lenin, she thought that

'Economics is the method; the object is to change the soul.' But unlike Lenin, she thought that by removing those tiresome financial regulations which stifled initiative and by suppressing the unions' demands for higher wages, the spirit of Britannia would soar.

Thatcherism is a set of sometimes contradictory attitudes held by its progenitor: she was a snob who resented class barriers, a highly successful woman who did nothing to help other women, a conservative who hated the countryside ('too untidy'), a moralist who sanctioned greed, and an ambitious political thinker who reduced policies to Manichean struggles between the 'dries' and the 'wets', black and white, good and evil.

She said, notoriously, that: 'There is no such thing as society.' Indeed it became her mantra. The rest of her statement was interesting: 'There is a living tapestry of men and women and people and the beauty of that tapestry and the quality of our lives will depend upon how much each of us is prepared to take responsibility for ourselves and each of us is prepared to turn round and help by our own efforts those who are unfortunate.' She ignored her qualifying clauses, the 'living tapestry of men and women', in favour of demonstrating that, while 'There's no such thing as society' might appear to be a figure of speech, it would be turned into a self-fulfilling proposition.

Its residue is an attitude that encourages us to regard human beings as units to be measured, counted, assessed and disposed of if they are of no immediate economic worth; that any social activity that cannot be shown to have a structure or a purpose that imitates the business of making money is imbued with self-doubt and insecurity; and that the very society whose existence she denied—those people who believe that we do things better together than we do alone—is corroded by the reductive logic of market economics.

Would reform of organisations like the NHS and the BBC have occurred without Thatcher's zealotry? Would the Murdochisation of the media have occurred without her vigorous (reciprocal) encouragement? Was the credit collapse the last sigh of her legacy? Was she a charismatic revolutionary? Did she change the syntax of Britain's politics? Or was she the Wizard of Oz—a confection of bombastic rhetorical flourishes?

During the height of her power, dreams of Margaret Thatcher were as common as dreams about the Queen. When Alan Clark was not enjoying lubricious fantasies about her, she used to appear in his dreams as his mother. When I was Director of the National Theatre I dreamt that I had a meeting with her during which I spoke without drawing breath to convince her that the arts were not a waste of time and money. My dream never came true but then neither did hers: according to friends, in her declining years she'd dream she was still Prime Minister.

The Monarchy

I wrote this at the request of the Guardian *in 2000.*

In a recent edition of a magazine there was a photographic feature which displayed the magnificent rulers, robes, retainers and regalia of some African states. One king was pictured being carried above the crowd like a god in a plywood model of a Mercedes car. The photographer, clearly anticipating the readers' giggles, pointed out that 'they are no more ridiculous or strange, surely, than a British Lord Chamberlain walking backwards before the Queen at a State Opening of Parliament' or, he might have added, a baroque gold coach drawn by six white horses containing a Queen dressed in a costume that would earn a good laugh in a pantomime, accompanied by a man who finished his naval career as a Lieutenant, dressed like a Christmas tree, in the costume of an Admiral of the Fleet.

A religion—according to the *OED*—is 'action or conduct indicating a belief in, reverence for, and a desire to please, a divine ruling power'. Few, I think, believe in the Queen's divinity, but many people, including the Queen herself, believe that she is divinely appointed, and it's hard to deny our resemblance to devout worshippers of a cult: we crook the neck, we bend the spine, we bob and curtsy, we metaphorically cross ourselves before the altar of monarchy. And just as religious faith defies the light of reason, so we are reluctant to examine the monarchy with anything more than an irritated shrug: well, who would *you* want as Head of State, Paddy Ashdown? Well, possibly not, but I wouldn't mind Mary Robinson, and I wouldn't mind electing one.

Is monarchy the English religion? Isn't it merely a fondly regarded old institution with a number of harmless admirers and old buildings like, say, the Church of England, which John Mortimer has compared to a 'well-intentioned old gent who doesn't care much for religion'? The similarities between the two institutions are close, but the monarchy has one distinct advantage over the Anglican deity: millions of people still appear to believe in it. Indeed, you could say that it's just about the only thing that, as a nation, we do believe in.

Every now and then—a royal marriage, the Queen Mother's birthday—we see a genteel public expression of this faith, and every time the Queen turns up at a hospital we see the literal evidence of its power: astonishingly, some people actually get better. With the death of Diana we saw an outpouring of passion that wasn't just the apotheosis of the *Hello!* syndrome nor was it the mourning for a fallen demi-goddess dying in the under(pass)world. For the thousands of people who threw flowers on the hearse, who streamed towards the shrines at Kensington and Buckingham Palaces in the early morning, who bore banners such as 'DIANA OF LOVE', 'WHEN IRISH EYES ARE CRYING' and 'DIANA, FAIRY GODMOTHER OF THE NEEDY COLOMBIANS IN MOURNING' it was something more: it was religious ecstasy. Some people described it as a revolt against the monarchy, but it wasn't: the new religion replaced the old, it was evolution not revolution.

When the heat of religious passion died down, we slipped back into our habitually tepid faith, curated by a priesthood of civil servants, constitutional historians, politicians, public figures and broadcasters who agonise about ritual, protocol and precedent and live in fear of *lèse-majesté*, while the blessing, the royal 'appellation', is invoked on all our public institutions, our lifeboat service, ambulances, hospitals, academies, charities, concert halls, and theatres, in order that they can serve as the rivets of our theocratic state. Day by day we are reminded that the interests of the monarchy and the public are incompatible: our army, our prisons, our police, our public broadcasting are hers not ours; we are subjects, not citizens, a congregation not a democracy.

All religions exist to give people a sense of a power greater than themselves, to give meaning to their lives, and to give continuity to them. An anthropologist would describe the way we express our Englishness—the sense provided by an unbroken association with our territory (green and pleasant land, sceptr'd isle, etc.) and with the hypothetically unbroken lineage of our royal family— as a religious phenomenon. Most societies imagine that there is a relationship between the people and the territory on which they live. The people need the land to remain fertile, so the health of the land and the people is, through ritual, made to appear to be synonymous. If the ruling lineage is deposed or if the royal family is infertile, they believe that the rains will fail or the crops will wither and die.

Despite the fact that Mrs Thatcher said it, it's unavoidably true that the family is a microcosm of society. Thus it's important that the family which presides over the land is seen as a model one, with larger houses and vaster and more enduring possessions than anyone else. The present royal family is conspicuously dysfunctional, which may confirm its position as a contemporary paradigm, but at least—and it's a wholly significant least—they've proved themselves to be fertile. (Tony Blair usurped the monarch's role by demonstrating his fertility while in office.) The royal family preside over the land partly literally, by owning hundreds of thousands of acres including Royal Parks, and partly by endowing their members or relatives with titles that speak of their metaphorical stewardship of Cornwall, Gloucester, Norfolk, Wessex, Westminster, Edinburgh, and so on. How many streets in your neighbourhood are named after our great painters, writers, sportsmen, or even politicians? Most of them are named after royal relatives whose names reflect their totemic (and sometimes real) hold over territory.

We know all these iconic signs are nonsense, we know that the 'unbroken' lineage of the royal family is a fiction, we know that the Queen doesn't protect us from floods or bankruptcy, and we know that the royals are frail, vulnerable and all too human, but we still don't feel confident enough to dispose of the monarchy, or even to begin to eradicate their presence from our streets and public buildings. No government will seriously tamper with the 'constitution' (whatever that is) precisely because they feel they are dealing with religious feelings—those atavistic fears of infertility. So we end up with the monarchy in the position of the monkeys on Gibraltar: a superstitious charm against the decline of our territorial integrity. As long as we feel like leaves in the wind, unable to control our destiny, we will crave something that is apparently immutable. But we will not grow up as a democracy until we refuse to be beguiled by myths and pageants and resist the consolation of the English religion. And of course having become a Knight of the British Empire, I'm a fine example of tenacious resistance to this consolation…

In Defence of the BBC

This is a conflation of two pieces that I wrote for the Guardian *in the wake of one of the BBC's periodic crises. The first was written in 2003, after a journalist, Andrew Gilligan, reported on the* Today *programme that a government briefing paper on Iraq and weapons of mass destruction had been 'sexed up', and David Kelly, a former UN weapons inspector in Iraq, had died. The Hutton Inquiry had been set up to investigate the circumstances surrounding his death. The second piece was written in 2004 after the Hutton Inquiry's report was published. It cleared the government of wrongdoing but strongly criticised the BBC, and lead to the resignation of the Chairman, Gavyn Davies, and the Director-General, Greg Dyke.*

I first worked for the BBC in 1978 when I became producer of a strand of exclusively new drama called Play for Today. *I have continued to work for the BBC in the years since, making films such as* The Imitation Game, Tumbledown *and* Henry IV Parts I and II. *I was a Governor for nine years from 1996 until just before the 'Gilligan Affair' in 2003.*

A few years ago an arts journalist and one-time BBC script editor, W. Stephen Gilbert, started a speech at the Edinburgh TV Festival with these words: 'There are three great lies in the world: the cheque is in the post, I won't come in your mouth, and the BBC is a public service broadcaster.' He was wrong about the BBC.

These words were spoken in the nineties, when the BBC cringed in fear of the three horseman of the new apocalypse—Money, Management and Marketing—and was failing in its attempts to square the circle of popular programming for a largely disenfranchised mass audience with its remit to inform and explain. The threat proved—for a while—to be an exaggerated one.

In spite of (and even to some extent because of) the rigours of the Birtist revolution, the BBC convincingly fought justified accusations of dumbing-down and made its case as a public broadcaster in the only convincing and effective way available to it—by making programmes that couldn't or wouldn't be made by any other British broadcaster, for which no 'demand' could be proven and which defied the bogus logic of 'market predictions'. Provoked by its unarguable success, the BBC was attacked on all sides: government, the Murdoch press, the *Daily Telegraph*, the *Daily Mail*, rival broadcasters and MPs opportunistically joined hands to demand that the giant was kneecapped.

It used to be said by the BBC's rivals, like a wistful compliment that might be paid by a philandering husband to his long-suffering wife, that the BBC 'exists to keep us all honest'. No longer; its opponents would rather see the wife obliged to sell them her favours and then be locked up in a nunnery. Commercial television, of course, exists to make money: this is not incompatible with making good programmes, but the first obligation of commercial television companies is to the shareholders, the second is to the advertisers, and the third is to the audience. The BBC exists to serve its audience: indeed, it has a duty to serve it, and the public is best served by making the best programmes, which is why its lapses so try the patience of its supporters.

No one should underestimate how difficult it is to make good TV programmes. We no longer sit down in front of the television at a particular time. We watch bite-sized time-shifted fragments with the remote control in our hands and the critic in us becomes an executioner. It's no longer possible, as those nostalgic for the BBC's role as the nation's educator wish, to dispense cultural directives and expect an audience to follow them, even if they were able to give expression to the huge plurality of voices clamouring to be heard. In addition it's clear that the virtuous practice of 'hammocking'—putting, say, an arts or political documentary between two popular programmes—is fruitless in the face of multi-channel television and the tyranny of the remote control.

Nevertheless, the fact that it's become more difficult to make good programmes, and far more difficult to persuade people to watch them, shouldn't be used as an argument for not making ones which have complexity and passion, an individual voice and a moral dimension, and offer up a commentary on the infinite messiness of being alive. Which might well be a prospectus for a programme on the Hutton Report, where the vulnerability of the leading participants has been so publicly and painfully paraded; none more so than the BBC.

If the BBC is being attacked from Downing Street, it's nothing new. A Head of Radio in the days of Thatcher told me that he went down to the foyer of

Broadcasting House to meet Norman Tebbit when he came to do an interview for the *Today* programme during an election campaign. As Tebbit came through the art deco doors he greeted the BBC dignitary across the acres of marble floor with a scream: 'You fucking cunt!' Little has changed since except that Downing Street has acquired a powerful propagandist in Alastair Campbell, who has frequently used precisely the same words about BBC executives.

During the Iraq War, Campbell relentlessly bullied and taunted the BBC: letter after letter, email after email, phone call after phone call of provocative, disingenuous, belligerent, abusive and unfounded accusations of coordinated and systemic bias against the Government. If there is one thing that has been proved beyond reasonable doubt about the Iraq War, it's that the BBC was innocent of these charges. Indeed a study from Cardiff University has shown the opposite: that of all news-gathering organisations the BBC was the most consistently pro the war.

By picking a fight with the BBC, Campbell grotesquely magnified the status of Blair's claim that Iraq could use weapons of mass destruction within forty-five minutes, and he probably helped to bring about his master's downfall. The claim has been subjected to minute scrutiny and exposed as no less flawed than the BBC's notorious 6.07 report on the *Today* programme—a claim based on a single unreliable source. Which of course is the premise of a large number of newspaper stories. Two sources? A rumour will do. A correction? Forget it. Trying to extract an apology from a newspaper is as difficult as taking a leg of an okapi from a starving lion, as I discovered last year when I was libelled by a broadsheet newspaper which constantly celebrates its independence. From truth perhaps.

And yes, the BBC does have to do better than that. It does have to be capable of demonstrating its scrupulousness and reporters do have to keep proper notes. How else do they expect their version of events to be confirmed when they are challenged? By bleating: 'Trust me, I'm a journalist'? John Birt was right to describe the 'Gilligan Affair' as the result of 'slipshod' journalism, even if his remarks were tinged by a whiff of *schadenfreude* and shadowed by the barely concealed subtext: 'It would never have happened in my day.' And was he, subconsciously of course, influenced by his desire to see Mark Byford, for whom he had so conspicuously lobbied at the time of Dyke's appointment, as Director General?

In spite of this I should say that I admire much of what John Birt did for the BBC, even if I often disagreed with his manner of doing it or, as his much-loved consultants would put it, his 'management style'. He made the BBC—and the public—recognise that receiving the licence fee meant a responsibility to all the licence payers, many of whom felt thoroughly disenfranchised from the existing BBC. Secondly, however ill-conceived in execution, he insisted that programme-makers were made (or allowed) to be responsible for their own budgets. Thirdly, with some prescience, he established the BBC's online and digital strategy. And fourthly, he initiated a strong, coherent news-gathering and news-broadcasting strategy. Recurrent factual inaccuracies are rare in BBC news reporting, which bears a special burden of responsibility in resisting the tendency to treat every political battle, accident, crime, triumph or disaster like an incident in a soap opera peopled by cartoon-like martyrs, villains and fools.

In the BBC affair the martyrs were Greg Dyke and the poor, hapless David Kelly; the villains were the Government and Andrew Gilligan; and the fools, naturally enough, were the Board of Governors. The truth, if that's not a word to be used with caution, is that there was a little of each category in all of the protagonists.

Until recently I was a Governor of the BBC. I resigned before the 'Gilligan Affair' in order to shoot a film, so I missed having my emails to fellow Governors published on the Hutton Report website. Had they been, I might have been caught complaining about the sporadic descent of BBC news reports into tabloidism, their frequent superficiality, their unhealthy flirtation with celebrity, their excessive concern with reporting sporting in preference to cultural events, and even their occasional lack of grammar. In short, any of the complaints that might be levelled against any newspaper any day by any reader. But whereas in every national newspaper it is easily possible to identify factual inaccuracies—often disguised as 'opinion'—it is rare in BBC news reporting. I sat on the Governors' Complaints committee for many years: there were very few complaints of misreporting and when there were—as there conspicuously have been in the case of Gilligan—they were impossible to defend because there were no written records: evidence of sloppiness rather than bias.

From the beginning of the Iraq War, the Government, through Alastair Campbell, accused the BBC of bias that was coordinated and systemic. Coordinated? The BBC? Is Number 10 so ignorant, naive or wilfully disingenuous that it imagines that the BBC News department, however ably managed—and it is—could persuade its scores of editors, let alone its hundreds of journalists, to adopt a unified and consistent attitude to anything but the obligation to be balanced and fair in their reporting? Nation may speak peace unto nation, but you'll never get the *Today* programme to cooperate with *Newsnight*.

It is not hard to see why these programmes vex the government. They are run and staffed by journalists in whose DNA is the ambition to seek out a 'good' story and promote it, and their star interviewers barely conceal their considerable (and arguably well-deserved) contempt for politicians. In that respect, however, they can only be said to be doing their duty in reflecting public opinion. In the case of the Kelly story, the 'good' story was clearly marred by bad reporting and worse writing, and the Governors' reaction to it was coloured by the attritional accusations of endemic bias from Downing Street.

If there is bias in the BBC, it is the bias of those who, however venal their ambitions and prejudiced their political philosophies, share the values of the organisation that they work for: a belief that the sum of the organisation is greater than the parts and that they are a part of an entire vision which is larger than themselves. The fact that this has often proved to be an inaccurate vision doesn't make it an inappropriate one. When I was filming my Falklands film, *Tumbledown*, for the BBC in 1980s, I was on a hill in Wales at night in the rain when a prop man said to me: 'I like working here, you get to make good programmes.' 'Here? In Wales?' 'No no,' he said, 'I mean at the BBC.' 'Here' was a territory of the mind, a heartland.

And in spite of the zealotry of Producer Choice, the half-baked Stalinism of Reorganisation of Priorities, the proliferation of pie charts, the multiplication of graphs of share and reach, the obsession with process over content, the irksome jargon that comes in the wake of focus groups and the obscenely excessive salaries and expenses paid to the senior executives, which make it no longer possible for them to speak in good faith about public service broadcasting, a heartland still exists in the BBC. Within that heartland resides a faith that it is still possible to make a TV programme for no other reason than the shared belief that it is worth making for itself alone rather than as a token in the ratings game. Could this be the subversive ideology that renders the BBC, according to Conrad Black, the 'biggest menace in Britain today'?

The corollary of those values—you might call them Reithian—are institutional characteristics that exemplify the character of its founder. As the historian Peter Hennessy has pointed out, however much they try to adapt, British institutions carry the imprint of the genetic code from the era in which they were conceived—in the case of the BBC, a tendency to official sanctimoniousness coupled to institutional inertia, and a reflex to respond to critics as fools or worse. Or, in the words of my friend the writer Tom Clarke, behaviour that resembles the Church and the Post Office.

But even if the BBC does retain a trace of that body language, the contrast between the Church and the Post Office couldn't be more dramatic. For all the odd errors, embarrassments, fits of complacency and self-congratulation, the BBC is an institution which still does triumphantly what it was set up to do eighty years ago. It's one of the few things in Britain that works. The Government is eager to see 'wholesale reform' of the BBC. Are they so frustrated by their inability to reform the NHS and so exasperated by their failure to turn round the educational system, that they are prepared to act like Lucifer: 'I cannot read, therefore I wish all books were burned'?

Many commentators speak wistfully of a desire to return to a BBC which would dispense high culture and scorn its ratings. This Reithian Land of Oz, if it ever existed, vaporised with the coming of time-shift recording, satellite broadcasting and the internet. Today's BBC has an obligation to look after the interests of the majority of its licence payers just as much as the small, highly educated, culturally literate elite, and as long as it does so it will be necessary to try to square the circle of popularity and high-mindedness. There will continue to be mistakes made, but if all this is done in good faith, the licence fee will be justified.

As a journalist observed, as a tactician Alastair Campbell was a genius, but as a strategist he was a fool. Of Greg Dyke you might say the reverse: his strategy, perhaps unwittingly, will preserve the independence of the BBC. This Government—no more (or less) callow, philistine, unprincipled and opportunistic than any other government of the last twenty-five years—will be cautious about dismantling the BBC after its independence has been made such a matter of public examination.

But in the later charter renewal it's possible that a confederacy of interests—the Government, the Murdoch press, rival broadcasters—might conspire to shrink the BBC into a British version of PBS—a subscription service. While that would succeed in drawing the teeth of BBC News, it would do a murderous disservice to the country's most important cultural organisation. Politicians consider that news constitutes the heart of the BBC; so, perhaps, do many journalists. They are wrong: news is a significant part of the BBC's anatomy but it's not its heart. Its heart is the drama, documentary, entertainment, history, science, nature, arts and leisure programmes, and it's in these areas that the BBC has made its case as a public broadcaster in the only convincing and effective way available to it—by making programmes that couldn't or wouldn't be made by any other British broadcaster.

Like other cultural organisations—the National Gallery, the Royal Academy, the Tate, the British Museum, the National Theatre—the BBC is among the few things in Britain that actually achieves what it's supposed to and if the Government allows their obsession with one small (though significant) area of one division of the BBC's output to poison their attitude to the remainder, they will not be forgiven by history. Could these words of John Ruskin's be etched on each red despatch box?:

> Great nations write their autobiographies in three manuscripts: the book of their deeds, the book of their words and the book of their art. Not one of these books can be understood unless we read the other two, but of these three, the only trustworthy one is the last.

The Iraq War

The commitment of the British government to send troops to invade Iraq—in the face of demonstrations numbering hundreds of thousands of people—was not the beginning of the end of my admiration for Tony Blair's Government; it was the end of the end. These four pieces were written for the Guardian, _the first of them in January 2003, the last of them in October 2004, when George Bush visited London. The invasion of Iraq started in March 2003._

I sit in one of the dives
On Fifty-Second Street
Uncertain and afraid
As the clever hopes expire
Of a low dishonest decade.

I don't actually. I sit in Elaine's restaurant on 2nd Avenue with a friend, but every word of Auden's poem 'September 1, 1939' seems painfully apt. The atmosphere in the restaurant is grave. Apart from a couple next door to us who are hissing abuse at each other, everyone is mute, their eyes on the television set which sits on a shelf above the entrance. When we walked into the restaurant it seemed as if all eyes were on us. But all eyes were focused just above our heads on the President of the United States, who was addressing his nation on the State of the Union.

Elaine's is famed for its dominant proprietor, its dour decor, its rude waiters and its reliable, if unchanging, food. It's a sanctuary for a certain kind of New Yorker, whose conversation is likely to be more about Lionel Trilling than Manolo

Blahnik. In London in such a place—say the Union Club in Greek Street—a television broadcast by the Head of State, the Queen's speech, would be accompanied by a sort of satirical obbligato. In Elaine's, the instinct to mock is tempered by a near feudal regard for the office of President and the gravity of his message.

Few people here doubt that war is going to happen, certainly not the management of the *The New York Times*, who are taking their reporters off hit-and-run accidents in New Jersey to give them training to deal with kidnap and chemical attack in desert conditions in preparation for their transfer to the war zone. But few people seem to feel that it will affect their lives. After all, Iraq is a long way off, only ten per cent of reservists have been called up, there's no prospect of the draft being introduced and, even though the nation is on 'orange alert', there's still little evidence of any more security precautions on the subway or in public buildings. Only those of us of a certain age who grew up in an 'old Europe'—impoverished, exhausted and visibly scarred by bombs—seem to feel dogged by a constant shadow of apprehension at the imminence of another war.

There is little dissent on television and the press offers little to fuel debate. The members of the Washington press corps act as courtiers to the President, offering sententious pieties, meekly endorsing childish oxymorons like 'clean war' and 'smart bombs', and camouflaging the terse word 'war' with the cloak of 'military intervention' and 'armed conflict'. When Colin Powell addressed the UN in the lobby of the Security Council, a copy of *Guernica*, the twentieth century's most celebrated reminder of the consequences of aerial bombardment, was covered with a large blue curtain. It was not 'appropriate', said a spokesman, for Colin Powell to talk about war in front of women, children and horses screaming with terror.

It's no surprise therefore that it's widely broadcast that the war will be short and painless—'rapid, accurate and dazzling' in the words of Christopher Hitchens. The US will be greeted as emancipators, rebuilding Iraq will be simple, the Arab world will not turn against the US and democracy will be strengthened. If this sounds like the plot of a Hollywood movie in which the good guys do the difficult things for the right reasons, it's probably supposed to. After the attacks on the Twin Towers the US Government consulted the movie industry on national strategy: if Hollywood had dealt with rogue asteroids and alien invaders it could unquestionably sort out Islamic terrorists. Having acted as strategists, the studio bosses have now reverted to their more familiar role as propagandists. 'Hollywood Rallies Round the Homeland,' said *The New York Times* recently. Movies will be 'positive', 'life affirming', 'on the side of right'. What the public wants, they say, is 'to see the bad guy gotten'.

If the move to war seems to us, the spectators, to be unrolling like a movie, is it any less so to the soldiers who are going to fight it? When I made a film about the

Falklands War, I was told by a number of veterans that they had watched war movies on the *QE2* on the way down to the South Atlantic. Their favourite films were *Apocalypse Now* and *Rambo* and, when they went into battle, the films were running in their heads. In spite of their training, they were shocked to discover that, although they might shout 'Action!', nobody was calling 'Cut!', and the blood, the wounds, the corpses and the ruined lives were all too real.

The probable reality of a war against Iraq is that the US will occupy Iraq, invoke the wrath of the Arab world, become a sitting target for Al-Qaeda, and complete the circle of Bin Laden's strategy when he bombed the World Trade Center. 'I and the public know,' wrote Auden, 'What all schoolchildren learn,/Those to whom evil is done,/Do evil in return.' It's a lesson that the American President might be immune to. He is 'often uncurious', according to the opportunistic ex-speechwriter David Frum, the man who coined the phrase the 'axis of evil'. In spite of Bush's lack of curiosity about the world he is, says Frum, 'courageous and tenacious', making him in Frum's view a 'great president' but, in mine, the possessor of a lethal amalgam of ignorance and aggressiveness.

I will fully support President Bush when he stands up and says this: 'My fellow Americans, we are going to war not only because we want to free the Iraqi people from the yoke of tyranny, take weapons of mass destruction out of the hands of evil murderers and enforce a settlement between Israel and Palestine, but also because I want to guarantee my fellow Americans the inalienable right to cheap gasoline, I want to protect the business interests of my colleagues in Government, and I want to secure another term as president.' It could only happen in the movies. Until then I am left with despair, a voice of protest and Auden's poem written fifty-three years ago.

> All I have is a voice
> To undo the folded lie,
> The romantic lie in the brain
> Of the sensual man-in-the-street
> And the lie of Authority
> Whose buildings grope the sky:
> There is no such thing as the State
> And no one exists alone;
> Hunger allows no choice
> To the citizen or the police;
> We must love one another or die.

Auden famously disowned the last line and until recently I felt indignant about his change of heart, like the woman I heard on the subway talking to her book: 'No no no no, you've been disowned, you fuck!' He changed 'We must love one another *or* die' to 'We must love one another *and* die', moving from wilful optimism to despairing resignation. Now I think he was right.

———•·———

The back of a New York taxi is a fair place to consider the coming war. Shut in a yellow metal box where there is no room for the usual human extensions such as legs and knees, tossed from side to side, bounced over manholes, potholes and dead rats, while the driver leans on the horn as if it had a magic power to dispel drivers and pedestrians, you reflect on how a nation which can't devise an efficient taxi or tarmac its streets beyond the standard of a regional city in the third world can believe this: 'We're approaching the point where we can tell the SA-10 that its target is a Maytag washer and not a missile site, and put it in the rinse cycle instead of the firing cycle.' The speaker was General John P. Jumper (sic), the Air Force Chief of Staff, an earnest evangelist of the fairytale notion of 'clean war'.

His brand of sublime self-confidence swells the flood of xenophobia that is now being addressed as much to French weasels as to Iraqi ragheads. Customers at McDonald's are wary of French fries and the widely respected columnist William Safire writes that 'Thanks to the populist pacifism of the German chancellor, the crowd-pleasing anti-Americanism and the blossoming of the perennial "peace movement", Saddam Hussein is convinced that he can persevere without fear of contradiction.' In addition, New Yorkers suffer from a 'stronger than ever' post-9/11 chauvinism, like the man I heard shepherding his three small children through Times Square: 'Guys, stay close, there's a lot of tourists and they don't know how to walk properly.'

After seven weeks in New York I have stopped flinching when people talk about the war as if it was an immutable fact, or even as if it were already in progress. Recently I met a group of postgraduate acting students at New York University. A student said to me, 'A lot of us are wondering: what's the point of being an actor on a stage in a time of war?' And I said something like this:

I agree that art is useless, but so is life, and it's precisely our awareness of the 'uselessness' of life that make us want to struggle to give it purpose, and to give that purpose meaning. We're told that we're engaged in a Manichean contest between 'Civilisation' and 'Terrorism' to create 'a new world order'. If anything is to change what we need is to understand ourselves better as well as understanding those who are different from us. With understanding begins change, and understanding begins by identifying oneself with another person: in a word, empathy. We need to put ourselves in the minds, eyes, ears and hearts of other human beings, as Tony Harrison put it in his Gulf War poem: 'Let them remember, all those who celebrate,/That their good news is someone else's bad.' To see and hear an actor on a stage, a character in a play, is to be invited to share someone else's view of the world and to be reminded of the scale and frailty of human beings—of the smell of mortality, if you like. And any work of art reminds the leaders that the led are not ciphers, that we are all 'I' not 'them'. And all the while as I'm talking I'm thinking: Do I believe this or is this self-serving propaganda? And then I went to the ballet.

Those of us who like the arts in general invariably have prejudices against particular art forms. For many years I resisted opera, unsympathetic to a medium which told its stories through music, character and narrative but almost invariably ignored the most basic demands of psychological reality. Then I came to accept that opera is a world like any other, with its own criteria and its own forms of truth, and that it was as fruitless to blame it for not being like theatre as it is to blame theatre for not being film, or a melon for not being an orange.

Nevertheless I still stubbornly retain a prejudice against classical ballet, whose vocabulary is so often so limited and inexpressive—neither sufficiently abstract nor sufficiently humane, remote from the contemporary world, engrossed in archaic conventions, danced by painfully angular women in organza tutus and wooden-toed pointe shoes lifted effortfully by men who strut their stuff in padded codpieces to music treated as a necessary but irksome accompaniment to the movement.

All of which was in my mind at the New York State Theater at the Lincoln Center as the dun-coloured curtain rose on a Balanchine ballet called *Concerto Barocco*, based on Bach's Double Violin Concerto. It started badly. The music was played at a leaden tempo, accompanied by hollow thuds from the stage as the female chorus (silk tutus, pink pointe shoes) landed slightly after the beat, moving, by the standards of a Broadway chorus line, with a careless lack of synchronicity. Then came the adagio. A female soloist crossed the stage ghosted by a male one. He lifted her seamlessly and, as the two dancers merged with the grace and weightlessness of leaves in an autumn breeze, my eyes pricked with tears, moved by the virtuosity of the two dancers and their unaffected beauty. In their ability to defy gravity, I saw the divine in the human form. And just as the divine can be rendered visible by art, so can the bestial: we can be made to look in the face of Caliban as well as Ariel.

But talking about art in the presence of war it's hard not to feel a sense of bathos. 'Art,' said Flaubert, 'needs white hands', and however much General Jumper may talk wishfully of 'surgical strikes' the hands engaged in war will always be dirty with blood, shit and dust. Bush has declared a 'fight for civilisation'. What civilisation? He should borrow his rhetoric from *49th Parallel*, made by Michael Powell and Emeric Pressburger, as a propaganda film, in 1941. Laurence Olivier played a French Canadian with an accent that would have scared a polar bear, Leslie Howard played the decent Englishman and the evil Nazi was, inevitably, played by Eric Portman. There's a scene early in the film in which Portman castigates Howard for the decadence of Western painting: the modernism of Matisse and Picasso, he says, will be swept aside by the new Aryan art, fine purebred men and women wearing lederhosen. At the end Leslie Howard chases Eric

Portman up a mountainside and corners him in a cave. There's an off-screen fist fight and this is how the dialogue goes: THUD 'That's for Matisse—' THUD 'That's for Picasso—' and THUD 'That's for me!'

'HE LOVES IT,' said the *Sun* front page admiringly of George W. Bush and war, and for many years so did I. I was born during a war, 'The War', my parents called it, as if there had been and would be only one. 'The War' was the time of my parents' lives; it wound up their emotional clock and it marked out the grammar of my childhood. They had had a 'good war' and spoke with a sort of impatient pity of those who had had a 'bad war'—in POW camps, wounded in action or, perhaps worse still, removed from the action in reserved occupations, condemned to be spectators rather than participants. Even as a child I could sense that it was one of the consequences of war that life would never be the same for those who were involved, but it took a lifetime to realise that the casualties were not always the wounded.

As a child all the games I played were war games. I fired sticks and mimicked the high stutter of machine guns in the woods, and flattened the long grass as I dive-bombed my friends with ear-damaging howls and flung my small body into the arc of heroic death. Or I sat in the cockpit of a large paratroop glider whose still intact but inert carcass lay in an orchard at my friend's house, wearing a gas mask as a pilot's helmet and taking turns to sit in the pilot's seat and steer the flak-torn fuselage through heavy bombardment towards its target. I have only to smell a bicycle inner tube to bring it all back.

From the age of eight to twelve all the books I read for pleasure were about the war, with titles that resonate like regimental mottos: *Boldness Be My Friend, Fortune is my Enemy, Reach for the Sky, Carve Her Name with Pride*... stories of escape from POW camps, of espionage and counter-espionage, of resistance and torture (pliers and fingernails). They competed with *Jane's Fighting Ships*, a guide of biblical authority to identifying naval ships, which qualified me precociously for a career spent at the periscope of a submarine. I loved the romance, the nobility, the extremity and the secrecy of war. War was a test of character and a proof of life; you became, as Rupert Brooke said, 'as swimmers into cleanness leaping'.

Then I renounced war, or my fascination with it, or at least replaced it with another, more hideous, fascination, with what Wilfred Owen described as 'the pity of war, the pity war distilled'. *The Wooden Horse, The Dam Busters* and *Odette: The Story of a British Agent* were replaced by Owen's poems, *Goodbye to All That, All Quiet on the Western Front* and A.J.P. Taylor's *History of the First World War*. I could see and understand nothing but the waste, the futility and the degradation of war. In war, I learned, everyone was a loser.

My conversion coincided with three events, two public, one private: the Suez adventure, that dribble at the end of the British empire; the hydrogen bomb, the perfection of mankind's ingenuity for destroying itself; and the legislation that ended conscription. I became part of the first generation in our century who wouldn't fight in a war and part of a substantial minority who believed that as a nation we should never again become involved in a war. This article of faith survived the Vietnam War, the Falklands War and the Gulf War. It was underpinned by an assumption that people are rational, that war is a flight from reason, that it engenders universal disgust and that society will flow towards enlightenment and decency as rivers to the sea.

Now I'm not so certain. This optimistic credo seems like colossal *naïveté*. While the historical models are invoked—the need to avoid appeasement, the duty to defeat dictatorship—the historical lessons are ignored. And in spite of all the information, the statistics, the analysis and the opinion, nothing changes about war except the speed with which we learn what is happening, or what appears to be happening, or what is permitted to appear to be happening. Nor, despite the preening rhetoric of 'smart weapons', 'surgical strikes' and 'clean wars', does much change in battle. Soldiers were fixing bayonets and using them in anger in the Falklands; in Baghdad and Basra they are fighting with small arms from house to house. And every so often, after a massive bomb falls in Baghdad and lights up the night sky like a premature sunrise, some commentator is on hand, as there has been since Homer, to talk of the 'terrible beauty' of war.

The beauty of war, if it ever existed, disappeared with the machine gun and the tank. But where is the 'beauty' of having your arm cut off by a broadsword rather than shot off by a heat-seeking missile fired by a soldier sitting in front of a computer screen? In modern war, soldiers die without the assurance that they are travelling to a soldier's heaven, or worse still are wounded and, on their return home, are ignored or reviled for reminding civilians, now uncomfortable about their haste to war and that they have to pay for building up the country they have destroyed. And yet the wars go on, each one with its more or less virtuous or more or less specious justifications. Why?

A US army officer said that when Afghanis understood why US forces were fighting the Taliban, it was the '*voilà* moment' for them. For me the '*voilà* moment' about war came while I was watching TV. After hours of homogenised 'rolling news', of reports from vicarious combatants ('embedded correspondents') talking with knowing assurance of desert strategy, rapid dominance and friendly fire, and with prurient awe of bombs, mortars, missiles and tanks, I realised that all this is happening because in some atavistic way most of us must have a desire for the rush of adrenalin, for the smell of napalm in the morning, an appetite for war indistinguishable from the one that fuelled my childhood passion for it: the great game, tin soldiers made real. In the story of mankind, war is the one unbroken subject.

Which is why, in this country, politicians have continued to be infected by what Anthony Barnett identified during the Falklands War as 'Churchillism', a virus which 'ensured that all parties were committed to a British military and financial role that was spun worldwide; it conserved the Westminster system when it should have been transformed... it ensured Westminster's allegiance to a moment of *world* greatness that was actually the moment when the greatness ceased.'

More or less the only people who don't seem to love war are the ones who do it, who are unimpressed by what an eyewitness of the Charge of the Light Brigade called 'the splendour' of it. 'I haven't come to Iraq to kill anyone,' said a captured US soldier, 'I've no argument with anyone, I was just doing my job.' As the historian Niall Ferguson has pointed out, in the First World War—The War to End Wars—'men kept fighting because they wanted to'. It's an extremely melancholy conclusion and it's surely the corollary of the observation of an ex-soldier, Ernest Hemingway: 'Never think that war, no matter how necessary, nor how justified, is not a crime.'

———————

A starched commentator intoned: 'It was the beginning and the end of imagination all at the same time.' I'm not sure I understand what this means any more than I understand what a 'war against terror' is, but I know that it refers to the Great Depression, that it's contained in the portentous voiceover in the film *Seabiscuit* and that it served as a useful inoculation against the visit of George W. Bush. As the promotional material of the film declares (and it doesn't lie) it is 'the story of a country whose dreams had been shattered and the people who found a hero that could achieve the unthinkable'. The 'shattering' was the Depression and the 'hero' was a racehorse. No, the horse didn't become president, merely achieved the improbable by appearing to cure blindness, end the Depression and spawn a bucketful of homilies, all derivatives of the flatulent mantra, 'You don't throw a whole life away just 'cause it's banged up a little'.

The platitudinous half-truths, the toxic sentimentality, the Capra-esque we're-all-little-guys-who-don't-know-we're-little-guys rhetoric is the emotional vocabulary that sustains America's notion of itself as the quintessential free society and kindles Blair's passion for the 'special relationship'.

Over forty years ago, Mary McCarthy said that 'the immense popularity of American movies abroad demonstrates that Europe is the unfinished negative of which America is the proof.' The finished negative could be said to be evident in the McDonald's, Burger Kings, Nando's, Baskin Robbins, Gaps and Kentucky

Fried Chickens that we see in every British high street; in the Levi jeans, Tommy Hilfiger T-shirts, Nike trainers, Calvin Klein underwear, NYC baseball caps that we wear; in the Buds, Becks, Coors and Miller Lites ('Democracy's Drink') in our pubs; in our cinemas and on our TV; and in the foreign policy of the unofficial fifty-first state of the Union. 'We were Britain's colony once, she will be our colony before she is done,' said a prescient US newspaper in 1921.

It started in the War when the native population, already softened up by the vision of the Promised Land offered by the movies, were subdued by hundreds of thousands of American soldiers who grafted their magazines, films, and music onto ours. As a contemporary US journalist observed, 'They so often seemed to treat Britain as an occupied country rather than as an ally,' and we became willingly, enthusiastically and comprehensively colonised. And for all that I grew up in a small village in West Dorset—or even *because* I grew up, etc.—I was ravenous for American comics, novels, music (rock 'n' roll and jazz), movies, TV, musicals and plays (which I read but never saw). I loved the energy and the optimism—the lack of Englishness I suppose—and if in 1958, when I was fifteen, you had asked me what were my three wishes, all three would have been to emigrate to America.

So I feel uneasy at my current resistance to American culture, which grows with every *Seabiscuit* that I'm fed. Like a member of the Académie Française, I find myself flinching when I hear people talking about 'taking a rain check' or 'ballpark figures' or 'getting to first base' or 'striking out'—terms taken from baseball, a game not even played by amateurs in this country. This hybrid English is a form of Hobson-Jobson, the lingua franca of Imperial India, whose legacy is in words like juggernaut, chicanery, curry, ginger, sugar, toddy, pyjamas, pundit and nirvana, the currency exchanged between the colonised and colonisers.

Imperial India must have been in the minds of the organisers of last Wednesday's pageant at Buckingham Palace [the State Visit of George W. Bush]. If there was one thing that it resembled, it was the Delhi Durbar of exactly one hundred years ago. Bush, standing on a platform designed to hint both at English chivalry and Mughal pageantry, played the part of the Viceroy, Lord Curzon. There was no longer any room to doubt that the reason for Blair's courtship of Bush was rooted not in realpolitik, but in nostalgia for our imperial past. Curzon could have provided Bush's text for the occasion: 'In the empire we have found not merely the key to glory and wealth, but the call to duty, and the means of service to mankind'.

Later that day I wandered past Buckingham Palace and my futile exasperation with the theatre of statesmanship was assuaged by the demonstrations. Not that they were, on the whole, less theatrical or much less futile. A demure-looking woman in her forties chatted amiably to police as she waved a placard that read 'BUSH IS THE MASTER CRIMINAL MASON UNDER THE COMMAND OF HIS

MASTER THE QUEEN THE HEAD OF THE CRIMINAL SOCIETY'. Another read 'BUSH UNWELCOME BLAIR UNREAL', while another sort of unreality declared itself in 'DEFEND YOURSELF AGAINST HOMOPHOBIC, MATERIALISTIC, IMPERIALISTIC BOLLOCKS'. A young man with a scarf wrapped round his head like a djellaba shouted, 'Your grandfathers died for freedom!!!', while another with a long bugle and a tattered Bible cried: 'O ye people here, have ye read my book? Yea a lion, a unicorn and a sea monster shall lie down together. Yea, it is written.' That would cover Bush and Blair, but who is the sea monster?

Helicopters jarred the air while every few yards police stood sentry duty, or sat in transit vans like battery hens until they moved into action with grateful enthusiasm to deal with the arrival of a smallish (about 300) Socialist Worker demonstration. 'GET BUSH! GET BUSH! GET BUSH! GET OUT!' was the chant; 'BUSH THE WORLD'S NUMBER ONE TERRORIST' was the written message. So no exaggeration there. A woman protester shouted, 'Bush and Blair should be assassinated,' and I felt discouraged, as I did the next day when I saw the statue of George Bush topple in Trafalgar Square: the gesture and rhetoric seemed as empty and contrived as the object of the parody. I found myself admiring the courage of a man who looked like a decrepit version of Fred Mac-Murray waving an American flag on a stick.

But scorn for the grand gesture, fear of folly, fear of commitment, love of even-handedness, gives comfort to our leaders. They applaud undemonstrative demonstrators because, they say, they are the evidence that protest is a part of our democratic heritage and our democratic privilege—the right and privilege to be ignored, of course. In the midst of the anger, the clamouring, the posturing, the hyperbole and the glibness, there was one protest which struck my heart with the force of an arrow—a large cheery girl had a message spread across her T-shirt: 'THIS MACHINE KILLS APATHY'.

General Sir Mike Jackson

After I'd written a few pieces for Sarah Sands when she was Deputy Editor of the Daily Telegraph, *she asked me in 2007 who I would like to interview. I chose to interview the man who was in charge of Britain's armed forces.*

———•——

To borrow from Neil Kinnock, I was the first Eyre in a thousand generations to get to university. In his case this had everything to do with enlightened educational policies and the introduction of free tuition (*o tempora o mores*). In my case you joined the army or navy because it was what you did: my father and maternal grandfather were naval officers, my paternal one a major, his father a colonel... and so on for receding generations.

I was born during a war. I loved the romance, the nobility, the extremity and the secrecy of war—a test of character and a proof of life. Then with the end of the British Empire (Suez), the end of civilisation (the Bomb), and the end of conscription, I renounced war's allure and became part of the first generation in our century who were not called upon to fight a war for their country, and part of a substantial minority who recoiled from our nation's involvement in any war.

In the world that I grew up in it wasn't uncommon to join the army because you couldn't do anything else. For much the same reasons I became an actor, a profession which had this at least in common with soldiering: I was required to dress up for work, was often involved in pointless routines, was subject to confused or conflicting orders, had to engender patience in the face of waiting tedium and endure frequent degradation with amused stoicism. At this point the analogy breaks down into preposterous and insulting bathos: the job of soldiers is to make war not to pretend to. Soldiers have to be prepared to kill and be killed on the instructions of elected politicians who act on our behalf.

As a director I have become engaged by Shakespeare's exploration of war. For him it's the activity that defines manhood in combat and educates women in grief. He describes battle as a distillation of fear, danger and exhilaration which leaves a vacuum that nothing in peacetime can fill. Soldiers and the profession of soldiering dominate his plays—Benedick, King Lear, Othello, Macbeth, Antony, Julius Caesar, Coriolanus, Fortinbras, Hamlet's father, Henry IV, and above all, Richard III, whose acrid contempt for peace poisons the air in his opening speech:

> Grim-visaged War hath smooth'd his wrinkled front
> And now, instead of mounting barbed steeds
> To fright the souls of fearful adversaries,
> He capers nimbly in a lady's chamber.

I am fascinated by the profession of soldiering: the strutting neatness, cleanness, pomp and order of the soldier's life in peacetime set against the blood that gets shed in foreign fields far from home. And the seductive panoply of uniforms, pipes, drums, marching, medals, men amongst men and the promise of adventure, set against its savage corollary—hidden from the recruit—of breaking the ultimate taboo against killing your fellow man. This fascination has led me from Shakespeare's protagonists to *Tumbledown* (a film I made about the Falklands War in 1987) and now to the Ministry of Defence to interview the man who runs the British army, General Sir Mike Jackson.

It's not the first time that I've been in the Ministry of Defence. I went in 1979, when I was producing a film about a boy soldier who was killed in Belfast, to seek the use of an army recruiting office in which to shoot part of the film. I met a plump Colonel who observed, somewhat injudiciously, that the problems of Northern Ireland could be resolved by lining the troublemakers up against a wall and shooting them. The current Colonel in charge of public relations ('Corporate Communications') is, mercifully, a tactful and shrewd man called David Norris.

Like all the soldiers I meet at the MoD, there is something dandyish about him in his civilian clothes—double-breasted suit, silk handkerchief in breast pocket, vermilion socks. When we pass through an open-plan office, a group of lightly tanned, fit-looking young officers are celebrating the departure (at 10.30 in the morning) of one of their colleagues with a glass of champagne. They're like dapper clones, jackets off, pale pink shirts and blue pinstripe suits, compensating for the lack of the peacock glitter of their uniforms. What amounts to a civilian uniform is highlit by the presence of occasional soldiers in combat uniform—boots and camouflage—walking incongruously, like actors in costume in the front-of-house lobby of a theatre, down corridors which are indistinguishable in their decoration from the new-look BBC: red walls, grey carpet, elegant signage.

There is much in common with the BBC and the army—their love of acronyms, their sense of hierarchy, their reference to holidays as 'leave' and job interviews as 'boards', their public service remit and their accountability to government. What the BBC lacks, and certainly envies, is the clear sense of mission, a rigorous command structure and a rigid enforcement of discipline, sanctioned by operational necessity.

I met CGS (the acronyms are catching) in his office, one in which the Chairman or Director General of the BBC would feel perfectly at home, a featureless room decorated with military prints and a gallery of black-and-white photographs of previous incumbents of the job, who look, in spite of their uniforms, identical to their broadcasting counterparts. General Jackson is less intimidating in the flesh than in his official photographs where, with his rakish beret, creased face, baggy, heavy-lidded elephant's eyes and teeth like battlements, he looks every inch the fighting man. In his shirtsleeves, his beret off and his baldness apparent, his uniform jacket with its red shoulder flashes and glinting braid laid over the back of a chair, he is more accessible but no less authoritative. It's a reflex for me as a director to think of how I would cast him: Nigel Davenport or Richard Johnson, perhaps—good actors both—but neither has the gravitas of the real thing.

If you consult ARRSE (www.arrse.co.uk)—'the army's UNOFFICIAL centre of reasoned argument, intelligent debate and bullshit'—you will find that Jackson is 'legendary for his drinking abilities, death stare and a face that suffered the hardest paper-round in NATO'. I can't testify to the first, can deny the second and am certain of the truth of the third.

He has a gruff, don't-mess-with-me, bass voice. He's direct and un-evasive, but shies away from anything that comes close to a personal question. Why did he join the army? 'No idea... It's impossible for me to answer that question. It's what I wanted to do.' And he's unsurprisingly unforthcoming about his work in intelligence: 'I only spent, in terms of working time, a very short period in intelligence.' He has an assurance, a self-belief—actors call it being 'centred'—that instinctively makes me feel frivolous, as if my occupation were a sort of game. Politicians never have this effect on me, but General Jackson joins a few farmers, medical consultants and Arthur Miller in my private catalogue of proper grown-ups.

Is the Homeric ideal of the Good Warrior—the man who makes a success of his death—an anachronism? 'No, I don't think it is,' he says; 'we still get young people joining the army for whom there's never really been any other option in their own mind… That's all they've ever wanted to do, for whatever, you know, whichever part of soldiering was ringing a particular bell.' But is that a search for heroism? Or merely a determination to test your masculinity? 'That's a rather un-British motivation it seems to me. You don't really see that. What you do see though is when the moment comes, soldiers rise to the occasion in the most extraordinary way. You've only got to look at the last operational awards—young Private Beharry with his Victoria Cross, and about a year before that, a young trooper in the household cavalry who won the George Cross—these are young men who find themselves in the most testing of circumstances and more than rise to the occasion with extraordinary courage. If by "a search for hero-ism" you mean going medal-hunting, no, that's not really how we are. Young men like it when you say, "Well how the hell did do you that?", "Just doing my job, sir, just doing my job. Anybody would have done it. Looking after my mates." There's an innate modesty.'

But what about the immodest ones? If courage in a private soldier is utterly admirable, is that sort of courage inconvenient in a commander? (I'm thinking of Colonel H. Jones in the Falklands and perhaps Colonel Tim Collins in Iraq.) Does the army have a problem dealing with the mavericks? 'I don't think we have a problem with it but it's true that soldiering can attract somebody with—how to put this?—a greater sense of adventure than the average.' But isn't that what you're encouraged to think when you join the army? The propaganda insists on a life of adventure. 'Oh, I'm not sure I would accept the word propa-ganda.' Well, the advertisements say 'THE ADVENTURE STARTS HERE', but the adventure is that you're being trained to kill and be prepared to be killed.

'Clearly you have to give the recruit the military skills which he—or indeed today she—will need when they join the field of arms. That's, if you like, the mechanical side of it. You've also got to inculcate into these youngsters a value system: it's the glue which holds the whole thing together. A value system places the emphasis on the team, not on the individual. You see, it's not a "me me" business. Of course, in today's world, with its greater emphasis on the individ-ual, that's a greater challenge than it has been in the past. You can't teach somebody how to be brave. It's impossible to do that… but from day one of your training, you are being taught how to do things on the battlefield, and it's inevitable that everybody will think "How will I do?"'

And here is a paradox—a painful one to him, I think—the courage of this war-rior, who was a paratrooper and sometime member of the SAS, has never been tested in battle: 'his' war was the Falklands and he spent it in the Ministry of Defence. When I remind him of this, he looks rueful. It should have been your war, I say. There is a pause. 'It should.' Have you ever been in action? There is another pause. 'I have never fought a conventional battle.' So have you ever shot a rifle in anger? 'Oh, yes, oh yes, and been bombed and buggered about but not in a force-on-force conventional battle, that I have not done.' If he hadn't denied it with a laugh—'Why on earth should I? I've been very fortunate'—I would say that, like a centre forward kept on the bench during a cup final, he was full of regret.

But isn't it one thing firing, I ask him, but another thing being shot at? He answers with an implacable British understatement. 'Yes, it's quite an interesting theory. But fear can be quite useful if controlled. Does that sound fair? Because your fear is telling you be careful. You've got to control that fear in such a way that you don't let it overwhelm you and you turn and run, and we can't have that... You have to overcome that fear and some people do in extraordinarily brave ways.'

But surely, I persist (assuming a Paxman-like interrogatory tone), training a sol-dier requires a sort of brutalisation. Would it be a calumny to suggest that? 'I think it would be quite wrong.' So you can't draw any sort of connection between young men being encouraged to be very violent in training and that violence becoming uncontrollable? He pauses judiciously. 'I think you have in the back of your mind certain incidents in Iraq?' Well, I am thinking that, I say. And I'm thinking of the maxim: 'Training doesn't produce soldiers, character does.' And I'm also thinking (although I don't say it) of a US unit who have christened themselves 'LONG-DISTANCE DEATH DEALERS' and I'm thinking too that a professional soldier is a professional killer and I'm thinking: What happens to you as a person when killing becomes a job?

'A young soldier has got to have not only the training, but the inner confidence, if necessary, to take the enemy's life. So it can be a brutal business, and we have to get that into them. This whole question therefore of the training regime is a very interesting one. We're still suffering the aftershocks of the Deepcut affair. There is a notion in some minds—not everybody's—that training a young civil-ian to be a soldier is, to quote your word, a brutalisation. That, I think, is quite the wrong way of looking at it but we often get the phrase "duty of care" thrown back at us, that we failed in our duty of care because these poor young people are dead... But it seems to me that there's another side to this "duty of care" coin which is probably even greater, in that if we do not properly prepare these youngsters with the physical skills and also mental robustness, we have failed in our duty of care in a rather more fundamental way.'

But these youngsters, who are often no more than seventeen years old, have been saturated with images of violence for years from films and TV, and are going into battle with these films running in their heads. They were the stars of their own odysseys of destruction—even of their own deaths. 'I wouldn't dis-agree with what you've said, but that is not, of course, what we're talking about here at all: it's the application of violence in an extremely disciplined way, not in a gratuitous way. We've got to be absolutely focused.'

So you ask soldiers to behave like responsible policemen and yet within a day you're telling them they've got to go out and kill and risk being be killed. 'It can be less than a day, very much less than a day at times. In Basra, at the front you were fighting, somewhere in the middle you were doing some peace enforcement of the area you'd recently taken, and at the back end you were delivering humanitarian aid. Soldiers have to be prepared to move from one level of the application up or down very quickly indeed, and it's not easy. We ask a great deal of these youngsters.'

Given that there's so much more reporting of the war—with TV and with embedded correspondents—and there's no end of fictional dramatisation of battle, doesn't it seem odd that the public seems so blind to what soldiering entails? To speculate, as the media did when the Black Watch were preparing to enter Fallujah, that the troops were nervous of engaging in combat seemed a preposterous misunderstanding of the soldier's job. Perhaps it's due to the lack of conscription or is it simply a desire not to know or to understand what is being done in our name? 'I think that there's some truth in what you say and I would wish it wasn't so. I mean, at the end of the day, we recruit from and serve this nation—that's our only purpose. We do, at times, seem to be not too well understood; why we do things the way we do. Well, it's not because we're perverse; it's because this is the distillation of decades, of centuries of experience. There's a reason for our insistence upon a disciplinary system for example, and it rests a little uneasily with today's world, but without it we're not an army, we're just a mob, a rabble.'

The army is an organisation whose conduct is based on discipline and tradition, like the Church, and, like the Church, or at least the Anglican variety, the army is subject to the pressures of modernisation. Leaving aside the development of technology—'Well, we have smart weapons, and frequently…' Frequently…? 'they're not as smart as you'd hoped, but there you are'—the army will always need 'boots on the ground'. Won't their wearers need to be managed just as much as they will need to be commanded? 'Part of soldiering has always been the whole logistic piece. Talk about the sort of management side and you can go back to Hannibal. No doubt he had to have cared about whether he had food for his elephants.'

So how do you modernise the army—let's say by amalgamating regiments— without scorning the soldier's identification with regimental histories and honours and all the tunes of glory that are so alluring to army recruits, just as ritual and liturgy is to applicants for the priesthood? And what about health and safety, and pay and welfare, and public relations ('a reflection of the modern world') and 'duty of care'? 'Yah, and we live in a more, what's the word I want, we live in a world where matters legal have grown very considerably in importance… a very litigious society. As an aside, the one part of the army which has virtually doubled in size over the last, what, fifteen years or so, is our legal branch—make of that what you will.'

As the General said, 'We can talk on this particular aspect for an hour or more,' but while I would have been happy to hear about the army's housekeeping, I was more eager to talk about the politics of going to war in the spring of 2003. It seems clear—at least to me—from the leaked Downing Street memo of July 23rd of the previous year that the Government had already committed to the action in Iraq, but I didn't say this quite to the General, mindful of his response to Michael Mansfield in the Bloody Sunday Inquiry: 'I hear what you are telling me, but this is surely a matter for the tribunal.'

I did, however, ask him the extent to which he was consulted: 'For any government which contemplates the use of force to achieve a political end, the first questions are: "Is it doable?", "Will you achieve this?" Because it could be worse to take the huge risk of applying force and failing, than of not doing it at all... After all the use of military force—to quote Clausewitz—is "politics by other means", and it's, if you like, the means of final resort. The violence, state violence, will always have a political objective. Always. You don't take these huge risks without a political objective.'

And should we have gone to war, was it just? 'I think, on the whole, the British people do understand that there is a difference between a decision to commit a military force and the execution thereof. In other words, the opprobrium, such as it is, against the Iraq War is not visible upon those who have to carry it out. It is visible on those who are making the decisions and that's absolutely right and proper. We catch some overspill, I think, if I can put it that way.'

For my generation, growing up in the shadow of the Second World War, Dr Johnson's adage that 'every man thinks meanly of himself for not having been a soldier' had sufficient truth to trouble the conscience. For the generation after, growing up in the sixties, it was meaningless. Now, I think, there's only one class of men who feel it: politicians. I can't help feeling that behind every ASBO, curfew and campaign for 'Respect', there's a lurking regret for the disappearance of conscription, and perhaps military service should be a basic requirement for holding political office. Then all politicians—male and female—might be that much less likely to devise political objectives, make the facts fit the policy, as they unquestionably did in Iraq, and commit us to a war whose justice is, at best, dubious.

Colonel Norris saw me off the premises at the MoD and as the car pulled away into Whitehall he raised his hand, somewhere between a salute and a wave. It was an eloquent metaphor for an army poised between the operational necessity of fighting wars and the desire to please a public reluctant to accept what their job is. It is a measure of how keenly the army feels this gap between actuality and perception that the head of the British army was prepared to spend three-quarters of an hour talking to a theatre director masquerading as a reporter. It might, however, have been a shrewd calculation on his part. A professional would surely not have neglected to ask him this question: Where *did* you fire those shots in anger?

Campaign Performance

The Financial Times—*at the time edited by Richard Lambert—asked me in 1997 (my last year as director of the National Theatre) to write about that year's election.*

I once saw a film of Churchill encountering a television camera. He was being introduced, with great reluctance on his part, to the notion of the party political broadcast. He eyed up the camera with the distaste of a dog inspecting a new variety of dog food, and spoke with the painful self-consciousness of a man who has been given the instruction: 'Just be yourself.' He had become an actor, giving an unconvincing performance of 'Winston Churchill'. Since then all politics have declined to the condition of show business, and all politicians have been obliged to become performers. They choose their costumes carefully, their decor fastidiously; they discuss their roles with their directors, their fellow actors, and their agents; they study their scripts, they rehearse, they put on make-up, and they give performances; they adapt their acting styles from the would-be intimacy of the small screen to the not-to-be-avoided histrionics of the public platform, and sometimes, often disastrously, they improvise.

Actors require us willingly to suspend our disbelief, to accept that what we know to be fiction is, at least temporarily, reality. Politicians expect something rather similar but more enduring, and we, the voters, are expected to give our consent. But we're at best reluctant and at worst intransigent about closing the circle of the illusion: the gap between content and performance is risibly clear, and we know all too well that, however little reality their public pronouncements possess, politicians are not participating in a dramatic fiction.

All of us, consciously or not, are actors—we simulate feelings we don't feel, we lie, we pretend to be what we aren't, and this latent, though well-rehearsed, skill lures us all, and politicians especially, to believe that if everyone does the actor's job in life, then anyone can apply it to their own profession. But it's exasperatingly difficult for an actor to find what the playwright and philosopher Diderot describes as 'the true point':

> An actor who has only sense and judgement is cold; one who has only verve and sensibility is crazy. It is a peculiar combination of good sense and warmth which creates the sublime person; and on the stage as in life he who shows more than he feels makes one laugh instead of affecting one. Therefore never try to go beyond the feeling that you have; try to find the true point.

It's difficult to achieve the 'true point' in life, which is probably why we give such extravagant praise to those who achieve it in art. To act properly, in life as in art, implies a moral dimension that makes us want actors (and politicians) to be exemplary beings. Is it any wonder that when politicians perform they seem, as Hamlet said of bad actors, as if 'some of nature's journeymen had made men, and not made them well, they imitated humanity so abominably'.

There's precious little of the Shakespearean about this election, even if the spirit of Polonius presides over the campaign: you might find an Iago in Peter Mandelson, a Malvolio in Brian McWhinney, a Cassius in Michael Heseltine, a Claudius in Lady Thatcher, an Enobarbus in John Prescott, a Lear in Edward Heath, and a Jacques in Tony Benn. Norman Tebbit might make a good Fool, and you could find plenty of clowns in all parties, but unless you include Roy Hattersley, who has the stomach for the role of Touchstone, if not the wit, they belong more to the circus than to Shakespeare.

You might wish more of the Mercutio than the Orlando from Tony Blair, and from John Major, whose taste for Cantona-esque metaphors defy parody, you might wish a little of the Berowne. You would wish in vain: the manifestos, like the New English Bible, have been filleted of figurative language, and if you were looking for an event with which to compare this spectacle of the bland leading the bland, you would not find your model in Shakespeare or Shaw, but in a convention for management consultants or the Eurovision Song Contest.

So how are the contestants doing? When John Major stepped up on his 'soapbox' at the start of the campaign—an object as far removed from its original function as a freemason is from a stonecutter—he looked as if he pined for the return of *Spitting Image*, so keen was he to mimic his model: one puppeteer appeared to operate his arms, while his hands flapped helplessly at their extremity and his voice appeared, in an ill-disguised piece of ventriloquism, to emerge from his ears.

When the Prime Minister is speaking impromptu before a small group he seems intelligent, authoritative, even, yes, witty: in a word, plausible. But put this manifestly mild-mannered man before a large audience and a television camera, and he booms from a lectern which helpfully tells us what he's doing—'BRITAIN IS BOOMING'—and, with a rising inflection borrowed from Olivier's Henry V but performed with all the flair of Roger Moore, he berates his opponent with the milky rhetoric of a primary-school headmaster: 'This is incompetence pure and simple!', he booms. Indeed.

Tony Blair grips the side of his lectern at press conferences with a white-knuckled intensity, like a survivor of a shipwreck gripping the gunwales of a lifeboat. The Tories say he's suffering from stage fright; this is wishful thinking. That he's frightened is clear, but as a performer it's a strength—he's aware of the endemic danger and folly of playing a leading role on the political stage. (Incidentally, in France they make a direct connection between politics and the theatre: they speak not of the 'corridors' of power but of the 'wings'.) 'I can see how, if you're not careful,' said Tony Blair a week or so ago, 'whatever public persona you have starts taking over your private being.'

It may be that Tony Blair's true persona is what you see, and what you see is what you'll get if he becomes Prime Minister. It may be that he's achieved a state of grace rare among politicians, that he's reached the 'true point', where honesty and expediency are held in balance. He appears not to dissemble; it's possible, therefore, that he may be rejected by the voters—audiences have a way of preferring Edmund and Iago to Edgar and Othello. If politics is thought to be a dirty game, what price the politician who is honest, decent and true?

'Honest' Paddy Ashdown's epiphany was celebrated with several thousand balloons of dubious hue at the Lib Dem Rally. He began his speech with a pale invocation of the ghost of Neil Kinnock, chiding Tony Blair like Hamlet chastising Gertrude, and, then, like a poor actor striving to stir his audience, indicated his concern for the future of the country with a whirlwind of flailing arms and earnest adjectives, combining simultaneously the 'best' and 'worst' of Yeats' poem—lacking all conviction and full of passionate intensity.

It is a thankless task being a leader of a party whose only advantage is moral superiority, even if the party does contain a higher proportion of conspicuously excellent MPs than the two main parties. There are precious few opportunities to assert his authority, but I eagerly anticipate each year the moment at the Cenotaph when Captain Ashdown (retd.) reminds his civilian colleagues, like a dance instructor demonstrating the correct posture for an old-fashioned waltz, how a leader should stand to attention and place a wreath, thus proving Diderot's thesis: 'He who shows more than he feels makes one laugh instead of affecting one.'

The mad Lear says to the blind Gloucester 'Like a scurvy politician, seem/To see the things thou dost not...' I wish we didn't so readily agree with him, and I wish too that we didn't (with much encouragement from MPs themselves, it has to be said) invariably slip into the cynical assumption that all politicians are on the make, endemically dishonest, riddled with narcissism, self-regard, shallowness, and vanity. Much of the same is said about my profession, but, unlike most politicians, we don't set out on our professional careers with the intention of making the world a better place, nor do we make claims of moral probity; we have, therefore, less capacity for the corruption of our souls. Coming from a world mired in make-believe, I am familiar with the problem that faces the actor after the performance is over. It's the same that the politician faces after the election: to know how to be oneself. If the whole world is to be show business, when does the mask come off?

In one respect politicians are different from us: they have to be more thick-skinned. I'm glad for his sake that John Major wasn't sitting in the pub in Gloucestershire that I was in last week. Across the bar I heard a woman with the sort of upper-class voice that carries across three counties, marinated in generations of Tory self-confidence: 'I'm just going to write bum bum bum on my ballot paper, and I don't care who knows it.' She wasn't acting.

The People's War

The Financial Times *had a series in 2004 on 'My Favourite Book'. This was my offering. Angus Calder, who was a friend when I was at Cambridge in the early sixties, died not many years later.*

I know there are people who read and re-read novels with the regularity of the passing of the seasons; I married one, but even her hunger for *Pride and Prejudice* may have been assuaged by producing a TV series of the novel. There are no novels which I consume with such bulimic appetite, not even my Desert Island Dickens, *Our Mutual Friend*, although when John Updike's *Rabbit* tetralogy was published in one volume I read the four novels as if they were one huge, uninterrupted, all-inclusive narrative. The only book I return to consistently (and obsessively) is a book of social history: *The People's War* by Angus Calder.

It was published in 1969, and I bought it at Singapore Airport, when I was travelling—I suppose now I would call it backpacking—in South East Asia. As I travelled through Vietnam, where the American presence sat on the country like Goya's colossus of Chaos, and through Cambodia, which had yet to learn the benefits of receiving the protection of the USA, I was learning through *The People's War* about a far-away country of which I knew little: my own.

For me the title alone was an allure and a provocation: alluring if you'd grown up reading little else but POW escape stories and spy sagas, and provocative if your education has been ballasted by the proprietary memoirs of generals, whose war was emphatically in the first person.

Much of the attraction of *The People's War* is archaeological, the excavation of a world whose relics were gas masks, ration books, air-raid sirens, Anderson shelters, allotments, Bakelite radios, bombed-out houses, just barely the world of my childhood, but all the more potent for being forever a lost domain.

Like any evocation of childhood, the book is filled with fables, anecdotes of figures who have the status of demons and giants of folklore. He writes of Lord Haw-Haw, making his last broadcast, roaring drunk at the microphone: 'You may not hear from me again for a few months. *Es lebe Deutschland!*' then dropped his voice to a whisper '*Heil Hitler*'; of Nye Bevan, whose oratory was often tinged, as a woman MP said, with 'cattish displays of feline malice'; and of Monty, 'The People's General', who believed that 'his soldiers were human beings and their lives were precious'. And of Churchill, petulant with a back-bencher after being defeated in a minor debate on equal pay for women, 'You have knocked me off my perch. Now you have got to put me back on my perch. Otherwise I won't sing', and stoical after his election defeat: 'Lord Moran spoke to him of the ingratitude of the people. Churchill's reply revealed that generosity of imagination that was always the strength of his weakness. "Oh no," he answered at once, "I wouldn't call it that. They have had a very hard time."'

But for all the anecdotage of the leading players, it's the people, through the medium of diaries and the Mass Observation surveys, whose story Calder tells. He describes their endurance and patience, and their cowardice, complaints and selfishness as much as their heroism and humanity. He writes of conscription, austerity, the Great Aluminium Scare, the Blitz, the Tube, the sewers, the blackout, the factories, the allotments, the mines, the civil service—and peoples them with air-raid wardens, evacuees, housewives, Home Guardsmen, landgirls, pacifists, soldiers, sailors, airmen and women and William Beveridge in a story which, with its dynasties, its reversals and its hint of a happy ending, reads like a compellingly elegant family chronicle. It's a family in which, as Orwell said, there are 'rich relations who have to be kowtowed to and poor relations who are horribly sat upon, and there is a deep conspiracy of silence about the source of the family income. It is a family in which the young are generally thwarted and most of the power is in the hands of irresponsible uncles and bedridden aunts. Still, it is a family. It has its private language and its common memories, and at the approach of an enemy it closes its ranks.'

In Angus Calder's family tale I discovered a way of looking at my own country that changed my thinking as much as any book I've read:

> After 1945, it was for a long time fashionable to talk as if something like
> a revolution had occurred. But at this distance, we can see clearly
> enough that the effect of the war was not to sweep society on to a new
> course, but to hasten its progress along an old one.

I found a book which could, to paraphrase Auden, teach the unhappy Present to recite the Past, and, to quote Auden, 'remind the management of something managers need to be reminded of, namely, that the managed are people with faces, not anonymous numbers.'

Towards the end of the book there's a photograph. Two sailors and two girls are standing in the fountains of Trafalgar Square, trousers rolled up to their thighs, water above their knees. One girl, her arms wrapped round the two men, a half-knotted tie lying between her breasts on her Lana Turner jumper, a sailor's hat cocked at a rakish angle on her dark hair, looks straight at the camera, mocking the photographer. The other, blonde and demure, floats her hands away from her body like a dancer, neither encouraging nor rejecting the sailor's hand spread over the side of her stomach. They all look tired, drunk, young, and guileless.

It is dawn, VE Day, after a night when plump women in aprons made of Union Jacks danced with pinstriped civil servants, strangers kissed, the young princesses mingled with the crowd outside Buckingham Palace, searchlights danced on the night sky, bonfires blazed in the streets, and, as Angus Calder says 'The New World, so to speak, sang out its appreciation of the Old'. For a moment the country, it seems, held its breath, and it's that moment which, against all reason and against all knowledge, haunts me as a sentimental memory as strong as the grip of my mother's hand.

So I return to this book, this litany of misery and hardship and endurance, for solace. I'm still unable to read it without feeling both nostalgia and pain for the unfulfilled promise of the world I was born into. I used to think this was just longing for the time when my life was all expectation and no disappointment; now it seems little more than a neurotic fixation.

Cultural Apartheid

I wrote this for the Guardian *in 2007, although I'd written on the same subject, in much the same way, several times before.*

The announcement from the Secretary of State for Culture, Media and Sport that 'We will work towards a position where no matter where they live, or what their background, *all* children and young people have the opportunities to get involved in top-quality cultural opportunities in and out of school' has left me wrong-footed. Like most people who write for this paper (and most who read it) I'm habituated to responding with vexed disgruntlement to any government initiative—those who believe that the world can be improved by government will never believe that it has been improved enough. But instead of responding with a reflex whine of 'too little, too late' I find myself wholeheartedly applauding a well-funded strategy that seeks to address exactly the problem that, by neat coincidence, I was drawing attention to in a recent interview in the *Observer*.

What I said in the interview ('Arts chief warns of cultural "apartheid"') I had said often over the last fifteen or so years, and my words—with the calculatedly provocative mention of 'apartheid'—had been dutifully reported in the arts pages. This time, through an editorial quirk, my words appeared on the news pages and therefore became news. What I said was this: 'My fears are that you enlarge the divisions in society between those for whom the arts are a part of life and people who think they are impossibly obscure and incomprehensible... I would use the word apartheid.'

All things being equal, the choice of going to the opera or ballet or theatre or gallery or bookshop is a free one, open to everyone. But all things aren't equal: the 'choice' of going to the theatre or the opera or an art gallery is a choice that doesn't exist for vast numbers of people in this country, who, if they feel anything at all about art, feel disenfranchised. This distinction—between those who enjoy the arts and those who feel excluded from them—amounts to an absolute divide. It seems like apartheid to me.

I know something of this feeling. I grew up in a rural backwater miles from any cinema, even further from any theatre, in a house where the paintings were of horses and the books were of war. At school I was more interested in maths and physics until—at the age of sixteen—I went on a school trip and saw *Hamlet* at the Bristol Old Vic. I had never read the play, barely knew of its existence and it was an epiphany. I was like the composer Berlioz who said after seeing a performance of the same play in Paris: 'Shakespeare, coming on me unawares, struck me like a thunderbolt. The lightning flash of that discovery revealed to me at a stroke the whole heaven of art, illuminating it to its remotest corners. I recognised the meaning of grandeur, beauty, dramatic truth... I saw, I understood, I felt... that I was alive and that I must arise and walk.' And at that time he spoke not a word of English.

I know now that the only argument for art is art itself, but I was grateful enough at that age to have my appetite for the real thing whetted by the programmes I saw on television. At that time—the early 1960s—the BBC, on its one channel, had regular (and good) programmes about painting and sculpture and music and literature, showed foreign films, staged Shakespeare plays, had live broadcasts from opera houses and West End theatres. The BBC was my cinema, my theatre, my art gallery and my library.

Making good television used to be much easier then. Expectations were low, and there was an amiable chaos which made for a warm relationship between the presenter, as it were, and the public. There was an energy drawn from knowing that if you were on television, you were addressing the nation as a whole. Television was a newish medium populated by a newly emancipated group of male middle-class university graduates whose energies in an earlier age might have been diverted to the Church, or the army, or the civil service. There was a homogenous culture, largely imposed from above; you could say you knew where you were then. If Huw Wheldon, or even Melvyn Bragg, told you it was good art, then it was, and it was good for you.

There is now, thankfully, a plurality of voices in our culture and if we are to have good television, it is important that these voices are heard. 'Art' is the expression of the voice of gifted individuals with a point of view. It used to be easier to identify these voices when there was universal agreement that, for instance, Keats was better than Bob Dylan. It's not quite the point to say that Keats is the better poet (after all, Chuck Berry's a better poet than Bob Dylan), the point is that it's no longer possible, or desirable, for television to dispense directives about culture and expect an audience to follow them.

Fifty years ago we might have been certain what we meant by 'culture', and if we agreed with T.S. Eliot we would have been certain of its decline: 'I see no reason why the decay of culture should not proceed much further, and why we may not even anticipate a period of some duration, of which it is possible to say that it will have no culture.' Of course it all depends on what you mean by 'culture'. Are we talking about advertising, sitcoms, body-piercing, Bollywood movies, stage musicals, *The Da Vinci Code*, house music, hip hop, rap, punk, funk, acid, jazz, or are we talking about the culture that Kenneth Clark, the art historian and father of the diarist, meant when he presented his massively popular TV series on Western Art called *Civilisation*. 'Popular taste,' he said, 'is bad taste, as any honest man with experience will agree.'

It's no longer possible to pretend that 'civilisation' means what it meant to a 'man of culture' in the 1960s—and it was almost invariably was a *man*. Culture is about what we think, what we do, what we buy, how we behave, how we entertain ourselves, our 'lifestyle', if you must. Culture is by definition an inclusive concept; art, however, is not. The word 'art' is not neutral. To talk of 'art' is to imply a sense of values, of taste, of standards and—because of educational disadvantages—the word is inevitably shadowed by the spectre of class.

So what do we mean by art? I'm neither qualified nor capable of defining the meaning of 'art' but I can offer a personal catechism:

> Art—good or bad, high or low—must have form, it must have shape— it's a way of knowing the world, of giving form and meaning to things that seem formless.

> A work of art has to have ambition beyond wanting to please the audience or appease fashion, a desire to examine the world—people or nature or society—and make it look or sound or seem new. A work of art should introduce something to the world that didn't exist before.

> Art is everything that politics isn't: politics generalises about people; art particularises. Art is about the 'I' in life not about the 'we', about private life rather than public life. Nevertheless, a public life that doesn't acknowledge the private is a life not worth having.

> There has to be a complexity about art but that's not the same as obscurity. There must be mystery, a sense of unknowability in a work of art—as there is in every human being. In art, reality must be given the chance to be mysterious and fantasy the chance to be commonplace.

The DNA of art is metaphor: that's the genetic cell without which nothing can be mutated by craft into art. Art strives towards the mythic—towards seeing heaven in a grain of sand. Art is unquestionably a form of magic, conjuring something from nothing—sounds from the air on a musical instrument, a human being in paint on a stretch of canvas, a world with a pen on a page of paper.

Art must be serious about itself. That doesn't mean that it can't be funny, but it means it can't be trivial. But seriousness alone—any more than sincerity alone—isn't enough in itself.

There has to be an element of pleasure in art, of sensual enjoyment—be it of a combination of sounds, of words, or textures, or of images. Art has to ravish the senses but not only do that. There has to be a moral sense. You have to be able to feel that the artist has a view that human beings possess a moral sensibility. That's not the same as the artist being a moralist—or being a 'good' person. The artist may be saying, 'This is how you should live your life', but it must be inferred not preached. Art is not polemic.

There must be passion in art. Passion gives us a sense of life lived more intensely, with more meaning—more joy, more sorrow. 'We are all under sentence of death, but with a sort of indefinite reprieve', said Victor Hugo. We can spend our period of reprieve in a state of listlessness, or we can fill the period of our death sentence with experience—lived experience or the experience we gain from art.

Art reflects, expresses, invokes, and describes the ambiguity of humanity. Whatever the form of art, however realistic or however fantastical, it offers up a commentary on being alive, on the infinite messiness of humanity.

Art doesn't improve our behaviour or civilise us. Art is useless. It doesn't clothe the poor or feed the hungry. It's as useless as, well… life, but it's precisely our awareness of the uselessness of life that makes us want to struggle to give it purpose, and to give that purpose meaning through art.

Art is a way of drawing us into a heightened awareness of other people's feelings and other people's lives. It enables us to put ourselves in the minds, eyes, ears and hearts of other human beings.

Any government has a hard job justifying expenditure on the arts—subsidising weapons of destruction is easier than subsidising weapons of happiness. The benefits are hard to quantify, and it is awkward but necessary to recognise that failure is an essential part of artistic creation; bad art will always exist beside the good. But it seems no more than logic to acknowledge—as our current Minister of Culture, Media and Sports James Purnell has—that the corollary of investing taxpayers' money in the arts must be to evolve a strategy that embraces both the departments of culture and of education to invest in the performers and the audiences of the future. It will enfranchise the victims of apartheid.

Shakespeare Had a Sponsor

The Financial Times *asked me, as Director of the National Theatre, to respond to an American journalist who had written a piece deploring subsidy to the arts.*

A financial journalist argued in an article titled 'Shakespeare didn't need a subsidy' for the abolition of arts subsidies. His argument was passionate, specious, provocative and ahistorical. It was an assertion of ideology, based on faith rather than evidence, and larded with the familiar pejorative adjectives of political fundamentalism: 'unnecessary', 'foolish', 'harmful', 'pernicious'.

The world of the arts is an alluring paradigm for the believer in the theocracy of the market. The dictates of artistic endeavour are very harsh. It's a Darwinian universe whose creatures are governed by the law of survival of the fittest: talent, skill, vision and willpower are the currency of this world and they regulate its fortunes ruthlessly. It is tempting, therefore, to think that the funding of arts organisations should be made to float on the same principle. In the case of the performing arts this is simply incompatible with survival.

The performance of a symphony requires upwards of eighty people, an opera sometimes twice that number, and while it may be cost effective to leave out the double basses in a performance of a Beethoven symphony, it will be music only to the accountant's ears. Whatever arguments may be made by small theatre companies desperate for survival, a Shakespeare play cannot be properly performed with fewer than fifteen actors. For better or worse, theatre companies through the ages of Euripides, Shakespeare, Calderón, Molière, Chekhov, Ibsen,

Stoppard and Kushner have relied on royal, state, civic, corporate and private patrons. They have also relied on the patronage of the public: those who live to please have to please to live.

When we speak of subsidy being provided for the theatre, we're not asking for the money to hear the sound of our own voices echoing in an empty room. There is no theatre in this country that treats with disdain the obligation to find an audience, or which is able to afford the luxury of dispensing with one even if it were thought desirable. Most of our theatres depend on box-office income for well over half of their revenue. At the National Theatre, unless we earn nearly £17m a year through our own efforts, we are faced, like Mr Micawber, with the result: misery.

If we want a theatre that takes artistic risks, sustains the best of tradition, develops new talent, feeds the commercial theatre, and does all this at seat prices which do not exclude all but the very rich, then we have no alternative but to seek state support. If we think all these aims are worthless, then I agree—let's dispense with subsidy.

We have been encouraged to look to sponsorship as a secondary source of income, and we have long accepted our mixed economy. Yet for all its exhortation the government has done little to encourage the sponsor. To cite the American model as a goad and inspiration is to ignore the much larger tax advantages, both personal and corporate, that it offers, and it's to be blind to the huge difference between a nation which believes in philanthropy out of gratitude or self-promotion or even guilt, and a nation that, apart from a few outstanding contributors, has no tradition of private giving.

It is possible to argue for subsidy on the grounds of cost effectiveness, or as a tourist enticement, or as a visible or invisible export; even, sometimes, on the grounds that there is a good return on the original investment in VAT, tax and savings on unemployment benefit. But if you justify subsidies on economic grounds alone, then you are asking for the arts to be considered as merely another commodity to be quantified, marketed and—eventually—privatised.

You can argue, rather as a nineteenth-century curate's wife might advocate distributing informative pamphlets to the deserving poor, for the social usefulness of art. But this takes away from art the very thing that makes it alluring; its mystery and its joy. Make art as accessible, both physically and intellectually, as TV or popular music, but don't rob it of its chance to enchant; don't exchange the wizard's robe for the coat of the social engineer. This view treats past art merely as a preparation for future art, with a single mission: to educate. It denies fantasy the chance to be commonplace, and reality the chance to be mysterious.

It's perfectly reasonable to ask why 'art' should be protected where popular culture is not, and it's not a comfortable question to answer. To reply that art is special because it is special is, to say the least, lame. I'd have to assert articles of faith which are no more (or less) demonstrable than a catechism of market ideology. I believe in art as a pursuit of excellence, as a pursuit of meaning, as a way of trying to make sense of the world, and of decoding its chaos.

We live in the first atheistic age in history, which asserts that man is capable of knowing and doing anything. We no longer respect what we don't know, and the more we want to control the world, the more despairing we feel when we find that we are unable to control anything outside our own homes. In this context, art offers the comfort of beauty, the mitigation of pain and the inspiration of hope.

I have to concede that much as I cherish these evangelical assertions, we've become victims of our own propaganda: we brandish our success and our indispensability while at the same time lamenting our decline and our poverty. This is confusing for a public which finds the principle of subsidy difficult to understand, and the motivation by forces other than profit impossible to believe. When British Telecom was privatised, a poll showed that the public thought that the company had become more accessible, was more democratic and worked more to their benefit than when it was owned by the people it served. We're confronted here by a formidably deep-seated scepticism about organisations that exist *pro bono publico*.

We can't be sure that we haven't created an artificial culture in which the relationship between artists and audience has been engineered and is based on 'obligation' rather than on free will, and in which indifferent talent is allowed to survive, but we must accept this danger as an occupational hazard, and not use it as a stick to beat the principle of subsidy, any more than we should cite examples of abuse of welfare payments as an argument for abolishing unemployment benefits. That there are sometimes bad plays and lifeless productions in our subsidised theatres is, in itself, no argument against subsidy.

Nor is it true that the success of the good plays in our subsidised theatres is in some way less authentic than the success of plays which have flourished on Shaftesbury Avenue. Any commercial manager would have envied the success of *The Madness of George III* and *Racing Demon*, but would have been both unwilling and unable to take the risk of producing them in the first place. A mutual dependency exists now between the commercial and the subsidised theatre; starve the one and you stifle the other.

'Any subsidies,' said the financial journalist, 'represent a judgement that all taxpayers should be required to support certain artists, living or dead, however much they may abhor their work. Such coercion is indefensible in a free society.' I live in a free society where I am coerced into subsidising mortgage payers, farmers, and company-car owners; I am compelled to pay for Trident missiles and military bands; I am forced to be a spectator at the pigs' trough of privatisation of public utilities while the health service and education are undernourished; I am obliged to condone the underwriting of the national economy by the arms trade; and I am pressed to provide public protection to an ex-prime minister during a book-promotion tour. I may wish devoutly to be exempted from these demands and pray for a more enlightened government at the next election, but I accept them, as I accept subsidy to the arts, as part of the price of democracy. And by the way, Shakespeare did have a subsidy—from King James, Queen Elizabeth and the Earl of Southampton.

Why the National Theatre Matters

I was asked by the Daily Telegraph *in 2013 to write about the National Theatre on the occasion of its fiftieth birthday.*

———•———

All successful theatre companies resemble each other; each unsuccessful company is unsuccessful in its own way. Successful theatres grow out of the obsessions and stubbornness of gifted and persistent individuals rather than government legislation or civic decree. The National Theatre exists largely because of four people: a radical bookseller, Effingham Wilson, who suggested in 1848 the need for a 'house for Shakespeare where the works of the world's greatest moral teacher would be performed'; a theatre critic, William Archer; an actor/playwright/director, Harley Granville-Barker, who together argued in 1904 that the art of theatre was being destroyed by greed, vanity and long runs—'the only remedy lies in a national theatre, with good endowment, good traditions, good government'; and a Quixotic Cockney busybody, Lilian Baylis, who was visited by Shakespeare in a dream in 1914.

'Why have you allowed my beautiful words to be so murdered?' asked Shakespeare. 'If they have been slaughtered,' she replied, 'the fault is not mine but the actors'.' 'You must run the plays yourself,' said Shakespeare. And at the Old Vic theatre for nearly twenty years she did just that, making Shakespeare an essential part of the repertoire, promoting the great actors of the era—John Gielgud, Ralph Richardson and Laurence Olivier—and engendering a climate in which national and local government could see the virtue of a National Theatre. After generations of prevarication, after changing the site and moving the foundation

137

stone so many times that the Queen Mother said that it should have been put on castors, a National Theatre company was set up at the Old Vic in 1963 under the leadership of Laurence Olivier, with the aim of moving to a new building on the South Bank.

It was another twelve years before the National Theatre on the South Bank opened its doors under the directorship of Peter Hall. The building was conceived with three auditoria—well, two: the Cottesloe was an afterthought—under one roof, each playing a rotating repertoire of three plays. This principle is at the heart of its activities and its source of artistic adventure. To have three theatres in one building is, to say the least, a noble project. It was the triumph of Olivier's will, his wilfulness, and his ambition. Olivier was once asked what his policy was for the National Theatre. 'To make the audience applaud,' he said. When the National Theatre was built, a 'dream made concrete' (a metaphor made literal), he was asked what he thought of it. He smiled wryly: 'It's an experiment.'

It's an experiment which has been a wild success. The building, designed by Denys Lasdun, is stern, elegant, forceful and ascetic. In its intentions and its realisation, it's a classical building, which won't go out of fashion. It represents a social and political utopia—an imagined age in which public funding for the arts would be virtually unchallenged and an age in which the 'art' theatre and the commercial theatre wouldn't walk hand in hand—this, after all, is a building so certain of its purpose, its commercial chastity and the respect of its audience, that it was built without any sign of any sort advertising its purpose on its exterior.

The building attracted a storm of hostility when it first opened, which Peter Hall deflected with remarkable grace and stoicism. The torrent of criticism was directed partly towards the building and partly towards the whole enterprise: inflated, grandiose, hubristic, it was said. But it's proved itself, if numbers are anything to go by, to be a genuine expression of popular desire. And, like all successful buildings, it's been colonised by the many hundreds of thousands of people who have visited it, worked in it and shared some sort of communal experience. Like worn paving stones in a cathedral, it's become humanised by use. It's acquired a heart.

Why does theatre itself matter? The attraction of theatre lies in its 'theatreness', those unique properties that make it distinct from any other medium: its use of space, of light, of speech, of music, of storytelling. It prospers under the logic of plot and it thrives on metaphor—a room becomes a world, a group of characters becomes a whole society. Everything about the theatre depends on the relationship of a performer to a group of spectators in the present tense. And it's the only medium which indissolubly has at its centre a human being: everything relates to the size of the human figure and the sound of the unamplified voice.

The National Theatre can only justify its existence by what appears on its three stages. To name its successes over the past fifty years is more or less to recite a litany of the landmarks of British theatre: classics, musicals, unknown old plays and unseen new plays, from *Rosencrantz and Guildenstern Are Dead* and *Equus*, to *This House* and *London Road*. I was lucky with my first outing—*Guys and Dolls*, the first musical the NT had ever produced, even though Laurence Olivier had toyed with doing it. A reviewer said of the show that 'it was as much fun as you can have legally'; if that was true for the audience it was doubly true for me. I became the NT's Director and had many other happy experiences—David Hare's trilogy about the state of Britain, *Richard III* with Ian McKellen, *King Lear* with Ian Holm, Tom Stoppard's *Invention of Love*, plays by Christopher Hampton, Tony Harrison, Ibsen, Tennessee Williams, Eduardo De Filippo and more. I had some disasters too painful to recollect and I discovered that to run the National Theatre you have to learn the opposite of schadenfreude (joy in other people's failure): you have to take pleasure and pride in other people's successes. I had the time of my life.

When I was running the National Theatre someone said to me, 'Oh, of course, you only put on hits.' I wish. What the statement implies is that there's a kind of second-guessing that goes on, that you decide in bad faith to put on plays because they'll be successful rather than because you think they'll be good. The National Theatre—like all other theatres that receive state subsidy (now only twenty per cent of the NT's income)—has no right to fail; it's rather that it has a right not to have to succeed every time. It's in that grey area between triumph and catastrophe that the hidden riches of the theatre lie. Writers, actors, directors, designers and audiences get the chance to experiment and to take risks and to learn without the penalty of absolute defeat that marks any enterprise in the commercial theatre that fails to hit the inner rings of the financial target.

What's more, the National Theatre has a research and development facility—the NT Studio, situated in The Cut next door to the Old Vic Theatre, which acts as an artistic laboratory not only for the National Theatre but for the theatre in the whole country. It's barely possible to name a single celebrated actor, writer or director who hasn't benefited from its existence. It's one of the hidden jewels of British theatre and one of the unseen dividends of public subsidy.

The National Theatre has defied its critics by proving that it's not an immutable bureaucracy or a cultural colossus riddled with institutional inertia. To state what ought to be obvious, it's demonstrated, to parody Gertrude Stein, that a theatre is a theatre is a theatre. It's existed to do work that, either by content or by execution or both, couldn't be performed or wouldn't be initiated by the commercial sector. It's provided continuity of investment, of employment and of theatrical tradition, at ticket prices which haven't been punitively expensive. In all its departments, it's acted as a benchmark of quality for the whole of our theatre, and, most importantly, it's provided many hundreds of thousands of people with countless evenings of exceptional theatre.

I was always inflamed by Margaret Thatcher's dictum that 'there's no such thing as society', because for me the National Theatre has always been a living refutation of it. It's always demonstrated a sense of common purpose and community. I am not being 'touchy-feely' here: all organisations—newspapers, churches, schools, hospitals, theatres, businesses, even governments—are nourished by unquantifiable things like morale and self-esteem. Within that heartland at the National Theatre resides a faith that it is still possible to put on theatre for no other reason than the shared belief that it is worth making for itself alone rather than as a commodity.

The endemic flaw in many cultural organisations is that they become more interested in themselves than in the people they exist to serve. For fifty years the National Theatre has defied this gravitational pull. It's been topical, fashionable and socially aware. What's more, it's always been conscientious about widening the social range of the audience and looking to the audiences of the future. In recent years the live cinema broadcasts and the Travelex £12 ticket scheme have conspicuously changed the profile all over the country, making the National more national.

'People say: "Ah, but the same young people who you're giving seats to at this very low price will go and buy a pair of shoes for three times the price",' Peter Brook once said to me. And then he added this: 'But shoes haven't let anyone down over the centuries and the theatre has.' The National Theatre hasn't let its audience down. It still does triumphantly what it was set up to do fifty years ago; it's one of the few things in Britain that does so.

Britishness

I wrote this piece for the Guardian *in 2005 at a time when immigration and identity were brewing up as hot political issues. It seems more topical now than then.*

I have recently tried to test my Britishness. 'Why should I pay for what I haven't used?' 'You have used it, the figures show.' 'They can't show what doesn't exist.' 'It exists here.' And on and on in Beckettian iteration as I failed to answer one of the recommended questions to be required of prospective applicants for a British passport: 'How do you pay a phone bill?' Is it purely coincidental that one of the other questions—'Who is the Prime Minister?'—is used as a test for incipient Alzheimer's disease?

A test of Britishness is as fruitless and elusive as a war against terror. What is Britishness? Something that can be politically expedient to invoke on behalf of Falkland islanders, 8,000 miles from Britain in the South Atlantic, but awkward in Scotland and embarrassing in Northern Ireland where, far from being the nation's glue, it's pepper dust in an open wound. Being British is a variable ideology. We're comfortable with being seen as a source of creative energy in fashion, pop music and TV comedy. We're occasionally proud (but often ashamed) of our sporting heroes, and we're chagrined by being celebrated for HP Sauce, Marmite, Oxford marmalade, red buses and pillar boxes, rotten teeth, 'Swinging London', 'Cool Britannia' and the heritage diorama from Normans to Windsors.

We're fond of our reputation for amiable eccentricity—talking about the weather, apologising when we're the victim, queuing in an orderly fashion, and of our birthright of unbroken traditions, individual liberty and parliamentary democracy. And we regard ourselves as reticent, pragmatic, decent and fair people. These qualities would have been acknowledged a hundred years ago on these islands, less so by the Boers or the Zulus in South Africa or most Indians in the subcontinent. They would have recognised reserve and pragmatism, certainly, but also self-repression, insularity, haughtiness, snobbishness and an obsessive concern with class and skin colour. They would have been familiar too with the bilious expressions of nationalism (rather than patriotism) of swaggering squaddies steeped in booze, with 'MADE IN ENGLAND' tattooed on their bellies.

In drink at least we're united—Scottish, Irish, Welsh, English: whereas the Russians become maudlin, the Italians mournful, the Germans militaristic and the French sentimental, we tend to get violent. Perhaps it's the corollary of our reticence. Or that less-endearing national characteristic: not liking foreigners very much, which is perhaps why we find it easier to define ourselves more by who we're not than who we are. For David Blunkett that's simple enough: we're not people who approve of forced marriages and genital mutilation. For me, for much of my life, I was not the person who belonged where I grew up and then—for six-and-a-half years in Edinburgh—I was not Scottish.

Until I was seventeen, my feeling for the Country with a large 'C' was almost exclusively derived from the country with a small 'c'. I grew up in the west of England, in Dorset, almost at the feet of the priapic figure of the Cerne Abbas giant in a landscape that defined Englishness almost to the point of parody: little churches, sandstone villages, valleys, hills, downland, and the barrows, lynchets, burial mounds, earthworks, ditches and standing stones of Celtic Britain: an enchanted landscape, Arthurian as well as Hardy country. I couldn't wait to get away from it: from the bucolic philistinism and what Evelyn Waugh described as 'the sound of English county families baying for broken glass'.

I felt no less of a displaced person when, forever conscious of my foreignness, I lived and worked in Scotland. I didn't feel homesick there—why would I? I didn't know where my home was—but I longed for a homeland. Even if my admiration wasn't indiscriminate, I envied the variety of Scottish cultures— Gaelic music and Sorley MacLean's poetry; the 'Lallens' world of John Knox, Queen Mary, Jamie the Saxth, the Jacobite Rebellion and the Age of Enlightenment, Walter Scott, the Saltire Society and ersatz folking and dancing; the tartan, haggis and bagpipe theme park, which annexed Burns as its patron saint and buried at least as great a writer, James Hogg; and the working-class cultural stew of sectarian football, comics, musicians and novelists—self-mocking, wild, satiric, anarchic, energetic, sometimes self-pitying and often despairing. I envied all of them their sense of belonging to something.

Now, if I belong to anything, it's to London or to Europe, and the only things that I feel are indissolubly 'British' are my feelings about the language and the landscape. If there's one part of the country that expresses that feeling with a sharp intensity, it's a place that's a mile or so from where I grew up: Eggardon Hill. It's an oval plateau above an escarpment that dips down hundreds of feet to woods and farmhouses and fields which stretch out to a hill called Golden Cap on one side, the sea beyond, and the Blackdown Hills of Somerset on the other side. Apart from a spider's web of electricity pylons tracing across the valley, the view hasn't changed since hedges and stone walls started to enclose the land in the eighteenth century, making private fields of common grazing ground. The edges of the hilltop are scored by a wide trench, whose sides rise steeply. This is not a violent accident of nature, it's a monument to man's occupation, and bears witness to its life as a hill fort and settlement, commanding the surrounding countryside with the assurance of an Aztec temple for over two thousand years.

Like all English landscapes, Eggardon Hill makes you examine the meaning of 'green'; it calls for a spectrum of its own. The prodigality of hues in our landscape is part of what gives rise to our language. It's set on a seam of Shakespeare, stuffed with dialect and courtly speech and foreign importations, supple, highly imagistic, highly idiomatic.

To regard landscape and language as my cultural DNA doesn't mean that I hanker for milkmaids, ladies cycling to evensong and warm beer. Even at the price of the Dianification of the nation, I'm pleased that the stiff upper lip has slackened and that self-confidence is replacing self-deprecation. And I accede without nostalgia to the definition of Britishness provided by Malcolm McLaren: 'It's about singing karaoke in bars, eating Chinese noodles and Japanese sushi, drinking French wine, wearing Prada and Nike, dancing to Italian house music, listening to Cher, using an Apple Mac, holidaying in Florida and Ibiza and buying a house in Spain. Shepherd's pie and going on holiday to Hastings went out about fifty years ago and the only people you'll see wearing a Union Jack are French movie stars or Kate Moss.'

My regret is solely that in the swamp of celebrity worship and marketing theology, and the apparently helpless desire to become the fifty-first state of the union, that there's one British virtue that'll be overlooked: tolerance.

Arts

Autobiography

I wrote this for the Guardian *when my diaries*—National Service—*were published in 2003.*

'We are alone. We cannot know and we cannot be known,' said Beckett in an essay on Proust. The makers of *Big Brother* will hoping that that the word doesn't get around, as will the publishers (but perhaps not the authors) of today's dominant literary genre: self-revelation. Beckett's truth is ignored every time an intimate, confessional, genital-warts-and-all account of a life is published in the hope of making the readers feel that far, from being alone and unknowable, they are part of a sentimental community in which envy is banished, pain is shared and everyone is part of a homogenous soup of humanity.

Autobiographies and memoirs are a literary form open to all: no skill as a writer is essential, just a modicum of experience and a dash of celebrity. The form achieved its apotheosis a few years ago in the publication of the autobiography of an emergent eighteen-year-old snooker player, Stephen Hendry. It was called *Nobody Knows My Name*. Most celebrities employ a professional ghost writer to help them to mediate their memories into prose, like an interior decorator translating a client's taste into furniture, fixtures and fittings. The amateur version, the DIY of autobiography, is the diary.

At some times in their lives most people have kept a diary. For teenage girls it's a more or less mandatory catechism of tastes and feelings; for boys it's more a litany of statistics. Adults record income and expenditure, dreams, lovers, weight losses, weight gains, cabinet meetings and sporting triumphs. Hoaxers write 'secret' diaries—Hitler's or Elvis Presley's—in the certainty that editors will be blinded by greed to the obviousness of the fraud. There's even a website—diaries.com—where you can share your 'personal' diary, and I've recently joined literature's B&Q by publishing *National Service*, a diary of the ten years that I was the Director of the National Theatre.

I used to be asked whether, like my predecessor Peter Hall, I was keeping a diary and would I be publishing it? I responded shirtily that I was but wouldn't dream of it. I can see that my answer now appears both sanctimonious and disingenuous, but it's what I thought at the time, a paradox in that I had started to write the diary some years before because I wanted to become a writer. The diary was my exercise book and, like all first-time writers, I wrote about the subject that I knew best and found most alluring: myself.

I didn't have a strategy. I wrote what overflowed from my mind at the end of the day or at a weekend, a solipsistic, Pooterish dialogue with myself. If I have a regret about my approach, it's not so much that I took myself too seriously and wrote too cautiously, but that I failed to record more of the inconsequential minutiae of life—conversations in corridors, phone calls, turns of phrases, faces in windows, changes in fashion, the price of petrol—that make a diary so distinctively unlike fiction.

I kept the diaries compulsively while I had little enough time for my day and night job and I stopped when I had ample time and no job—when a feature film which I was due to direct in the autumn failed to get financed. I was left with a continent of unexpected time to transcribe my diaries from my biro-written A5 black notebooks to my laptop computer. I had written a sizeable book (word count 190,000) which, in spite of a stuttering narrative, had a beginning, a middle, an end and a single tone of voice. Could it, should it, be published? Was it wise to put myself up for inspection? Was it dignified to offer advertisements for myself? Was it proper to betray confidences? My wife thought not; others disagreed, but encouraged by friends and by the publisher, Liz Calder, I went ahead.

'Confession is an act of violence to the unoffending,' as Tom Stoppard says in *The Invention of Love*. In going ahead I had to recognise that there would be some people who, in finding themselves involuntary contributors to my book, would feel that their work was underappreciated, their friendship unrecognised, their conversations misrepresented. Worse still, perhaps, they might find themselves left out of the story. My friend Nicholas Wright (who encouraged me to publish), said that I couldn't help offending people, 'even if it's just saying that they part their hair on the right side and it's really on the left.' Or I could damn a life with a single entry like Auden's example of a diary which said: 'In the evening went to a party at Mr Afnere's. Very slow—small rooms, piano out of tune, bad wine and stupid people.' What of all the evenings at which the diarist *wasn't* present?

When the piano was tuned, the conversation feverish with intelligence, the wine superb?

Whatever their merits, all diaries are self-vindicating, full of evasions, self-justifications and self-recriminations: *quand je m'accuse, je m'excuse.* But there's always a fascination—for the reader as much as for the author—in looking back at the blind and unknowing past in terms of the present. A diary is a literary anomaly: it can't be rewritten with the triumphant irony or wisdom of hindsight. It can only shaped or improved by subtraction. In my case there wasn't extensive editing, at least on the grounds of libel or gratuitous insult, because I had been restrained—even with myself—in objectifying most of my more disturbing, louche, disloyal, violent and ungenerous thoughts. I surgically removed the malign bits that remained—possibly, some would argue, thereby draining the journals of whatever attraction they might have possessed. Even though I had written without the desire to please or appease, I can see now that I lacked the steel in the heart that Graham Greene deemed necessary to become a writer.

The biggest frustration for me in editing was that I couldn't change the way in which I appeared to—no, *did*—amplify, exaggerate and magnify misery, while minimising happiness. I think I give the impression that I had a miserable time at the NT, infected by melancholy. It wasn't the case: it's a weakness in the writing. Happiness can only be done by exceptional writers, and even Tolstoy funked it. 'All happy families resemble each other; each unhappy family is unhappy in its own way.' What a cop-out. What is most interesting in diaries is what is interesting in art: the description of specific words or actions that cause hurt or insult or joy or delight. Happiness is generalised: a mood of contentment, a state of satisfaction, an absence of pain. Happiness writes white.

King Lear

This was a lecture I gave to the Royal Society of Literature in 1998.

'We wish we could pass this play over, and say nothing about it. All that we can say must fall short of the subject, or even of what we ourselves conceive of it.' That's not me speaking—it's Hazlitt, and not an unfair description of how I felt once I'd committed myself to directing *King Lear*.

To stage *King Lear* is to begin to trifle with an indivisible part of our cultural heritage, to toy with our genetic make-up. When you approach a new play as a director or an actor, you carry no baggage, you are free of opinion. With a Shakespeare play you arrive with pantechnicons: you cross continents of critical prose. When I thought about the play I felt as if I was balancing the summit of an inverted mountain on my skull.

I started by taking a frail defensive position: it's only a play, I said. But as my confidence grew I began to realise that far from being a life-preserving reductive position, it was the only proper position to take—and not just because I'm a theatre director. I became aware of the comparative rarity of commentators—all convinced of the greatness of the work on the page—to concede, or perhaps even to understand, the singularity of Shakespeare's genius. Shakespeare was writing plays not for publication or reflective analysis, but for a medium that only exists in the present tense, a medium which depends for its success—at the moment of performance—on the skill of the actors and the imagination of a willing audience.

Shakespeare is often referred to as a poet, and a poet of variable abilities—as if to describe him as a playwright and to judge him as such is to risk some sort of intellectual infection. Even such a keen theatregoer as Dr Johnson could only view him through the prism of poetry: 'Shakespeare,' he said, 'never had six lines together without a fault.' Johnson's successors are all around us, many of them holding distinguished positions in English-speaking universities. One of them— a Professor of English at a London university—boasted in a newspaper column recently that she didn't need to see any production of *Lear* in the theatre—and in particular *my* production; her friend had been to see it and had emailed her response: 'No sequins. They all took their clothes off, shouted and died.'

People who write plays choose an extraordinarily difficult medium. When it comes off it's little short of a miracle. Plays are about the spaces in between the spoken word, as much as about speech itself; about how people react as much as how they act. The playwright has to balance revelation against concealment, has to animate character through action rather than description, has to juggle relationships, plot, entrances and exits by sleight of hand, and has to consistently engage the attention of the audience at the moment of performance.

Poetry is applied to plays, not as Dr Johnson seemed to think, like a sort of decorative paint, but as an expressive tool that gives a greater pulse, momentum, and distillation of thought and feeling than prose—but it's no less a medium for delineating individual character. If Shakespeare had wanted to write his plays in prose he would have been more than capable of it—as a glance at the 'Willow' scene in *Othello* will confirm. To appreciate Shakespeare thoroughly is to believe in him as a writer who wrote for the theatre in verse as a matter of choice, which is why the wonder of *King Lear* lies not only in its profundity but in its accessibility. To believe in the theatre is like believing in religion: you have to experience its effect rather than discuss it—which is part of what makes it so much more difficult for me to describe the making of a production than to do the thing itself.

I have been a director for over thirty years and by the time I decided to do *King Lear* I had directed at least two-thirds of Shakespeare's plays, but I had always fought shy of *Lear*. About twelve years ago—just before I started to run the National Theatre—I was asked by Joe Papp to direct it in New York with George C. Scott. 'Are you ready for *King Lear*?' he asked combatively. I obeyed my instinct. 'No,' I said, 'I don't think I am.' But until recently I didn't know why.

The first production of *Lear* that I saw was Peter Brook's production with Paul Scofield in the early sixties. Since this was almost the first Shakespeare production I'd seen I had no sense at the time of its iconoclasm or its historical importance. I barely knew the play, and I was knocked sideways by its savagery, its bleakness, and its extraordinary prescience. I've come to know Peter Brook well in the last ten years, and not the least of the challenges when I came to direct *Lear* was the certainty that I would have to confront his criticism of my production. A few years ago, in Paris, walking across Les Invalides, I started to talk to him about the play. It seemed unapproachable, he said, until you start to think about it as a play about a family. Oh yes of course, I said. There's a Persian proverb: the way in is through the door, why is it that no one uses it? Exactly, said Peter—who had probably coined the proverb in the first place.

With a Shakespeare tragedy it is not even worth looking for the door until you have an actor to play the protagonist who is prepared to travel through it. I can't say exactly what made me decide to approach Ian Holm, but the fact that he was approaching sixty-five and was an actor for whom I had boundless admiration and considerable affection had something to do with it. But at the time it could have been construed a Quixotic decision—after all, Ian had hardly been on stage for fifteen years after an attack of stage fright, and had not played in a Shakespeare play for thirty-five years. But I followed my instinct and he was intrigued. He didn't say yes, and he didn't say no. How does one play an eighty-year-old man? he said. I had just worked with Georg Solti—eighty-two at the time, still conducting at the height of his powers, still dominating every gathering, still playing tennis. Look at Georg Solti, I said.

Ian had one condition, and it was a condition that concurred with my desire: to do the production in the National's smallest auditorium, the Cottesloe. About five years before this I had done a production in the Cottesloe of *Racing Demon*, a new play by David Hare about the Church of England. This play had about thirty separate scenes, varying from small domestic interiors to the nave of a large cathedral. With the designer Bob Crowley, we devised a way of staging the play on a cross-shaped stage that was minimalist, and allowed the necessary and sufficient conditions for each scene to flourish, and for every scene to flow seamlessly into the next. That's how Shakespeare should be staged, I thought.

It's a commonplace to observe that Shakespeare has a 'filmic' style; but only by providing a staging that allows a seamless cut from the end of one scene to the beginning of another can we begin to experience it—for instance, the cut, in the cinematic sense, from Edmund's 'The younger rises when the old doth fall' inside the house, to Lear, Kent and the Fool on the heath in the storm; or from Kent's soliloquy in the stocks to Edgar escaping from his pursuers. These scenes are simply robbed of their power unless the pulse of the verse—and the action— is allowed to beat unbroken. And, as in so many other Shakespeare plays—*Hamlet* and *Richard III* to name but two—the vertiginous speed and the breathless plausibility with which events develop are a crucial element of the descent into disaster. We have all sat down to a family meal that has descanted from geniality to savagery before the pudding's been put on the table.

We have to keep rediscovering ways of doing Shakespeare's plays. They don't have absolute meanings. There is no fixed, frozen way of doing them. Nobody can mine a Shakespeare play and discover a 'solution'. To pretend that there are fixed canons of style, fashion and taste is to ignore history. We have to aim at re-establishing the relationship between actor and audience that had existed in Shakespeare's theatre, and I don't personally believe we can do this by looking for a synthetic Elizabethanism—a sort of aesthetic anaesthesia, involving the audience in an insincere conspiracy to pretend that they were willing collabora-tors in a vain effort to turn the clock back. We have to use scenery not to decorate and be literal, but to be expressive and poetic. It must also be specific; it must be real; it must be minimal and it must be iconographic: the cart in *Mother Courage*, the nursery in *The Cherry Orchard*—or the table in my production of *King Lear*.

Armed with a provisional commitment from Ian Holm, I started to think seri-ously about the play in August of 1995. I was helped, if it's not too cruelly ironic a way to describe it, by being in the country for three weeks looking after my wife after she'd had an operation for peritonitis. It was an unusually hot sum-mer, and we'd sit on our terrace looking out over a Gloucestershire valley reading *King Lear* by sunset and candlelight. Only one copy, so we huddled together, while my wife affected not to mind that I insisted on reading the best parts.

I started to develop a sense of what the play meant to me, and the truth of Peter Brook's remark about the play started to gather force: a play about family, about fathers and their children, about children and their fathers. There are two fathers in the play—one with three daughters, the other with two sons. Both receive a brutal education in parental love, both in a sense being made to see through blindness. I began to realise why I had shied away from the play until now: I didn't know enough about the subject matter, but with the death of my parents I was no longer a child: I was an orphan, a grown-up, and a parent myself—and I was ready to understand *King Lear*.

I realised my sympathies had shifted with time. When I was young I saw two terrible daughters abusing a man more sinned against than sinning. Now I was no longer prepared to judge: all were to blame, all could be forgiven.

I was working in New York in the autumn of 1995. So was Ian Holm. Once a week, on a Sunday evening, we would meet at a restaurant and talk about *Lear*. We talked of fathers, of children, and of kings. Of parental tyranny, different only in scale from the political variety. We talked of old age, and we talked of mad-ness. That's the easy bit, said Ian.

If we get the beginning right, we said, it will all fall into place. We must think of the habit of power: a man who never has to ask for anything, a man who only says 'thank you'—possibly for the first time in his life—on the edge of death, when a button is undone for him. And I have two thoughts, said Ian, about the storm. Oh so do I, said I. You speak, he said. Real rain is the first, I said. Ian nod-ded. And the second, I said? He must be naked, Ian said. And I nodded; anything less than 'unaccommodated man' would be dishonest. I know of no other actor who would have suggested this, agreed to do it—but more importantly have made it seem so inevitable, so unself-advertising, and so deeply shocking.

When I got back to London I started work with Bob Crowley. You have to start somewhere—and Bob and I invariably start with the bare space: the stage. With Shakespeare you always need, in some form, to replicate the space for which he wrote his plays: you will always need two entrances, the equivalent of an 'inner' stage or the ability to change immediately from one part of the stage to another, and you will invariably need an upper level. In our case we had already decided on our traverse stage with entrances at both ends, and a balcony at one end that completed the three sides of the Cottesloe's upper level. To progress beyond that we needed to move beyond the abstract into the specific. What would we put into the space?

I used to be entranced in chemistry lessons with an experiment involving a saturated solution of iridescent blue copper sulphate and a piece of thread. The object was to grow a crystal of copper sulphate, which after a few days could be lifted from the liquid and turned in the light like a precious jewel. But to grow the big crystal you needed a tiny piece on the end of the thread. It's the same with designing a production: the design has to coalesce around an object—an architectural feature, a room, or a piece of furniture.

I had a clear view of how I wanted to stage the first scene: a long table around which the family sat with Lear at the head of the table. An image of order, of hierarchy, of family, one that would resonate for everyone in the audience—a family meal, a family meeting, the king's cabinet. We talked around this and then tried to see how useful a table could be in the rest of the play, how we could get rid of it, whether its advantages outweighed its disadvantages.

We started to understand that the play depended on a world of what Tony Harrison would call the 'versuses' of life: the home and the heath, comfort and privation, soft clothes and nakedness, riches and poverty, interior and exterior. We talked of the stark horror of being locked out of your own home by your children, and this led us to a certainty that we needed walls and doors, a sense of being inside, protected from the elements, and a sense of being outside, exposed to wind and rain and mud and nature. And we thought of Robert Frost: 'Home is the place where, when you have to go there/They have to take you in.'

A week or so later I was in Paris, and I met up in a brasserie with our lighting designer, Jean Kalman. I was explaining the stage that I'd reached in discussion with Bob. I stood two menus up to demonstrate the way in which we wanted the traverse space to be bounded by walls at each end, and then how we wanted an empty space, a disappearing interior. Why don't the walls collapse, he said, when the storm begins? Like this, I said, as the menus flopped down on the table. Like that, he said, like a kabuki wall; the storm blows Lear's world apart.

So Bob developed the collapsing walls: two huge flats with large double doors within them made of the strong, lightweight material used in the floors of planes. We wanted the audience to feel a visceral fear when the walls fell and the thunder cracked. We talked of warm colour for the interior; mud, rain, wind, for the heath; and a world beyond that—the chalk world of Dover, a *tabula rasa*, like a world after the bomb. And we talked of the play beginning with an eclipse of the sun—a diminishing disc presiding over the space as the audience trickled into their places.

We wanted to create a world on stage that was consistent within its own terms, specific but ahistorical, that didn't lean on specious notions about the look of pre-Christian Britain, eschewing woad and Iron Age jewellery. In short, the design of the set and the costumes had to serve Shakespeare's imaginative universe: all expression and no decoration.

I began to edit the text. Even if you were to take the position that you were going to perform every word that Shakespeare wrote, you still have to make a decision between two palpably imperfect versions: the Quarto and the Folio. It seems probable that Shakespeare started the play in the autumn of 1605—when there was an eclipse of the sun, and the Ur-play, *The True Chronicle History of King Leir*, was published. We know that Shakespeare's *King Lear* was first performed on Boxing Day in 1606. It is fascinating to look at the source play and identify what Shakespeare added to the story: Lear's madness, the storm, the Fool, the second family—the entire Gloucester subplot.

It seems that the Quarto—the first printed version, which appeared in 1608—is further from what Shakespeare wrote than the Folio, printed in 1623. It is possible that the Folio was printed from the prompt book, and is a version corrected by the author. If that is the case then there are inexplicable anomalies: for instance, the Folio doesn't have the 'joint stool' scene, the brilliant account of Lear's declining madness in which he tries his imagined daughters before a court consisting of Kent, Edgar and the Fool. The Folio also includes what in my view is a completely bogus speech of the Fool, the prophecy of Merlin. So dubious is this speech that when I asked Michael Bryant if he would play the Fool he agreed on one condition: that he didn't have to do that speech.

Any director of a Shakespeare play has to make a number of choices about cutting the text, prompted perhaps by anxiety about the performance length, perhaps by anxiety about comprehensibility, perhaps even to suit a directorial conceit—in both senses of the word. I cut a little for length largely in the fourth and fifth acts, and perhaps 100 lines on the grounds of comprehensibility—largely the Fool's obscurer jokes and the wholly untranslatable parts of Edgar's Poor Tom speeches.

I decided to put the interval after the 'joint stool' scene, at the tail end of the storm. This meant starting the second act with the short, sharp shock of the blinding of Gloucester, which had the effect of ending the first half with Edgar's speech:

> When we our betters see bearing our woes,
> We scarcely think our miseries our foes.

That became a pre-echo of his speech at the end of the play:

> The weight of this sad time we must obey;
> Speak what we feel, not what we ought to say.

I had decided to place Edgar on stage at the beginning of the play, watching the eclipse of the sun, establishing him in the mind of the audience perhaps as a thinker, a rationalist, a student scientist. Apart from inserting Edgar at the start of the play, I made no changes to the content or position of his speeches, but this did not prevent one critic from castigating me for employing Edgar as a choric character when, according to the critic, Shakespeare intended nothing of the sort. Perhaps not, but honesty compels me to point out that Edgar consistently steps outside the action to comment on Lear's madness in the storm and at Dover, on his father's blindness and on his brother's villainy.

Actually, I'm fairly sanguine about critics, even if I sometimes feel after a bad notice that the appropriate fate for the critic is what they did to the dead pharaohs before embalming them—having their brains drawn out with a long hook. I know of no practitioner in the theatre who doesn't suffer, painfully and unphilo-sophically, from bad reviews. At the moment when you are most tired, vulnerable, optimistic and subjective, and your work is the centre of a Ptolemaic universe, who can deal with a bargain-basement Galileo telling you that the sun doesn't go round the earth? Which is why there's some truth in Garrison Keil-lor's observation that the only acceptable review is a headline that reads: 'Hail sun god, rise and lead thy people.'

I started to cast the production in the autumn of 1996, and rehearsals were to start in January of the following year. If politics is the art of the possible, casting is the art of the available. There is much talk about luck in the theatre; on first nights we wish each other 'good luck' with the earnest solemnity of explorers about to cross the Antarctic. The truth is that, apart from the luck of the chem-istry of a particular audience, luck has nothing to do with it: talent, passion, hard work, and collective endeavour are the less than mysterious ingredients. As Peter Brook has said: there are no secrets apart from the fact that there are no secrets.

The luck in a production is in obtaining the right actors at the right time. They're often not the actors that you first thought you wanted or indeed first offered the parts to; they just prove themselves during rehearsals to be, well, the only actors you can imagine playing the parts. It's been my experience that some projects are blessed and some are not; you cannot legislate for luck. This bleak empiricism is neither a comfort nor a curse: it's a fact.

When you cast you start with certain givens derived from your understanding of the play—the demands of the characterisation and of the play's dynamics. With *King Lear* you under-cast at your peril: there are eleven parts which need to be strongly played, anything less will dilute the power of the play.

I was convinced that part of the play's meaning lay in the sense of the young needing to be liberated from the oppression of the old—the universal feeling of the child towards the parent. This led me to the conviction that there were four old men in the play: Lear, Gloucester, Kent and the Fool. It may be pointed out that Kent says in answer to Lear's enquiry that he is forty-eight. This, I was convinced, was intended as a joke, and I was reassured that it was consistently received as such by the audience. Having cast Ian Holm, I had to cast three of his peers, which of course meant that I would be casting three actors who would consider themselves plausible candidates for the part of Lear. It is a tribute to the generosity of Tim West, David Burke and Michael Bryant that they agreed to play the parts; it is also, of course, a tribute to the remarkably high esteem in which Ian Holm is held by his colleagues.

In the weeks leading up to rehearsals I ruminated about the play, and here are some of my ruminations culled from my notebook:

> The play is a symphonic variation on love: family love, parental love, brotherly love, sisterly love, sexual love. Love flouted, love refused, love suppressed, love unrequited. Lear at the beginning sees himself as the fount of patriarchal love.

> How is Kent disguised?

> Lear is lonely; he really wants to know if he's loved for himself.

> Lear wants to be young again: no cares, no responsibility. He just wants to hunt, eat, drink, and knock around with the lads.

> Lear's madness is not senile dementia, even if it has characteristics of it. He goes mad and recovers. His madness is an overload of remorse and pain and anger. It's a purging.

> People love Lear: Kent, the Gentleman, Cordelia, Gloucester, the Fool, Albany. He is not a tyrant except in Goethe's sense: 'An aged man is always a King Lear.'

> Kafka on his father: 'Often I picture a map of the world and you lying across it. And then it seems as if the only areas open to my life are those that are not covered by you or are out of your reach.'

Virginia Woolf on *her* father: 'Why had he no shame in indulging his rage before women?'

Should Gloucester recognise Edgar during the storm, and then deny it to himself?

Is the hovel a pig pen?

What was the mother like? Did she die in childbirth, having Cordelia?

Edmund is a total nihilist; shocking even today. He feels nothing except the pain of exclusion.

If we can make sense of Edgar we make sense of the play. I've cast Paul Rhys; I know he can do it.

From *A Thousand Acres*, a novel based on *Lear*: 'It was exhilarating talking to my father as if he were my child, more exhilarating to see him as my child.'

Should France and Burgundy have foreign accents?

Why are Gloucester and Edgar so gullible, or would we all react like that?

Lear initially sees everything in terms of price, of number, of capital; gradually he's made to construe his relationships in terms of feelings.

Senile men often talk dirty: Lear's obsession with sex in the mad scene.

Lear's division of the kingdom is all fixed *before* the scene begins. It's not even a real test of love—as they all know. None of them has a choice.

Lear never looks at servants; that's why he doesn't recognise Kent.

The play is about being human. No more, no less.

I stood on the cliff at Eype in Dorset. Six foot away from the edge I couldn't hear the sea. At the edge it's hypnotically strong; I deny the urge to throw myself over.

And so on, until rehearsals began. They have to begin somewhere, and this began with a meeting of the cast, and a reading of the play. I talked a little and my words drifted like incense over a group of actors who, regardless of their mutual familiarity, were at that stage united only in their nervous anticipation and social unease. I stood like a heron, rigid with anxiety, and offered the cast a few simple precepts, as much to remind myself of the guidelines as to inform the cast:

1. You may be daunted by a play that appears to be about everything. At this moment it may appear to be a mountain that is inaccessible and unscaleable. But trust your own knowledge of the world: this is a play about two fathers—one with three daughters, the other with two sons. Everyone is an expert on the subject of families.

2. Believe that the writer is a playwright who understands what he is doing. However great Shakespeare's genius, it doesn't help to treat him as a sort of holy fool, or a messianic seer. He was a playwright, and an actor, and a theatre manager. He was utterly pragmatic; his plays would not and could not have worked if they had been shrouded in obscurity and abstract conceits. And remember that in spite of the play being in verse, each line is characterised. No two characters speak the same.

3. Treat the verse as an ally not as an enemy. Look at the scansion, the line endings, the line breaks, the changes of rhythm: they are all aids to understanding the meaning and how to convey it.

4. Don't make judgements on the characters. Let us—and the audience—discover what the moral scheme of the play is. Don't describe anyone as good or evil; let us decide on the basis of their actions.

5. Rely on the evidence of the text, not on speculation, or psychological theory, or conceptualising, or spurious historical research.

6. Try to be simple; trust that Shakespeare is trying to do the same, however profound, eloquent and complex is his intention. Be specific: all good art is derived from specific observations, all bad art from generalisations.

7. Our job is to discover and animate the meanings of the play: its vocabulary, its syntax, and its philosophy. We have to ask what each scene is revealing about the characters and their actions: what story is each scene telling us? We have to exhume, examine and explain: line by line, scene by scene. We have to understand the mystery of the play—in the light of that understanding.

Then we read the play, not apologetically as often happens at a first reading, but following Ian's example, with daring and ferocity. Ian did what he said he would do: I'll just… do it, he had said. And he did. Then for a few days we sat around and talked. Partly as a means of trying to gain purchase on the mountainside, partly as a way of putting off the moment when the actors stand up and you start to draw on the blank sheet of paper, and partly as a way of finding out about each other. We talked about religion, about money, about monarchy, about hierarchy, about living conditions, about crime and punishment, about the climate, about the geography, about the food, about the clothes. All assertions had to be supported by the evidence of the text; everyone had an equal voice in the discussions.

And then we started from the top: standing-up rehearsals. Painfully slowly we examined each line, each move, each relationship, each character—however apparently insignificant. All actors work at different speeds, some alarmingly quick and instinctive, others exasperatingly slow and methodical. There are as many 'methods' of working as there are actors, and, unless they are subject to the collective discipline of an expressionistic production or of a musical, most actors will work like scavengers, picking up ideas, images, 'business', and occasionally, like panhandlers, pure gold. A rehearsal has to be a time when actors can experiment, invent, explore, discuss, dispute, practise and play, and it's the job of a director to create a world—private and secure—where this activity can go on without fear of failure.

For the first week or so of rehearsals I felt overwhelmed by the size of the task; I had never done anything so difficult or so physically draining. I didn't feel physically prepared for it. But Ian was like a fit dog gnawing at the bone. It took nearly three weeks to work through the play from beginning to end, blocking out each scene, chipping away like a sculptor with raw stone. At that stage I decided to have a runthrough, so we could all feel the power of the play in the light of what we'd learned about it. We sat round in a circle; some actors read their parts, others performed them. Some stood up for their scenes in the middle of the circle, some remained seated. We did the play without a break: two hours, forty-five minutes. It was thrilling: fast, clear, intensely moving.

The process of rehearsal defies conventional description. Only a Proustian narrative could do justice to the countless steps forward and back, the nudges of excitement, the nuances of insecurity, that mark the growth of the organism of a production. It is all in the detail: the physical minutiae of speech and gesture and movement—whether it be the blinding of Gloucester, the seduction of Goneril, the fight between Edgar and Edmund, or the death of Lear himself. Some scenes took weeks to evolve: the arrival of the knights in Goneril's house, for instance, where we were trying to create the mixture of licensed anarchy and sycophancy that characterised the court of the king of rock 'n' roll, Elvis Presley. Other scenes fell into place easily—the last scene for instance. I responded to Albany's demand to 'bring forth the bodies' by suggesting out of practical expediency that Goneril and Regan's corpses be wheeled on by a single soldier with a trolley, since there wouldn't be enough actors to carry them on with stretchers. Only during rehearsal with the trolley did it develop into an object that acquired an iconic resonance, bodies piled like lumber and the broken-hearted Kent, in a last gesture of loyalty, dragging off Lear and his daughters as if for burial, the victims of a domestic holocaust.

Of course there were problems. Every actor had a day or two or three when they doubted their talent or the way they were playing a particular scene or speech. Ian was anxious about his voice sustaining through rehearsal, let alone performance. He would not rehearse at anything but full pitch, for eight weeks, six hours a day, and he made it impossible for any of us to work any less energetically. And I was constantly concerned that the arc of the play from the blinding of Gloucester to the death of Cordelia should be sustained without a loss of momentum: helter-skelter, a descent into hell.

The week before we went onstage I spoke to Ian about the production. Well, I said, it's too early to celebrate. It *was* too early, and we were approaching the precipitous moment when the production had to be lifted up like water in the palms of one's hands and decanted into the Cottesloe theatre. There we encountered a new set of problems: how to make the wind machines work (they didn't); how to extend the rain over the stage (it couldn't); how to light the storm; how to make everything audible and everything visible to an audience surrounding the action on three sides.

For me the most exciting part of the production is always the first time an audience sees it, even though it's often disappointing, and sometimes catastrophic. But this was one of those nights that Lorca might have described as possessing *duende*: hugely charged, highly emotional.

I talked to Ian just before the performance. 'I think I know how to do the "Howl" speech,' he said.' 'Ah,' I said. 'See what you think,' he said. And he did know how to do the 'Howl' speech. He carried Cordelia's body on—always an anxiety for every Lear—and instead of putting her down before he spoke, he stood with the body in his arms and howled at Kent, Albany, Edgar and God. The four 'howls' emerged as an order, a command, the indictment of a father and a curse—don't be indifferent to my suffering. We weren't; and not for the first time in the evening I found myself brushing tears from my cheeks with the palm of my hand, professional objectivity long since cast aside.

I don't know what makes one production soar like a bird of paradise, and others, embarked on with just as much optimism and care, fall like dead sparrows from the nest. I know that I was part of an enterprise that did manage to be more than the sum of its parts, and I know that that is at the heart of every successful theatrical enterprise. Nothing will come of nothing.

Richard III

I wrote this as an introduction to a new edition of the play published by the RSC in 2007.

I came to know tyranny at first hand through visiting Romania. Over a period of nearly thirty years I watched their dictator, Ceausescu, graduate from being a malign clown to a psychotic ogre. His *folies de grandeur* consisted of razing villages to the ground in order to rehouse peasants in tower blocks, sweeping aside boulevards because the streets from his residence to his office were insufficiently straight, building miles of preposterously baroque apartment blocks which echoed in concrete the lines of Securitate men standing beneath them, and led the eye towards a gigantic palace which made Stalin's taste in architecture look restrained. They ran out of marble to clad the walls and the floors, and had to invent a process to make a synthetic substitute out of marble dust; and there was never enough gold for all the door handles of the hundreds of rooms, or the taps of the scores of bathrooms. It was a palace of Oz, built for a demented wizard, costing the lives of hundreds of building workers who, numbed by cold, fell from the flimsy scaffolding and were brushed away like rubble, to be laid out in a room reserved solely for the coffins of the expendable workforce. There was a photograph of Ceausescu that showed only one ear, and there's a Romanian saying that to have one ear is to be mad. So another ear was painstakingly painted on the official photograph. Such are the ways of great men.

The language of demagoguery in this century has a remarkable consistency: Ceausescu, Stalin, Mao Tse Tung and Bokassa shared a predilection for large banners, demonstrations, and military choreography, and the same architectural virus; totalitarianism consistently distorts proportion by eliminating human scale. Mass becomes the only consideration in architecture, armies, and death. The rise of a dictator and the accompanying political thuggery are the main topics of Shakespeare's *Richard III*, which could be said to be a handbook for tyrants—and for their victims. I directed the play with Ian McKellen as Richard in 1990 for the National Theatre and took it to its spiritual home in Bucharest early in 1991.

For a director, working with a designer can often be the most satisfying and enjoyable part of a production. You advance slowly, day by day, in a kind of amiable dialectic, helped by sketches, anecdotes, photographs, and reference books. The play starts as a tone—of voice, or colour, and a shape as formless as the shadow of a sheet on a washing line; through reading and discussion and illustration, it acquires a clear and palpable shape. When I started working on *Richard III* with Ian McKellen and the designer, Bob Crowley, I had no definite plan about the setting. We never sought to establish literal equivalents between medieval and modern tyrants. We worked simply, day by day, reading the play aloud to each other, and refusing to jump to conclusions.

Some actors start with trying to establish the details of how the character will look, some with how they will think or feel. It was said of Olivier that he started with the shoes; with Ian McKellen it's the face and the voice. I have a postcard he sent me when we were working on *Richard III*—a droll cartoon of a severe face, recognisable as his own, with sharply receding hair, an arrow pointing to a patch of alopecia; at the throat is a military collar, above the shoulder the tip of a small hump. He is a systematic, fastidious and exacting actor; each word is picked up and examined for its possible meanings, which are weighed, assessed, discarded or incorporated. In rehearsals he is infinitely self-aware, often cripplingly so. His waking, and perhaps sleeping, dreams are of how he will appear on stage—his position, his spatial relationships with the other actors. But in performance that inhibition drops away like a cripple's crutches and he is pure performer. All the detail that has been so exhaustively documented becomes a part of an animate whole. In sport, in a great performance, there must always be an element of risk, of danger. The same is true of the theatre. I wouldn't say there is not a good or even effective actor without this characteristic, but there is certainly no celebrated one.

As Ian, Bob and I talked, a story emerged: Richard's occupation's gone. He's a successful soldier who, in the face of great odds, has welded a life together in which he has a purpose, an identity as a military man. His opening speech describes his depression at the conclusion of war, his bitterness at the effeminacy of peace. He's a man raging with unconsummated energy, needing a world to 'bustle' in. This hunger to fill the vacuum left by battle is the driving force of the play. It has a deep resonance for me. When I made *Tumbledown*, a film about the Falklands War, I saw this sense of unfulfilled appetite at first hand in people who had fought in the war and were unable to come to terms with peace. The experience of battle is a profound distillation of fear, danger and exhilaration; nothing in peacetime will ever match it, and those who are affected by it are as traumatised as those who have been wounded, who at least have the visible signs of trauma to show for it. Soldiers are licensed to break the ultimate taboo against killing; some of them get the habit.

Richard has had to fight against many odds; he is the youngest son, coming after two very strong, dominant, assertive brothers—and he is deformed, 'unfinished'. His eldest brother, Edward, is a profligate, and the spectacle of his brother's success with women is a sharp thorn in his flesh. The age, no less than today, worshipped physical prowess, and Richard is accustomed, though certainly not inured, to pejorative terms like 'bunch-back'd toad'; he has heard them all his life. We know that he is deformed, but the text repeatedly tells us he is a successful professional soldier. We have to reconcile the two demands of the text. Olivier's interpretation has become central to the mythology of the play, but the deformity that he depicts has never seemed to me plausibly compatible with what Shakespeare wrote. Ian McKellen played Richard with a small hump, he had chronic alopecia, and he was paralysed down one side of his body. These three handicaps taken together were sufficient to account for all the abuse he attracts and for his still being able to serve as a professional soldier. Experience shows that even slight deformities are enough to inspire revulsion; modern reactions to disability haven't changed very much in this respect.

It is clear that Richard has been rejected from birth by his mother; she says so unequivocally to Clarence's children, and her words of contempt spoken to her son in front of his troops confirm this. It is impossible to escape the conclusion that Shakespeare is attempting to give some history, some causality, to Richard's evil.

The design of the production emerged empirically. We started with an empty model box, and put minimal elements into it—rows of overhead lamps to create a series of institutionalised public areas, a world of prisons and cabinet rooms and hospital corridors as well as palaces and areas of ceremonial display, set off against candlelit areas of private pain. We drew some parallels with the rise of Hitler, but these were forced by Hitler himself; his rise shadows that of Richard astonishingly closely, as Brecht showed in *Arturo Ui*. Specific elements of Hitler's ascent to power, or Mosley's to notoriety, were echoes that bounced off a timeless sounding board. The play is set in a mythological landscape, even if it draws on an apparently historically precise period; I say 'apparently' because Shakespeare treats historical incident with little reference to fact—incidents are conflated, characters meet whose paths never crossed, Tudor myths prevail.

Tyrants always invent their own ritual, synthetic ceremonies borrowed from previous generations in order to dignify the present and suggest an unbroken continuum with old traditions. Hitler played up all the themes of historical resti-tution. Napoleon, the little man from Corsica, designed the preposterous Byzantine ceremony which is represented in David's painting. Most of English ritual, our so-called time-honoured ritual, is not very old either. The order of the last British coronation, in 1953, had been almost wholly invented by Queen Victoria. Putting Richard in medieval costume in the coronation, as we did, was a way of showing how tyrants like the authors of the Thousand Year Reich would have us believe that medievalism and modern time coexist; the past is consistently made to serve the needs of the present.

Richard III is so much a one-man show in our acting tradition that the miseries visited on women by the male appetite for power tend to be ignored or obscured. The female characters are as strong as in any of Shakespeare's plays. The legacy of men's cruelty is swept up by women who have been educated by the experi-ence of grief. They have caused pain to Richard and they are taught by him to suffer: Elizabeth—proud, arrogant, and abusive of him—loses her brother and her sons; the Duchess of York—sealed in her own self-importance, openly con-temptuous of her son—loses another son and grandchildren at his hands; Lady Anne—blinded by her grief and her hatred and seduced by him—loses her self-respect and, finally, her life. Only Queen Margaret needs no education at his hands; 'Teach me how to curse my enemies,' says Elizabeth to her. Their mod-els in our times are only too obvious: the women who wait in Chile and in Argentina for news of their sons who have 'disappeared', and the mothers I saw in Romania shortly after the Revolution, putting candles and flowers in the streets on the spots where their sons had been killed. The play is called *The Tragedy of Richard III*, and it is the tragedy of the women that is being portrayed.

The crude villain of melodrama has managed to overrule a play of considerable political subtlety. Richard does not appear in an untainted Eden; his England is the world of realpolitik. Clarence and Edward have both committed crimes in the civil wars, Clarence even admitting his guilt to the Keeper; Queen Eliza-beth's family are greedy parvenus; Buckingham, Stanley and Ely are all morally ambiguous. At the beginning of the play Clarence has just been capriciously arrested; such behaviour may be exceptional and outrageous, but not unprece-dented. What right have any of the characters to call Richard a villain?

Hastings, the Prime Minister, is a politician's politician, expedient, and amoral—when he is told of the impending execution of his political enemies, he can't fault this transparent abuse of justice; within minutes he is himself under sentence of execution. 'The rest that love me, rise and follow me,' says Richard, and at this point self-preservation takes over from courage, morality, or political expediency. We all hope that we will never have to face this choice; it takes formidable courage to say 'no' when the consequence is imprisonment or worse; and where there is a crying need for reform, it's easy enough to agree that minor infringements of liberty are a small price to pay for the benefit of an able leader. We are comfortably insulated in our unchallenged, liberal, all-too-English, assumptions.

The play ends with the triumph of Richmond—a young man, almost a boy, in the hands of mature soldier-politicians who are promoting him. It is essential for their purposes that he succeed, and he is equally determined to show that he can succeed. I set his first entrance against a backdrop of a peaceful country village, in Devon, in fact, near where I was born, the England of 'summer fields and fruitful vines'. If I was asked what I thought Richmond was fighting for, it would be this idealised picture of England. It was more than a metaphor for me; it was a heartland.

When I took my production of *Richard III* to Romania a year after their Revolution, familiar landmarks in Bucharest were obscured entirely by the snow, and the people were unrecognisably changed from the years of oppression. Though some claimed that nothing had altered, the mere fact of being able to say this openly contradicted what they were saying. A stagehand said he wasn't at all frightened of being killed in the Revolution; after all, better to be dead than how it was. A small pixie-like woman was helping at the theatre; she was slightly retarded but had some English. 'Are you happy? I am happy,' was her refrain. Like many others she was homeless, and lived in the theatre, where at least she could get hot water. Outside it was often one hour of hot water a day.

At the end of the last performance I went onstage with the actors and made a speech, starting through an interpreter. She was shouted off: 'English! English!' they chanted and I continued in English. I told them the production had come to its spiritual home, that this sort of cultural exchange was the only true diplomacy, and thanked them for their hospitality. They didn't want us to go, clapping rhythmically and incessantly, but we walked offstage slowly, blinking back tears. As we left the stage a man walked up to us and handed a note and a bouquet to one of the actors. The note read: 'Nobody can play Sir William Shakespeare's plays better than his English people. I've seen with your remarkable help that somewhere in England Sir William Shakespeare is still alive. Thank you. Signed: a Simple Man.'

Hedda Gabler

This was for the programme when I directed the play at the Almeida Theatre in 2005.

It's a paradox of great plays, which are great on account of the profound speci-ficity of their characters and actions, that we try to compress them into neat, autographed theses, hoping that our mark on them will be as lasting as hand-prints on drying cement rather than sand in the incoming tide. We provide ourselves with generalised conceits—*King Lear* is 'about' fatherhood, *Richard III* is 'about' tyranny, *Hedda Gabler* is 'about' the position of women—which shrivel the beguiling complexities and ambiguities that have drawn us to the plays in the first place. Great plays are great precisely because, to borrow King Lear's words, they show us the 'mystery of things' rather than serve as tools for polemic or guides to good living.

That Hedda is a victim (tragic or not) of her gender and social conditions—and of her own self-destructiveness—is unquestionable, and it's quite reasonable to conscript her to the ranks of fighters for the freedom of women while charac-terising the men in her life as her oppressors; in short, to argue that the play is 'about' feminism and patriarchy.

But part of what is so alluring—and daring—about *Hedda Gabler* is its wit, its unexpected lack of solemnity, its defiance of an audience's expectations, its reluc-tance to conform to reductive theory. Is there any other dramatic heroine who possesses such an extraordinary confection of characteristics as Hedda? She's feisty, droll and intelligent, yet fatally ignorant of the world and herself. She's snobbish, mean-spirited, small-minded, conservative, cold, bored, vicious; sexually eager but terrified of sex, ambitious to be bohemian but frightened of scandal, a desperate romantic fantasist but unable to sustain any loving relationship with anyone, including herself. And yet, in spite of all this, she mesmerises us and compels our pity.

Hedda can't even succeed in dominating the centre of the universe she has created: in the thirty-six hours of the action of the play she realises that, as a mere wife of an academic, she's powerless, imprisoned by her prospective motherhood and indentured to a cruel man as his mistress. Suicide is the only way out, a final, awful, 'grand gesture'.

'The title of the play,' said Ibsen in a letter, 'is *Hedda Gabler* rather than *Hedda Tesman* [her husband's name]. I intended to indicate thereby that as a personality she is to be regarded rather as her father's daughter than as her husband's wife.' Hedda's father was a general, with the status if not the wealth of an aristocrat, and, according to Ibsen's notes, Hedda was born when her father was already an old man and had left the army in slightly discreditable circumstances. Hedda, an orphan (perhaps the mother died in childbirth), is left to vindicate her father's reputation. 'She really wants to live the whole life of a *man*,' said Ibsen, but, of course, as he said in his notes for *A Doll's House*: 'A woman cannot be herself in modern society. It is an exclusively male society, with laws made by men and with prosecutors and judges who assess feminine conduct from a masculine standpoint.'

Which might suggest a schematic creation of a character, but Hedda seems a creation as ambiguous and unpredictable as anyone you might meet in life—and, in the case of a Hedda, avoid. And to her creator she, and indeed everyone in the play, were as real as if they had lived: 'Finally, in the last draft, I have reached the limit of my knowledge; I know my characters from close and long acquaintance—they are my intimate friends, who will no longer disappoint me; as I see them now, I shall always see them.'

That quality of even-handedly creating characters who seem to exist independently of their maker is not one that I, at least, have often ascribed to Ibsen. It's more, well, a Chekhovian quality and perhaps it's a confession of ignorance (or banality) that for many years I thought a liking for Chekhov and for Ibsen were incompatible: you declared yourself for one party or the other. 'Ibsen is an idiot,' said Chekhov, and in my infatuation I was prepared to agree with him. But compare these two statements:

> 'It was not really my intention to deal in this play with so-called problems. What I principally wanted to do was to depict human beings, human emotions, and human destinies, upon a groundwork of certain of the social conditions and principles of the present day.'

'You are right in demanding that an artist approach his work consciously, but you are confusing two concepts: the solution of a problem and the correct formulation of a problem. Only the second is required of the artist.'

And then answer the question: which is Chekhov, which Ibsen? (The first is Ibsen.)

When I was working with the conductor Georg Solti, I asked him what he regretted most: 'Not being able to say sorry to Shostakovich for having underrated him and thought of him as a lackey of the state.' I've often felt I'd like to apologise to Ibsen for my prejudice. I have a temperamental inclination to Chekhov because of his mordant wit and wordliness, his doctor's eye and his talent for transforming experience of life and love into art. But in fact, at least as far as *Hedda Gabler* is concerned, Ibsen was doing the same thing. 'The essential thing,' he said 'is... to draw a clear distinction between what one has merely experienced and what one has spiritually *lived through*; for only the latter is proper material for creative writing.'

It's both pointless and prurient to behave as if there's a linear equation that connects life (particularly love life) and art, but in the case of *Hedda Gabler* there's no question that events in Ibsen's life were a catalyst to his creative process, a crystal of lived experience around which the play coalesced.

In the summer of 1889, when he was sixty-one, Ibsen was on holiday in a South Tyrolean village. He met an eighteen-year-old Viennese girl called Emilie Bardach and fell in love. He had dedicated himself to his art like a monk, for 'the power and the glory', and he'd renounced spontaneous joy and sexual fulfilment. Emilie became the 'May sun of a September life'. She asked him to live with her; he at first agreed but, crippled by guilt and fear of scandal (and perhaps impotence as well), put an end to the relationship.

Emilie, like Hedda, was a beautiful, intelligent, spoilt, bored, upper-class girl with 'a tired look in her mysterious eyes', who wanted to have power and was thrilled at the possibility of snaring someone else's husband. The village in which they met in the Tyrol—Gossensass—was mentioned specifically in an earlier draft of the play when Hedda and Loevborg are looking at the honeymoon photographs in the second act, and fragments of dialogue in Ibsen's notes from the play appear to be derived directly from his conversations with Emilie.

But, if Emilie was the inspiration for the character of Hedda, Ibsen himself—consciously or not—contributed many of her characteristics. With his fear of scandal and ridicule, his apparent repulsion from the reality of sex, his yearning for an emotional freedom, Ibsen might have said of Hedda, as Flaubert did of Madame Bovary: '*Hedda, c'est moi.*'

There were two entirely unconnected events which occurred last year that drew my attention to the play. I was sitting in a dentist's waiting room reading an interview in *Hello!* magazine with a rich posh young woman who was celebrated for being celebrated. She craved attention and yet had no talent for anything but self-advertisement and was quoted, without irony (never the strong suit of *Hello!*), as saying: 'I'm afraid I have a great talent for boredom.'

Mmmm, I thought, Hedda Gabler lives. The same evening I went to a fine production of Eugene O'Neill's *Mourning Becomes Electra* and saw an actress, Eve Best, who seemed born to play Hedda. With the sort of credulousness typical of a reader of *Hello!*, I took the synchronicity as a sign that I should do the play and got myself commissioned by Robert Fox and by Michael Attenborough at the Almeida Theatre to do a new translation.

The best way of understanding a play is to write it—even if that means merely typing a script yourself or copying it out in longhand. It obliges you to question the meaning of every word, speech, gesture and stage direction. Arthur Miller once said to me: 'You know what I used to do years ago? I would take any of Shakespeare's plays and simply copy them. Pretending that I was him, you see. You know, it's a marvellous exercise. Just copy the speeches, and you gradually realise the concision, the packing together of experience, which is hard to do just with your ear, but if you have to work it with a pen on a piece of paper, you see that stuff coming together in that intense inner connection of sound and meaning.'

Which is what I've tried to do in this version of Ibsen's great play. It can't properly be called a 'translation' because I speak not a word of Norwegian. I worked from a literal version, and I tried to animate the language in a way that felt as true as possible to what I understood from it to be the author's intentions—even to the point of trying to capture cadences that I could at least infer from the Norwegian original. But even literal translations make choices and the choices we make are made according to taste, to the times we live in and how we view the world. All choices are choices of meaning, of intention. What I have written is a 'version' or 'adaptation' or 'interpretation' of Ibsen's play, but I hope that it comes close to squaring the circle of being close to what Ibsen intended while seeming spontaneous to an audience of today.

Sons and Lovers

This was written as an introduction to a new edition of the novel published in 2010.

It's not hard to imagine a teenager of today hesitating at the prospect of reading a novel by D.H. Lawrence. His stock is low. While his poetry is admired, his paintings are scorned, his plays largely unperformed and his novels neglected. What's more he's reviled for his supposed fascism and sexism. I can't think of Lawrence as being bound by any 'ism' nor can I think of him as anything but a genius. His poetry has a wonderful specificity and he's one of the very best—and least celebrated—English playwrights. His novels have a voracious ambition to embrace passion and ideas, aspiration and desperation. 'There is no such thing as sin,' he said. 'There is only life and anti-life.' They have a curiosity about the place of sex in our lives and an undaunted determination to examine it. And they give a rare picture—clear and unsentimental—of working-class life. But perhaps his stock is rising: an American friend told me recently that her seventeen-year-old nephew was reading *Sons and Lovers* and had pronounced it 'pretty cool'.

When I was seventeen, in 1960, the Lawrence novel that I was eager to read was *Lady Chatterley's Lover*, largely on account of the fact that I'd heard it had explicit descriptions of sex which included the naming of parts. That I knew this, was due to the fact that Penguin Books had published the first unexpurgated edition and had been prosecuted for it under the Obscene Publications Act, which aimed to punish books which had a 'tendency to deprave and corrupt those whose minds are open to such immoral influences'. A recent change in the Act, however, had made it possible for publishers to escape conviction if they could

171

show that a work was of literary merit. An array of expert literary witnesses testified to its merits and, with his memorably absurd line that the book was not the sort 'you would wish your wife or servants to read', the prosecuting counsel failed to convince the jury and the publishers were acquitted.

When I eventually got hold of a copy of *Lady Chatterley's Lover* I was surprised. Far from finding it lubricious, I found it a sometimes grave, sometimes droll, often earnest, novel that was partly about sex—or at least the differing attitudes to sex of men and women—but as much about class and culture and politics. Moreover the descriptions of sex were neither simple nor mechanical. Far from it, Lawrence was representing the *complexity* of sex—the power and fascination of it as well as the 'ridiculous bouncing of the buttocks, and the wilting of the poor insignificant, moist little penis'. It's a novel about people who are living in a world bruised by war and by 'mechanised greed', in which regeneration would only be possible through honest sexual relationships where the body and mind became inseparable. It's an argument he had set out fifteen years earlier in *Sons and Lovers*.

Sons and Lovers is autobiographical but it's not Lawrence's autobiography, though it's easy enough to conflate the two. The setting—'Bestwood'—is unmistakably Eastwood, where he was born and grew up and his father was a miner. His mother, like Gertrude Morel in the novel, married beneath her class, and her marriage had the characteristics of the Morel's marriage: an early passion declining into mutual resentment ('in her heart of hearts, where the love should have burned, there was a blank'). Lawrence's first job, as in the novel, was as a clerk in a factory which made surgical appliances. And in Miriam and her family, it is not hard to recognise the Chambers family at Hagg's Farm and the real life Jessie, who had the same role in Lawrence's life as Miriam did in Paul's: 'Miriam was the threshing floor on which he threshed out all his beliefs.' Jessie Chambers fiercely contested the characterisation of Miriam and the complexion that Lawrence had put on their relationship. The further he became removed from the real events both in time and in the several drafts of the novel, the more he became concerned with a fictional rather than historical truth. The novel was drawn, rather than based, on his life.

Here's his description to his publisher of his scheme for the book:

> ...as her sons grow up she selects them as lovers—first the eldest, then the second. These sons are *urged* into life by their reciprocal love of their mother—urged on and on. But when they come to manhood, they can't love, because their mother is the strongest power in their lives, and holds them. As soon as the young men come into contact with women, there's a split. William gives his sex to a fribble, and his mother holds his soul. But the split kills him, because he doesn't know where he is. The next son gets a woman who fights for his soul—fights

his mother. The son loves his mother—all the sons hate and are jealous of the father.

It's possible that this was a *post hoc* rationalisation—after all, the first title for the novel was *Paul Morel*—but as a description of the novel's emotional landscape it can't be bettered. Some people infer, both from the novel—'wherever he went her soul went with him'—and from Lawrence's stated intentions, that Paul Morel (and Lawrence himself) was in the grip of an Oedipus complex. With that dubious, reductive label, a character becomes a condition. It also fails to embrace the subtlety with which Lawrence creates the context of Mrs Morel's love for her son: 'She went into the front garden, feeling too heavy to take herself out, yet unable to stay indoors. The heat suffocated her. And looking ahead, the prospect of her life made her feel as if she was buried alive.' Entombed in her loveless marriage she lives vicariously through her sons, first William, then Arthur, then Paul. When William dies ('Oh, my son, my son!' Mrs Morel sang softly, and each time the coffin swung to the unequal climbing of the men: 'Oh my son, my son, my son') she grows into herself and becomes mute until Paul draws her back: 'His life story, like an Arabian nights, was told night after night to his mother. It was almost as if it were her own life.'

The battleground where Gertrude contends with her sons is sex. She is jealous for their attention and bitingly chides them when they take interest in women, or at least in strong women, the women who want to take control of her sons, the women who 'leave me no room, not a bit of room'. Miriam is the principal object of her resentment, and Paul is torn between love for his mother and desire for Miriam, which is finally unsatisfactorily consummated: 'She had the most beautiful body he had ever imagined... and then he wanted her, but as he went forward to her, her hands lifted in a little pleading movement, and he looked at her face and stopped... She lay as if she had given herself up for sacrifice.'

It will come as a surprise to readers new to *Sons and Lovers*, schooled to think of Lawrence as a priapic anti-feminist, that the novel presents an almost reverent attitude to women and, far from being concerned with sexual indulgence, is concerned with sexual shyness and virginity, 'the misery of celibacy'. Lawrence writes about the confusion in men and women about sex, the frequently child-like behaviour of men in the face of sexual desire, the ignorance and fear: 'He was like so many young men of is own age. Sex had become so complicated in him that he would have denied that he could ever want Clara or Miriam or any woman that he *knew*: sex desire was a sort of detached thing, that did not belong to a woman.'

It's common to mock Lawrence as the progenitor of the Bad Sex Award for his writing about sex, but are his descriptions of sexual passion—largely devoid of the geography of limbs and the exchange of bodily fluids—really less vivid than ones which are anatomically and mechanically detailed? 'He sunk his mouth on her throat, where he felt her heavy pulse beat under his lips. Everything was perfectly still. There was nothing in the afternoon but themselves.' Isn't that beautiful? In his writing about sex, Lawrence is the opposite of pornographic; he tries to anatomise feelings that are outside the realm of objectivity; he's always concerned with trying to parse the mystery of the relationship of the physical to the spiritual, instinct to reason, passion to love.

When Paul makes love to Clara Dawes there's a release—'the baptism of life, each through the other'—but there is still an unresolved inequality that troubled Lawrence throughout his fiction and his life:

'Do you think it's worth it—the—the sex part?'

'The act of loving, itself?'

'Yes; is it worth anything to you?'

'But how can you separate it,' he said. 'It's the culmination of everything. All our intimacy culminates then.'

'Not for me,' she said.

He was silent. A flash of hate for her came up. After all, she was dissatisfied with him, even there, where he thought they fulfilled each other. But he believed her too implicitly.

'I feel,' she continued slowly, 'as if I hadn't got you, as if all of you weren't there, as if it weren't me you were taking—'

'Who then?'

'Something just for yourself. It has been fine, so that I daren't think of it. But is it *me* you want, or is it *It*?'

The need to resolve this inequity became a credo in Lawrence's writing: 'I believe if men could fuck with warm hearts, and the women take it warm-heartedly, everything would come all right.'

Like the passage above, much if not most of the debate in the novel is portrayed in dialogue rather than prose. In fact, the spine of *Sons and Lovers* is the dialogue, the arteries too, for the blood of real life pulses through every spoken word. The dialogue is often italicised and capitalised for emphasis like a playwright determined that his lines are correctly heard; but then Lawrence was a very good playwright. Of his eight plays his masterpiece was *The Daughter-in-Law*. As in his novels, its themes—if you can describe anything as subtle and organic as 'themes'—are sex, class, dependence and freedom, all couched in the language of a mining community, whose speech is both authentic and poetic. 'I wish I could write such dialogue,' said Bernard Shaw. 'With mine I always hear the sound of the typewriter.'

Listen to this—it's just after the birth of Paul when his father, back from the mine with his face black and smeared with sweat, stands at the foot of the bed:

'Well, how are ter, then?'

'I s'll be all right,' she answered.

'H'm!'

He stood at a loss what to say next. He was tired, and this bother was nuisance to him, and he didn't quite know where he was.

'A lad, tha says,' he stammered.

Throughout *Sons and Lovers* (and all his plays), Lawrence shows a love of the physical, the way that men and women use their bodies to work, or wash, or eat, or touch or avoid each other. He physicalises the dialogue too, invariably using dialect to achieve authenticity and delineate class distinctions. It provoked many of his middle-class readers and is a further reminder of how few English writers write with authority about the working class. 'Why don't you speak ordinary English?' says Lady Chatterley to Mellors. 'AH thowt it WOR ordinary,' he replies.

Lawrence is good on the natural world too, the sounds of birds and animals, the 'chock-chock' of a gate closing, the smells of the railway and of flowers—'the scent made him drunk… the beauty of the night made him want to shout'. He's not without wit too. The description of the visit of William's fiancée, Lily (a bit of a 'bobby-dazzler'), to the Morels' house is a wonderful set piece about the awkwardness of introducing a girlfriend to the family, observed from every point of view. The whole book is threaded through the silvery glint of distinctive observations—'they had the peculiar shut off look of the poor who have to depend on the favours of others' and 'it is curious that children suffer so much from having to pronounce their own names'—which have a vigour and accessibility that makes the novel feel, nearly 100 years after its publication, as if it were written today.

Lawrence's writing is always concerned with what it means to be modern, what it means to live in an industrial age, to hold on to your own self when everything conspires to obliterate it. He writes about all kinds of love—physical and spiritual—but shows how love is bound up inextricably with class and with society. There's a kind of doggedness about the conclusion to *Sons and Lovers*, with Paul sacrificing his relationship with Clara in order to be alone: 'himself, infinitesimal, at the core of nothingness, and yet not nothing'. He calls out to his mother in suicidal despair, 'But no, he would not give in.' He endures, as Lawrence endured in the face of extraordinary difficulties in his life and work—poverty, controversy, condemnation and illness. 'We've got to live,' he said. 'No matter how many skies have fallen.'

The Smoking Diaries

I wrote this as a preface to a collected edition of Simon Gray's diaries published in 2013.

———•—

'Piero de Medici had the sculptor make in his courtyard a statue of snow, which was said to be very beautiful,' said Vasari in his *Lives of the Artists*. I'm fond of this story, apocryphal or not. Michelangelo's Snowman. It might well have been his greatest work but, like a theatre performance, you had to have been there to have seen it: it was unreproducible. Theatre only lives in the present tense: writing and acting for theatre is the art of feigning spontaneity. What could be more spontaneous than this:

> My plan is to get down some thoughts and memories of Alan, but I don't think I can start today, not with the pigeons hopping, and the little birds with yellow chests, etc., one of which is now sharing my drink. Best let it happen if it happens, tomorrow perhaps or later in the week, let it sneak up. Today the thing is just to be here, back here at the usual table, my yellow pad in front of me, free to go wherever— although I think I must make a pact with myself to lay off the subject of my age, and my physical deterioration, it's really time I outgrew all that, it's not becoming in a man nearing seventy, although I must confess that now I see those words on the page, 'nearing seventy', I find myself gaping at them.

This reads like dialogue in a play, part of a monologue spoken directly to the audience. In the course of his extended soliloquys the nature of the speaker is

176

revealed little by little as a not-quite-solipsistic, sometimes bitter, often loving, amiable, humane, vulnerable, intelligent, droll, melancholy, curmudgeonly protagonist called 'SIMON GRAY'—an almost entirely convincing characterisation of the writer Simon Gray.

If I say 'almost' it's because what Simon achieves is so beguiling and so difficult. The passage above (from the beginning of the second volume of *The Smoking Diaries*) is like Paul Klee's drawings: the pen never seems to leave the paper. Taking a line for a walk—Klee's famous description of drawing—is easier than writing. You can sketch a line following the brain's instructions in real time, but you can't write words as fast as they occur to you. It takes a good actor to convince you that the words he's speaking have just come to mind; it takes a virtuoso writer to give the same impression on the page. 'Hold on!' Simon tells the reader as if we—or he—were getting the wrong idea about what he's saying. Or 'No!' when he wants to contradict himself. Or '…wait until fresh and vigorous, vigorous? Hah! Well, until fresh, fresh? Also hah!' when he's trying to dissect the past or giving a cautionary message to his audience:

> but it's never too late, it is always said, never too late to change. Oh yes, it is… I would certainly go forth and do good in the world, if only my vices would let me. Alas, I am what I am, alas. Know what I mean?

He writes as if memories and the act of recording them are occurring simultaneously, achieving spontaneity with an artlessness that's supremely artful.

If the *Diaries* are a series of dramatic soliloquies, they're accompanied by their stage directions. The scene is always set meticulously: weather, architecture, furniture, supporting cast, who are often the cats, Tom and Errol, the dogs, George and Toto, and always the wife, Victoria. And the location of the action—the act of writing—is always described. It's on planes, 'I'm only going on like this because we're on the verge of taking off'; at a desk in Suffolk, 'It's now three in the afternoon, my lights are on, the rain is drizzling down, and I'm cold'; in a bar in Barbados, 'Can I, in all conscience, keep my table at the bar while I have lunch in the restaurant?'; a café in Crete, a hotel room in New York, or a smoker's table on the pavement in Holland Park Avenue.

Once the scene is set, like an actor tackling a long soliloquy, Simon fills his lungs (ironic for a would-be ex-smoker) and words fly out of him as if he'd discovered the secret of circular breathing: on cricket, tyranny, racism, sharks, rats, dogs, cats, flies, DTs, childhood, sex, murder, friendship, death, the power of fiction, lesbian fantasies, Harold Pinter (his temper and, more surprisingly, his gentleness), C.P. Snow, Simon Callow, Alan Bates, Tom Stoppard, Nathan Lane and more. It's the literary equivalent of the way in which thoughts come unbidden into your mind when you're lying half-awake in the early morning or drifting unmoored during the day.

The momentum of the *Diaries*—what I suppose you could call the 'plot'—is provided by the successive renunciations of Simon's greatest pleasures: alcohol and smoking. 'Start stopping smoking NOW' is an injunction that proves as painful to follow as the prospect of renouncing life itself:

> in short –
> in short
> and in short
> I am afraid.

Simon's writing for the theatre is invariably warm and approachable—a paradox given that his tone is sharp, his politics unregenerate, his central characters often rumpled wrecks whose alcohol intake is auto-destructive and whose nicotine consumption is probably poisoning half the street. His early plays were grotesques in the style of Joe Orton, but then he appropriated the classicism of Racine. We see a character in a room: doors open, people enter and leave and, by a remorseless accumulation of incident, that character's doom is sealed.

His plays have an ascetic, classical, conservative form yet contain (or restrain) characters whose emotions spill out in a prodigal disorder. The form of the *Diaries* is unrestrained but are no less plays than his plays, even though they feature a sole protagonist whose emotions, of course, spill out in a prodigal disorder. It seems odd that there aren't more playwrights, besides Alan Bennett and Michael Frayn, who take to prose in the intervals between plays, given that those intervals tend to be long. Writing a play is so precariously difficult; it's the literary equivalent of juggling with crockery in a high wind while tightrope-walking over a deep gorge. Character and story have to be revealed through action rather than description and have to be introduced by sleight of hand. Confrontations, love affairs, battles, deaths and births have to be engineered as if each action inevitably and effortlessly followed another and—hardest of all—an audience has to be left with the impression that the characters exist independently of the writer and that the play has come to life spontaneously.

Some novelists think that writing plays is an easy option: the literary landscape is littered with the corpses of novelists' plays that were dead at birth—Joyce's *Exiles*, Virginia Woolf's *Freshwater*, William Golding's *The Brass Butterfly*, Muriel Spark's *Doctors of Philosophy* and, notoriously, Henry James's *Guy Domville*. On the opening night, like many playwrights, James was too nervous to watch his own play, so he missed the reception of the line 'I'm the last, my lord, of the Domvilles' to which a wit in the gallery responded 'It's a bloody good thing you are!' He arrived backstage during the curtain calls and, reassured by applause for the actors, stepped onto the stage and was drowned by a tsunami of booing.

It's a story that Simon would have relished. He falls with masochistic gusto into riffs about the agonies of a playwright ('a combination of fool and criminal') watching his own play:

I feel like a criminal forced to sit with the jury and witness my own crime, witness myself committing it, and then showing it off. One of the things that might strike people as odd, but doesn't strike me as odd, which is the oddest part of it, is that my sympathies, no, more than my sympathies, my whole digestive system and nervous tract, are with the jury, at least its hostile members.

Or there's the story that he tells of a drunken director who 'stumbled down the aisle and tumbled over the seats, often with a lighted cigarette in his mouth'. Things go from worse to terrible and 'of course, the producer, who was devoted to the play, made periodic attempts to fire the director but was thwarted by the director's agent, who pointed out that the playwright had director approval, and as the playwright and the director were one and the same, it would be a question of asking him to fire himself, which he was unlikely to do, as he got on so well together.' When I first read this my simmering smile erupted into a bark of laughter.

And what joy there is in his account of trying to type up his day's writing when the letter 'h' on his typewriter had started sticking, leading to an h-less paragraph about the loss of his 'ligtness of touc'. The writing is crafty—moments of pain are subverted by explosions of comedy; and the whirling free association never becomes wearisome because it's spiced with irresistibly vivid turns of phrase— a woman has 'a voice you could grate cheese on'; a pile of dead insects looks like 'toast crumbs'; the loss of a friend is 'a bit of grit in my inner eye'. For all that he's voluble, irascible and wholly unclubbable; he's always wary of boring you.

Wit and spontaneity prevents *The Smoking Diaries* from ever being infected by the Pooterish tone that tends to afflict any conversation with oneself. With Simon there's always self-mockery or self-condemnation, or at very least self-disgust—'I've just re-read the above paragraph. It is disgusting.' Often with diarists evasion, self-justification and self-recrimination amount to self-defence but Simon's confessions aren't larded with self-pity. Memories, such as of his girlfriend—or to be more accurate 'his first fuck'—are anatomised for their reliability, and the narrator is interrogated and found wanting:

You had no sex with her?
That's it. Yes.
What form did this no sex take?
When I'd peeled my trousers down to my knees, and rolled my underpants down to my trousers' crotch, I lay on top of her and bucked about, yelping.

Or, writing about his mother, he charges himself with neglect:

I... thought about the kind of son I was, who would deprive his dying mother of a few more minutes, that's all she'd claimed... I still don't know why I wouldn't stay.

The problem with most diaries is that, if true, they're never quite true enough. Cocteau said that 'A journal exists only if you put into it, without reservation, everything that occurs to you.' Simon follows Cocteau with somewhat more wit and considerably less self-regard in writing frankly of sexual desire, failure, fantasy and jealousy; of his loneliness and of what he regards as his nastiness:

> The truth is that I'm nastier than I was at sixty-two and so forth, back and back, always the less nasty the further back, until I get to the age when I was pre-nasty, at least consciously, when the only shame I knew was the shame of being found out, which was when I was, well, about eight, I suppose.

He writes too about his addictions. Ill health may have forced him to give up alcohol and smoking but he couldn't resist the addiction of writing, even at 3 a.m after a sleeping pill, two co-proxamol and a Broadway opening night.

Under the whole book runs a strong but barely sounded obbligato: the love for his wife, Victoria. Perhaps it's this that prevents him from writing more biliously—'unchoke me from this hatred that comes on me like a sickness more and more…'—but his invocation to himself doesn't inhibit him from describing the *New York Times* theatre critic as having 'an unhappy prose style, aiming to be simultaneously colloquial and elegant it comes out here snobbish and there vulgar, and sometimes both in the same sentence' in a marvellously drawn and painfully recognisable passage about putting on one of his plays—*Butley*—on Broadway.

Simon's *Diaries*—like Pepys' and Virginia Woolf's and Joe Orton's—give the feeling of a life spilling out indiscriminately, innocent of self-censorship, as if the life is being lived through the diary. He takes life as he finds it, without seeking to improve it or to moralise about it. 'The moral is: you can learn nothing from experience, at least in my experience.' There are few who can write about their experience with such charm, such honesty and such self-knowledge.

Being and Nothingness

Astonishingly—at least to me—I was invited to write an introduction to a new edition of Sartre's extended philosophical essay in 2000, shortly after I'd directed my adaptation of his play Les Mains Sales.

In this country Sartre is as unfashionable as loon pants, so it's hard for us to imagine a world in which, as the novelist Iris Murdoch said when she briefly met Sartre in 1945 in Brussels, 'His presence in the city was like that of a pop star. Chico Marx, who was there at about the same time, was less rapturously received.'

When I was a student in the 1960s, Sartre didn't quite have poster status—his pipe, glasses and air of bad temper kept him off walls that celebrated Che, Brigitte Bardot and James Dean—but few student bookshelves lacked a (largely) unread copy of *Being and Nothingness*, his 632-page exegesis of existentialism. From the little I read of it, I understood only what suited me, but, as I was growing up in a world still scarred by the Holocaust, Hitler, Stalin and nuclear warfare, it wasn't hard to grasp a philosophy which was predicated on the absolute absence of God. And if I understood Sartre superficially, I understood him sufficiently to corroborate my feelings of confusion about my sexual and political identity: 'First of all, man exists,' he said, 'turns up, appears on the scene, and, only afterwards, defines himself.' That seemed to describe my condition pretty accurately, and his argument for the reality of 'nothingness' hit the mark as far as student life was concerned.

If Sartre's philosophy remained more talked about than read, his novels were popular (*Roads to Freedom* was serialised by the BBC) and his plays were much performed. In fact, it was practically a legal obligation in the sixties for student drama groups to perform *Huis Clos*. Sartre was attracted to the theatre because theatre thrives on metaphor—a room becomes a world, a group of characters becomes a whole society—so plays tend to be about how we live and why we live. In the theatre Sartre was obliged to characterise and animate his philosophical and political propositions, test theory against flesh and blood. And he was obliged to condense and distil his ideas. 'The metaphysician who could not say anything unless he said everything was compelled in the theatre to give his message briefly,' said Iris Murdoch, 'and as Sartre unfortunately could not *do* everything, as opposed to *thinking* everything, he found the theatre, where he had undoubted talent, a sympathetic place to drop in to.'

His play, *Les Mains Sales* (*Dirty Hands*), was first performed in 1948. It's a *noir*-ish political thriller, set in a fictional East European country ('Illyria') in the dying days of the Second World War. A young man is commissioned by a revolutionary Socialist party to assassinate the leader of a rival faction, who is held to be diluting the party's principles by joining a coalition with liberal and right-wing parties in order to form a government. Not long after the Labour landslide of 1997, I decided to adapt the play for the Almeida Theatre in North London. What attracted me to it was partly the topicality of the debate between means and ends and purity and opportunism, but as much its exploration of class, of sex, and of growing up. Like Hamlet, Hugo, the play's protagonist, grows up to grow dead.

My version of *Les Mains Sales* (which I christened *The Novice*) coincided with the peace negotiations in Northern Ireland and with rancorous bickering between Old and New Labour. 'Principle', 'pragmatism' and 'power-sharing' were words that rained down from all directions, while the metaphor of 'dirty hands' was invoked on a daily basis. Sartre's play seemed once again a play for today just as, it seems to me, *Being and Nothingness* is a philosophy for today.

The universe which Sartre's philosophy describes is a familiar one to any contemporary reader in the West: a meaningless, godless and depersonalised world in which the words 'ennui', 'angst' and 'alienation' are much more current than hope and compassion. But nevertheless, says Sartre, it's a world in which we have free will: we are responsible for our actions and are the sole judges of how they affect others. But that free will is curbed by the fact that our awareness of ourselves prevents us from ever truly being 'ourselves', so we play at being ourselves and become 'inauthentic'.

To behave 'authentically' is to understand that we can make and remake ourselves by our actions and thus become what our acts define us as being. To talk rather than act is moral self-deception—'*mauvaise foi*' (bad faith)—which involves our behaving as insensate things rather than 'authentic' human beings. In bad faith, we evade responsibility by not exploiting the possibilities of choice; in short, by not being fully human.

In *Being and Nothingness* Sartre doesn't present a total system of belief or a user's manual to life, but for me, in spite of being barely literate in philosophy and in spite of his sometimes barely penetrable technical vocabulary, he provides a top-ographical account—a moral template—that helps me navigate some of the more shadowy paths of my existence. And for all his pessimism, in asserting the absolute nature of the individual Sartre defies the inhuman determinism of the contemporary world, where every day we are told that we are 'wired' to do this or that by our genetic make-up, or by the pressures of society, or the structures of economic systems. Sartre presupposes that our lives require a basis in reason but declares that the attempt to uncover that basis is a 'futile passion'. Oddly I find some comfort in being told this: that we can never hope to understand why we are here and that we have to choose a goal and follow it with passionate con-viction, aware of the meaninglessness of our lives and the certainty of our deaths.

For me Sartre's concern with our disposition to evade responsibility and to lie to ourselves—our 'bad faith'—is as active a notion as when I first came across it. And in an age where we appear to believe nothing except celebrity, I can't think that a writer who says that we define man only in relation to his commitments is entirely redundant.

I hope the publication of *Being and Nothingness* does something to revive interest in a writer whose philosophy in Britain has become as unfashionable as his fic-tion. What's more he's frequently reviled as a misogynist: the writer Angela Carter once asked, 'There is one question that every thinking woman in the Western world must have asked herself at one time or another. Why is a nice girl like Simone de Beauvoir sucking up to a boring old fart like Jean-Paul Sartre?' But just before Christmas a few years ago, I arrived in Paris on the Eurostar. To my astonishment, the magazine kiosks were plastered with photographs of the boring old fart: Sartre had been resurrected as man and philosopher by the pop-ular savant, Bernard-Henri Lévy. Later I heard that there was to be a Place Sartre-De Beauvoir near his favourite café, Les Deux Magots, and that Richard Attenborough was said to be making a film about Simone de Beauvoir's affair with Nelson Algren with Sartre as the third corner of the amorous triangle. Fame indeed. People might even start to read his books.

Making *Iris*

Iris was a feature film I made which starred Judi Dench, Jim Broadbent, Kate Winslet and Hugh Bonneville.

———·•·———

There are good films and there are bad films. They are all difficult to get made. And then there are British films. This is the story of how one British film came to be made.

March 1999. I'm rehearsing *Amy's View* by David Hare in New York with Judi Dench, who has just won an Oscar for *Shakespeare in Love*. I ask her what she's going to do next. She says she's been asked to play Iris Murdoch in a film based on John Bayley's books about their life together and her death from Alzheimer's disease. She asks me if she should do it. I say yes and opportunistically offer myself as a director. I imagine an enterprising British producer has bought the film rights but discover that they have been bought by Hollywood: John Calley of Sony Pictures. I know John from his enthusiastic (but doomed) attempts to release *Tumbledown* (a BBC film I directed about the Falklands War) theatrically in the US. I contact him and lobby through all available channels.

November 1999. I'm in New York again, filming an interview with Arthur Miller for my TV series *Changing Stages*. In the early evening I meet John Calley in the St Regis Hotel: tea and scones. He asks me to direct *Iris* and we discuss possible screenplay writers. 'Why don't you write it?' he says. 'You know about these

184

things' (the 'things' being Alzheimer's disease). I say I'll think about it, and we discuss possible British producers; I suggest Robert Fox.

December 1999. John urges me to write the screenplay myself. I accept but then decide that solo directing and writing is a shade too hubristic for me, so I recruit Charles Wood (who wrote *Tumbledown*). Judi is only available in the autumn and there will be some scenes (swimming in the river) that we will have to shoot in the late summer. So the theory, which everyone says is impossible, is to deliver the screenplay in May, go into pre-production in August and shoot in late September. John says that if he likes the screenplay there won't be a problem. But I can't start working full time on the film until the end of April, so we have very little time. Charles and I think we can achieve it between the two of us.

January 2000. I tell a writer friend what I'm doing. 'The job is to make the audience cry,' he says. Ah yes. Charles and I now have contracts. We map out the screenplay: the film will begin and end underwater; it won't be a chronicle of an illness, but a story of a relationship (*Enduring Love* might be its subtitle); there will be two tenses: present and the past; it will be unsentimental, funny (?), and the actors playing Iris and John will also play their young selves.

April 2000. Charles emails me a draft, to which I then add and subtract scenes and email it back. We both have the same screenwriting software, which formats in a universally acceptable manner (i.e. it's American), and we write as if sitting on opposite sides of a desk, sixty-five miles apart: Charles in Oxfordshire, me in West London.

May 2000. I deliver our screenplay to John Calley. It opens with these words: 'JOHN BAYLEY and IRIS MURDOCH are in their sixties and seventies, and throughout the film they remain the same age. In the scenes set in the 1950s the other characters are the ages they were at the time.' I hear back from John. He doesn't like it at ALL: too many flashbacks, too confusing, the idea of the old people playing their young selves doesn't work, so if we're thinking of filming this year, forget it. Give me a week, I say. A sleepless night follows, in which I reconstruct the screenplay, simplify and reshuffle the flashbacks, and allow for young and old actors. I ring Charles in the morning in a state of demented excitement. We work on.

June 2000. We deliver the new draft. John Calley loves it. We meet at The Dorchester Hotel. There are no problems, we will film it this year, with a budget of, say, $20m. It will have wide distribution and reach a large audience. We discuss actors who might play John Bayley. It's a glorious sunny day and I walk though Hyde Park marvelling at the painlessness of it all.

July 2000. A silence of about three weeks after which a call from John. His 'people' are not happy about it, not happy at all. 'This is not the sort of film we make.' Ah. 'But we're going to try and make it through Sony Classics (their small-films division), but the budget will have to be around $10m.' Ah. A long and very detailed critique of the screenplay follows, fairly cogent even if fairly depressing: 'John Bayley needs to be more more rootable... For those beyond the ken of Oxford, their life there is utterly alien... etc., etc.', but it's a 'potentially moving, intelligent, unsentimental movie.'

It seems Sony Classics will only put up $5m. Will the BBC or Channel 4 come in as a partner? I call Alan Yentob and David Thompson (Head of BBC Films). It's possible; they want to read the script. Channel 4 have read the script but don't want to know: it's 'old fashioned', apparently. Sony Classics' passion now seems to be waning: the $5m budget would have to *include* a contribution from the BBC. With the commitments that John has made for fees to Judi, me, Charles, the book rights (predicated on a $20m budget) and the lawyers' fees, the cost of the film is grotesquely top-heavy. To shoot this year we have to resolve the budget problems by July 31st.

August 2000. The deadline has passed and John is 'putting the project into turnaround', i.e. they aren't going to make it. But he says that I can buy the project off Sony. Excellent! I just need to find $238,000. I ring Scott Rudin, who, as Bruce Robinson says in his memoir of life in the screen trade, produces practically every movie made in the US. I've known Scott for many years, have worked with him in the theatre and he's occasionally asked me to direct films.

Scott, Robert Fox and I meet in London, The Savoy this time. Scott has read the screenplay and is fired up: he has a million suggestions for the script. He counsels taking our time: the problems with Judi's availability will apparently take care of themselves. He says that he can make it with Paramount, budget $12m. Job, apparently, done. Meanwhile Judy Daish, my long-time agent, has talked to another of her long-time clients, Anthony Minghella, to see if he would be interested in being involved with the film with his partner in Mirage Films, the veteran director/producer Sydney Pollack. Anthony is enthusiastic but, I tell him, it seems that we're going to make the film with Paramount.

September 2000. It seems that Paramount isn't interested. A flurry of negotiations. The BBC is keen to be involved: they will buy rights to show the film on TV and distribution rights in the UK—i.e. the rights to show the film in UK cinemas. Anthony Minghella introduces the British/German/US film financiers, Intermedia, to the project: they will distribute to everywhere except the US and the UK. Scott now brings Miramax on board: they will distribute in North America.

Like all films, *Iris* will be financed on money advanced against possible sales (including film, TV and video) in three 'territories': Britain, North America, and the Rest of the World. Films are not financed on whim or speculation, but on the basis of quasi-scientific estimates made by sales representatives. Let's say you are trying to raise money against possible sales in Australasia: your sales rep in South Korea will guess at how much the film might take. You add up your estimates from your share of world territory, that's the money you have to make the film. This one's a hard sell: no car chases, no fights, no special effects, no extraterrestrial beings, just a love story between oldish people, Alzheimer's disease and Judi Dench.

We now have the possibility of nearly $7m and with it the certainty of eight producers—the last six of them 'Executive': Robert Fox, Scott Rudin, Anthony Minghella, Sydney Pollack, Guy East (Intermedia), David Thompson (BBC) and Tom Hedley (the publisher who sold the book to John Calley). Oh yes, and Harvey Weinstein, who produces (or at least distributes) as many films as Scott. They're rivals: both large men, two sumo masters.

In order to make the film we—actors, producers, director, writers—will have to take 'deferred payments'. This is a comically optimistic oxymoron: no one ever receives deferred payments. What it means is that you do the job for very little on the promise of your full fee when the film goes into profit, but 'going into profit' is as rare as—well, a successful British film.

Will this be a British film? We budget in dollars, we talk of 'greenlighting the project', of 'scouting for locations', 'making a movie' and 'watching the dailies', even though less than a third of our money comes from the US. When I made *Tumbledown* for the BBC we were told by a prospective American co-producer that the Falklands War was a 'parochial subject'. All too true of *Iris*, I'm afraid, but I'm stubbornly determined not to make the film any less English.

October 2000. We are supposed to start production in the third week of November. I deliver another draft (our seventh) to Scott, who responds with several pages of detailed notes. I spend a day with Anthony talking through the script. He asks a series of searching and thought-provoking questions. I distil the notes from Scott, Anthony, Guy East, David Thompson and their several advisers, and Charles and I divvy up the work to be done.

November 2000. The budget has shrunk to $6m. It's a huge sum by any reasonable standards, but the making of films doesn't adhere to any reasonable standards. A scene set in Lanzarote (sun, sea, massive contrast to English light and an agonising/comic scene at Gatwick Airport) becomes a scene on Southwold beach. The shooting schedule shrinks from forty-five days to thirty-nine. We are not starting in November; now it's to be January, but as yet the green light is still at amber.

December 2000. The BBC, now the majority investor, have provided us with money to keep us going and are going to cashflow the film. I get another three pages of notes from them. Charles and I digest these, both feeling by now terminally churlish. We have to be wittier at the beginning and sadder at the end apparently. We embark on another draft. Each time we finish one we say: this is it, we've really got it right, and each time there is more to be done. We're now on draft ten.

We decide to offer the part of John Bayley to Jim Broadbent. He's enthusiastic about the script; his only problem is that he is in Rome shooting *Gangs of New York* for Martin Scorsese. They are unable to guarantee a stop-date for him: stalemate. Judi is due to film *The Shipping News* in Newfoundland; her dates are wholly incompatible. Both her film and Jim's are Miramax films, so there is hope, but not certainty, of cooperation. Robert suggests that Kate Winslet would make a good Young Iris.

January 2001. We're still hoping and waiting: no bad news, no good news. Robert now seems to be in a state of perpetual meeting with the BBC, Intermedia and lawyers, or on the phone to Scott, who is in semi-permanent conference call with Miramax to try and sort the log-jam with Judi and Jim's dates. I'm present at some of the meetings and on some of the calls and have to fight hard not to shout: PLEASE JUST GIVE US THE MONEY AND LET US GET ON WITH IT!

Kate has accepted: universal jubilation but no more money. Judi is going to do three weeks on *The Shipping News*, then five weeks with us, then back to *The Shipping News*. In order to fit between Judi's dates we'll have no room for error and will have to work mostly six-day weeks. I'm really worried: her husband (ill for eighteen months) has just died and she's worn out from grief and looking after him. No progress on the Jim front; in despair I fax my editor friend Thelma Schoonmaker, to see if she can intercede with her director, Martin Scorsese. He says we *will* have Jim, but his executives are somewhat less convinced.

February 2001. We are in pre-production at Pinewood even though the light is still flickering between amber and green. We're like castaways on a desert island waiting for the sign of a ship on the horizon: waving, screaming, lighting bonfires, despairing, hoping. Our production office is situated within an archipelago occupied by *Tomb Raider*, a film which had been shooting for over three months, is still shooting now, and is supposed to be released in mid-June. The line producer tells me that his allocation for transport is larger than our entire budget. They might have got Angelina Jolie as Lara Croft but I don't mind: I've got Judi Dench and Kate Winslet as Iris Murdoch and I've almost got Jim Broadbent as John Bayley. I want to cast Hugh Bonneville as Young John but Scott is resistant: he doesn't know him.

Pinewood is Britain's most celebrated film studio, but it's not, as Fellini said of Cinecittà, a 'temple of dreams'. Its grandeur, such as it was, now has an air of dispiriting shabbiness. While the films of Fellini, Visconti, Antonioni, Bergman, Truffaut, Godard, Malle et al., were being made, Pinewood was host to James Bond and the early *Carry On* films. They are celebrated in a corridor of fame decorated with faux blue plaques celebrating Hattie Jacques, Peter Butterworth, Sid James and Kenneth Williams, Barbara Windsor and Bernard Bresslaw.

March 2000. I'm feeling like the old Fry's Five Boys chocolate ad— DESPERATION, PACIFICATION, EXPECTATION, ACCLAMATION, REALISATION: IT'S FRY'S!: Jim is going to be available and we have the green light. We even manage to get him back from Rome for a day to do a readthrough in my kitchen. It's terrifying: Judi, Jim, Kate, Hugh and two other actors— Samantha Bond and Kris Marshall—to play the other parts, Charles and five of the producers round my kitchen table. We celebrate our good luck in having these wonderful actors (Scott is bowled over by Hugh) and decide, of course, that we need more script changes, and more cuts to fit the schedule.

April 2001. My friend Stephen Frears recommends seeing a good film before one starts filming (on the grounds that it might rub off?), so I go to the video shop:

'Have you got *Fanny and Alexander*?'

'Do you mean *Fanny and Elvis*?'

'No, *Fanny and Alexander*.'

'*Fanny and Elvis* is good.'

Barely a year after we had a first draft, we're shooting: we've had a charmed life.

May 2001. Thirty-nine shooting days later we've finished filming and, like an astronaut released from a capsule, I re-enter the earth's atmosphere. After weeks insulated from the routine and obligations of daily life, I start reading newspapers, stop eating sausage, bacon, egg and fried bread at seven o'clock each morning, and discover that an election is taking place.

The film is shot, but that's barely half the story: we just have the stone from which the film is carved. Months of editing, screening, composing, recording, mixing, grading, testing, all the while listening to an inexhaustible flood of (sometimes conflicting) opinion and changing, changing, changing, has to come to an end, our cash exhausted.

December 2001. The film has its premiere in New York. It goes down well—tears and applause. How did it go in the UK? I'm asked at the party by Harvey Weinstein. I tell him it's opening in London in January. 'Watch out,' he said, 'They eat their own over there…'

Filming Fiction

Notes on a Scandal, *starring Judi Dench and Cate Blanchett, was a film I directed in 2006.*

———·•·———

In an inversion of the usual procedure, the driver of a white van screamed 'ACK-SHUUUUUN!' and the director cried 'TOSSER!' I am, or was, that director and I was standing on the knuckle of the roundabout at the bottom of Archway Road, waiting for the woman recently voted by C4 viewers the Best British Actress of All Time to appear at the wheel of an ageing VW Golf below the Victorian iron bridge which has been christened—for good reasons—'Suicide Bridge'.

I was shooting a film of Zoë Heller's novel, *Notes on a Scandal*, and over the weeks of the shoot—mainly in streets, houses and schools in North London— I was made vividly aware (not for the first time) of the scorn in which the public hold the activity of filming. Not the actors, of course, and certainly not Judi Dench, but on the streets of North London, she is either unrecognised (disguised in a short wig as a frumpy schoolteacher) or approached with the deference and affection reserved for a deity.

But while Judi Dench is revered, the crew are occasionally reviled. Their intrusive presence and privileged occupation is all too conspicuous, as is their perceived arrogance in forcing reality to give way to fiction. A few malcontents jump in front of the lens shouting 'I'm on TV!' and a drugged young man in the Kentish Town Road threatens with me with assault: 'Are you going to give me a part? I'm good, really good.'

But real indignation is reserved for the unwieldy procession—trucks, trailers, caravans, generators, cherry-pickers—that invades a street or a park like an occupying army and departs as suddenly as it arrives, leaving behind, in spite of scrupulous clearing-up, the film crews' characteristic spoor of polystyrene coffee cups and strips of gaffer tape. 'Are you gypsies?' asked a woman when we were camped out in Finsbury Park.

Mostly the London public appear bored by film-making. They're sated with the sight of pavements bulging with people in anoraks who divert their traffic and rob them of parking spaces. Or they're saturated with knowledge of the process of film-making either from DVD 'making of' extras or from their own efforts at home with video cameras. But in spite of this they remain forever mystified at the effort that it takes to record a fraction of a fragment of a scene in a film. The most frequent words that you hear when you're filming in a street are not 'tosser' or 'wanker' but 'Why does it take so many people to make a film?'

I find myself time after time asking myself the same question, and even though I'm only too aware of the essential role of each member of the crew, I'm still awed by the extraordinary degree of artifice that is required to simulate reality in order, paradoxically, to make fiction. We cosmeticise streets and houses. We make them look dirtier or older than they are—disguising their TV aerials, changing the profile of their chimneys, 'breaking down' their paintwork, 'distressing' their façades (and often their owners). We populate the streets with extras (to avoid the legal and physical peril of being accused of filming people without their consent); we introduce huge lamps when nature fails to provide sunlight; we make rain and snow. In short, we play God.

At the tip of this colossal inverted pyramid, stuffed with technology and manpower, there is a camera at the end of whose lens, perhaps no more than a few inches in diameter, is a small, vulnerable, variable, gifted person—an actor, whose image will be recorded on a rectangular piece of film a few centimetres wide, twenty-four times a second. At this point—the sharp end of film-making if you like—everything the director does is an attempt to confound or subvert the artifice of it all.

In Truffaut's (very romantic) film about film-making, *La Nuit Americaine*, the director (played by Truffaut) lies awake, racked with pain and doubt. 'Is my film alive?' he asks himself, and every film director confronts the same question. In an attempt to give life to their film, directors of drama often mimic documentary; they make actors mumble to simulate the incoherence of real speech, the camera shakes and wobbles, the picture slips in and out of focus, the editing is raw. These are all devices which conspire to give the impression that events have occurred spontaneously and a film crew has been lucky enough to be there to film them.

But pretty soon these efforts to create a heightened sense of realism decline into mannered stylistic tricks. Directors are forced to find another way to suggest the appearance of reality, and they have to confront the immutable truth that reality will always mock the way that fiction seeks to tidy up chaos and provide a passage through the fog. Perhaps the shout of the Archway critic of film-making wasn't far off the mark. Real life will always rebuke its fictional counterfeit.

Guys and Dolls

The Guardian *asked me to write about* Guys and Dolls *on the occasion of the first West End production of the show after my own at the National Theatre in 1982 and its revival in 1996.*

———•—

Theatre directors are given to talking about the 'relevance' of a play, generally to offer superfluous justification for doing a popular classic that gives actors good roles, is a joy to perform and sells tickets. Some shows defy 'relevance' and, regardless of their insights, exist solely to give pleasure: Shakespeare's comedies, Mozart's *Marriage of Figaro*, Wilde's *The Importance of Being Earnest*—works that combine wit, joy and generosity of heart in an irresistible and wholly accessible fashion.

Guys and Dolls can be added to this list. It's one of a clutch of musicals that for twenty-odd years—from 1940 to 1966, from *Oklahoma!* to *Cabaret*—sat in perfect equilibrium with the appetite of the audience, the talent of the performers and the taste of the time. It was a form of theatre that, uniquely, could be said to have crossed class barriers.

Impossible to patronise, these shows are supreme examples of dramatic art and address the emotional experience of an audience directly and without inhibition. In this they're peculiarly American—devoid of irony and cynicism and full of wilful optimism. But the best of these shows, the wittiest, the most joyous and the most devoid of mawkishness, is *Guys and Dolls*, which is, as a friend unhelpfully told me when I was about to direct it, 'so good not even a director could mess it up'.

My own attempt to mess it up started in the middle of 1981 when I agreed to join the National Theatre as an Associate Director. Faced, as is any director of the National Theatre, with feeding the yawning maws of the Olivier theatre, Peter Hall plaintively asked me if I could think of doing a 'major popular classic'. Years later I asked Nick Hytner the same thing in very much the same tone. 'Yes,' he said, 'I'd like to direct *Wind in the Willows*.'

Not much of a struggle there, but when I told Peter Hall that I'd like to do *Guys and Dolls* he was rather more cautious in his response. I was the latest in a long line of claimants who had wanted to direct it at the National. Olivier himself, encouraged by his literary adviser, Kenneth Tynan (who described it as the 'second-best American play', the best being *Death of a Salesman*), had planned to direct the show and play Nathan Detroit at the Old Vic in 1970. He had cast it and dance rehearsals had begun when his coronary thrombosis nipped the production in the bud.

Peter Hall's caution was prescient. His decision to stage an American musical brought forth a clamour of criticism: the National Theatre was dropping its standards; it was going commercial; the piece wasn't good enough to earn its place in the NT's repertoire; it would be treated patronisingly, like opera singers making excursions into popular culture; or the actors, singers, dancers and musicians simply wouldn't be good enough. In deciding to do it, Peter Hall was taking a risk that Sky Masterson would have approved of and I was the guy who had bet him I could make the Jack of Spades jump out of the pack and squirt cider in his ear.

Like most Broadway musicals the genealogy of *Guys and Dolls* is chequered with miscarriages, divorces and forced marriages. Two producers, Ernest Martin and Cy Feuer (who for a while ran the music department at Paramount Pictures) began with the smart idea of making a musical from *The Idyll of Miss Sarah Brown*, a short story by Damon Runyon, whom I'd encountered at the age of twelve when I asked my father why he referred to his overcoat—a loudish, belted, tweed coat with bulky, padded shoulders—as Big Nig. 'Read *More Than Some-what* and you'll find out.'

Guys and Dolls is without the savage undertow of most of Runyon's stories in *More Than Somewhat*—it's a 'Fairy Tale of New York', more Runyonesque than Runyonese—but the tone of its world is still recognisable as his creation. He wrote in the historical present tense, which, while much imitated, has never been used better, of people he hung around with. He idolised prize-fighters, regarded racketeers as his friends and loved money ('it's ninety-nine per cent of everything') though he had difficulty holding on to it. He wrote about characters ('to hell with plots') who were ruthless, vicious, psychotic, foul-mouthed and invariably criminal, and he purged them of their malign qualities with the grace and wit of his literary style.

The two producers mentioned their Runyon idea to Frank Loesser, whose Broadway success *Where's Charley?* they had overseen, and commissioned an adaptation from a screenwriter called Jo Swerling. His abortive script was abandoned when Frank Loesser appeared with four completed but uncommissioned songs. A radio sketch-writer called Abe Burrows was then approached to write the book and the hugely successful playwright George Kaufman to direct the show. By the time they had started work Loesser had completed the entire score.

Considering that *Guys and Dolls*, like the best book musicals, is essentially a play with music where the songs are a logical extension of the dramatic situation, it's a glorious irony that almost all of them were written before the dialogue. It merely serves to highlight Loesser's genius as a dramatic lyricist. The one song added during the out-of-town tryout was a song that Loesser used to perform as cabaret at parties, a strip-club pastiche: 'Take Back Your Mink'.

When Abe Burrows started to write the book he was briefed by Kaufman. 'Make it funny,' he said. 'But not too funny,' added Loesser. Abe Burrows made it funny, but if I were looking for the catalytic talent that made *Guys and Dolls* so successful, I would lay six to five on 'The Great Collaborator', George Kaufman, for supplying narrative rigour. 'Musicals are not written, they're fixed' runs the adage, and Kaufman fixed it to perfection. He felt so strongly that *Guys and Dolls* was a play interrupted by music that he looked on most of the songs as 'lobby' numbers—every time a song started he sprinted to the lobby for a cigarette. Abe Burrows once overheard him, mid-sprint, mutter: 'Good God, do we have to do every number this son-of-a-bitch ever wrote?'

Loesser had been born in New York, the son of a piano teacher. His older brother was a successful concert pianist and musicologist, but Loesser turned his back on classical music and taught himself the harmonica and the piano. He sold newspaper advertising, served writs, drew caricatures, wrote journalism, played piano in nightclubs and, after a failed Broadway show, went to Hollywood, where he wrote lyrics for songs for over sixty films before being lured back to Broadway.

Frank Loesser was like a Runyon character: he was boastful—when he told composer Jule Styne that he'd have to look for a new lyricist he said, 'You've been spoiled, there's no one like me'; he was sometimes violent—he once flattened a soprano for failing to hit a top note, then remorsefully compensated her with a diamond bracelet; he was often misanthropic, and he was frequently sentimental. 'I'm in the romance business. Which song made you cry?' he would say.

All musicals are love stories. *Guys and Dolls* has two of them, one romantic, one comic, but it's the comic one—between Nathan Detroit and Miss Adelaide— that's the better written. And it's hard to find any example in the canon of Broadway musicals of writing that describes character, advances plot, makes you laugh and touches your heart more than 'Adelaide's Lament'. This is how she mourns the loss of her fiancé of fourteen years:

> So much virus inside
> That her microscope slide
> Looks like a day at the zoo!
> Just from wanting her memories in writing
> And a story her folks can be told
> A person can develop a cold.

Loesser's own favourite song in the show was 'My Time of Day'. It was autobiographical: he got up very early—around four-thirty—had a Martini and a cigarette to get himself going, wrote from five to eight and then went back to sleep. The best time for him was the 'dark-time... When the street belongs to the cop/And the janitor with the mop/And the grocery clerks are all gone/When the smell of the rain-washed pavement/Comes up clean and fresh and cold/And the street lamp fills the gutter with gold...'

It was his second wife, Jo Sullivan (the first was known as the 'evil of two Loessers'), who told me of her husband's love of the dawn, and it was Jo—who starred in his last show, *Most Happy Fella*—who, as his executor, granted us the rights to stage the show and permission to make some minor script changes and re-orchestrate the score for a band of fifteen. I started working on *Guys and Dolls* at the National Theatre in the autumn of 1981 and, off and on, with gaps of many years, the production ran for the next seventeen years. Most of the best times I've ever had in a theatre have been watching it and working on it.

A critic described my production as a 'love letter to Broadway'. If he was right, it was both a celebration and a wake of a world that I never knew. Someone who did know it, and worked there during the late fifties, was our choreographer, David Toguri. He died a week before the show closed in 1998 after a long illness. Every step, every gesture, every action in the show was in some way illuminated by his spirit and by his personality: he brought joy to everything he did.

People say to me, perhaps ingratiatingly, that it's too soon to put on another production of *Guys and Dolls*. I don't understand this: there should *always* be a production of *Guys and Dolls* in London—indeed, I'm astonished that no party has touted the need for an Act of Parliament to guarantee it. If I have any churlish feelings at all about a new production, it's a sense of envy: it doesn't seem fair for them to be paid to have so much fun. As Bob Hoskins said on more than one occasion when we were rehearsing: 'This beats working.'

The Pajama Game

I wrote this for the programme when I directed the show for the Chichester Festival Theatre in 2013. It subsequently moved to the West End in 2014.

The Pajama Game was the first musical I heard—I say 'heard' because until now I've never seen it, or at least only in the rather unsatisfactory 1957 film which starred Doris Day. It was one of the first albums ('long playing'—i.e. 33rpm) that my sister owned and, like it or not, I was obliged at the age of twelve to listen to the British cast of the West End production until I knew the score backwards. I've been haunted by it ever since. I had never seen a musical in a theatre. I had never seen a play in a theatre. So, for a while, until she bought *My Fair Lady* and *West Side Story* and I bought Bill Haley, Tennessee Ernie Ford, Buddy Holly and Tommy Steele, the vinyl version of *The Pajama Game* was the centre of my musical and theatrical universe.

The pedigree of *The Pajama Game* was impeccable—its collaborators were all, or became so, the aristocracy of Broadway: George Abbott, Richard Adler, Jerome Robbins, Hal Prince and Bob Fosse. The dialogue and construction—the 'book'—were in the hands of George Abbott, who was writer or director and sometimes producer of a host of hits including *Pal Joey, On the Town, Where's Charley?, Call Me Madam, Damn Yankees* and *A Funny Thing Happened on the Way to the Forum*. Abbott directed *The Pajama Game* as well as writing the book. A tall—6'6"—authoritative, even imperious, figure, supremely well organised, brisk and unsentimental, he was known universally as 'Mr Abbott'. While he was opening two shows on Broadway—Leonard Bernstein's *Wonderful Town* and

198

Rodgers and Hammerstein's *Me and Juliet*—he was drawn to a subject that seemed to his friends about as promising as plague or paedophilia: a union dispute in a pajama factory in the Midwest.

Abbott based his script on a novel called *7½ Cents* by Richard Bissell, who had worked as a manager in the family's pajama factory in Dubuque, Ohio. The story followed the progress of an ambitious young man from Chicago called Sid Sorokin. Here's how Bissell describes the shop floor of the factory:

> It is mighty cheerful in a garment plant going wide open. The lights are bright and the sewing machines are working out themes by Stravinsky; it's warm and lively; the blonde tabletops gleam; the needles are punching their way to glory 4,500 stitches a minute. Telephones are ringing, the elevator gate is banging, voices are raised and the whole room is filled with women, all shapes and sizes, fat, thin, possible, impossible, goofy, semi-goofy, happy, sad, bouncing brunette, silver threads among the gold, slap-happy bobby-sock kids, old grousers with eight kids, and then the queens, always about two or three queens on each floor.

And here's how he describes Sid—unhappy in his new job—when he comes to the town in which the novel is set:

> When I woke up in the morning, even before I had my eyes open, I knew I wasn't in Chicago any more. No, not in Chicago, or South Chicago either, or in Gary or Hammond. These small towns smell different entirely… Life, as the man says, is funny. One day you are in Gary High School practising clarinet cadenzas for the orchestra and trying to get a date for the dance with Marie Kowalski of the beautiful dark eyes, and the next thing you know you're standing over in a foreign state looking at a window at some crummy old pump factory.

Bissell's writing is acerbic, dry and droll. The thriller writer, Elmore Leonard, cited him as an influence on his writing: 'He wasn't trying to be funny. That was the main point. I thought that's the way to do it.' This is a the sort of thing that he meant:

> 'Well, Myrna's baby died!' screams one, feeding elastic into the automatic short-length cutter.
>
> 'Pre-matoor, wasn't it?' screams the other.
>
> 'No, I didn't hear that.'
>
> 'I heard it was pre-matoor.'
>
> 'It was only five months.'

'Yeah, I heard it was pre-matoor.'

'No, five months.'

If Bissell was the inspiration of *The Pajama Game*, its godfather was unquestionably Frank Loesser, the composer and lyricist of *Guys and Dolls* and *How to Succeed in Business Without Really Trying*. Loesser worked in the Brill Building, the New York song factory at 1650 Broadway, where scores of songwriters, music publishers and song pluggers had their offices. Loesser was arrogant, and sometimes cruel, but he was also generous and took an interest in young composers. In 1950 he brought together two young songwriters who were also working in the Brill Building—Richard Adler and Jerry Ross—and became their publisher and mentor.

Adler and Ross were an improbable combination—Adler was the son of a concert pianist and a debutante from Alabama; Ross was the son of Russian immigrants and former child star of the Yiddish theatre. Encouraged by Frank Loesser, Adler and Ross started to write for the theatre. Their first effort was an unsuccessful revue but with their second collaboration, *The Pajama Game*, they hit gold. Their next show, *Damn Yankees*, opened the following year and had a similar success but soon after—at the age of twenty-nine—Jerry Ross died of a lung disease.

Until now I was unaware that Loesser, probably at the behest of his friend, George Abbot, had written two of the best songs in *The Pajama Game*—'There Once Was a Man' and 'A New Town is a Blue Town'—without receiving a credit. I'd like to think it was Loesser who was responsible for suggesting that the choreographer should be a young dancer called Bob Fosse, if only because Fosse later returned the favour by saying: '*Guys and Dolls* is the greatest American musical of all time.' True, of course.

It was actually George Abbott who was Fosse's champion. With the confidence of a man who had nothing to worry about his reputation, he consistently championed newcomers. When he was working on *Me and Juliet* with actress Joan McCracken, she asked him to consider Fosse as choreographer of *The Pajama Game*. She told Abbott that he was very young, very ambitious, and very talented—oh, and she was married to him. Fosse was then twenty-five, on his second marriage, a dancer who had tried to match the early Fred Astaire by working in cabaret as a double act with his first wife, and had then gone to Hollywood to become a director. Instead he had become a frustrated contract player for MGM and had been cast in a small part in the film of *Kiss Me, Kate*. The choreographer was Hermes Pan—Astaire's choreographer—who was persuaded by Fosse to let him do his own choreography for a number that he performed in the film with Carol Haney—later cast as Gladys in *The Pajama Game*.

Abbott was impressed by Fosse and his work and was ready to give him the job, but one of his fledgling producers—a young ex-stage manager called Hal Prince—needed convincing: 'How do we know he can do a Broadway show?' he asked, 'He's never done one.' It was agreed that, as a back-up, Abbott would ask Jerome Robbins to stand by in case things went wrong with Fosse. Jerome Robbins, although only thirty-five, had choreographed at least four shows with Abbott and was the crowned King of Broadway Dance. At Fosse's expense, he extracted punitive conditions for being his understudy—a handsome royalty and a credit as co-director. 'What do I care about the credit,' said Abbott, 'People will know that I did it.'

Fosse's routine for 'Steam Heat'—Carol Haney's number—had all the hallmarks of what became his signature style: bowler hats, rolled shoulders, turned in knees and sharply sexy gestures. Although what he did was borrowed from many sources—the cakewalk, burlesque, vaudeville, Jack Cole (the father of 'jazz dancing'), Hermes Pan and Fred Astaire—the way he put it all together was unmistakably his own. When the show was in previews Abbott wanted to cut 'Steam Heat' because he thought that it slowed down the narrative. If Jerome Robbins made a single contribution to the show it's that he persuaded Abbott to leave the number in.

The show opened on May 13th 1954 at the St James Theatre. It ran for three years and won countless awards. Apart from Carol Haney as Gladys, Janis Paige played Babe, John Raitt was Sid, Eddie Foy Jnr was Hines and Haney's understudy was a young actress called Shirley MacLaine.

In her memoir, *Sage-ing While Age-ing*, MacLaine tells this story:

> They gave me the understudy job, but I never had a rehearsal. I had thought Carol would go on with a broken neck. Then a few nights later, Carol sprained her ankle… When I arrived at the St James, across the stage door stood Jerry Robbins, Bob Fosse, Hal Prince, etc. 'Haney is out,' they said. 'You're on.' I couldn't believe what I was hearing. 'I'm on? Without a rehearsal?'

> There I was, waiting in the wings, when the announcer said Carol Haney would be out and I would replace her. There were boos from the orchestra to the second balcony… I did drop the hat in 'Steam Heat'. I lost it in mid-air, and said, 'Oh shit,' right out loud. The first few rows gasped and crossed their legs, but I got through the rest of it without falling into the pit. When the show was over, I took my bows with the other two 'Steam Heat' dancers. The audience stood up. Buzz Miller and Peter Gennaro peeled off and left me in the centre of the stage to bask in the audience's appreciation.

MacLaine rang her brother, Warren Beatty, and told him to get some people over because she was on. That's how the movie producer, Hal B. Wallis, came to be in the audience that night. He signed her on the spot to Paramount Pictures for a five-year contract.

Shirley MacLaine didn't, sadly, appear in the lacklustre film of the show that was made three years later. Doris Day, who was then top of the charts with Sammy Fain's *Secret Love*, was cast as Babe.

In the mid-fifties the songs you'd hear in the theatre were the ones you'd hear sung in the street or on the radio. Rosemary Clooney's version of 'Hey There' was at number one in the US charts for several weeks, while Archie Bleyer's cover of 'Hernando's Hideaway' was at number two, and Patti Page's 'Steam Heat' at number nine. With the arrival of rock 'n' roll that easy transfer from musicals to the hit parade started to dissolve and so did the book musical: the new music couldn't carry narrative and character. What's more, the implacable optimism which underwrote the Broadway musical for three or four decades withered in the face of the growing awareness that the US was engaged in a major war in a faraway country in Asia which was causing an increasing number of American soldiers to be sent home in coffins.

The Pajama Game opened in London at the Coliseum on October 13th 1955 and ran for a year and a half. Unlike many of the Broadway transfers of the period it didn't import American stars. Joy Nichols and Edmund Hockridge, Australian and Canadian respectively, led a company that also starred the comedian Max Wall as Hines and a young dancer called Elizabeth Seal as Gladys. It did the trick for her too: she became famous overnight.

Music

Simon Callow used to be the monthly columnist of Gramophone, *and when he retired he bequeathed his column to me—via James Inverne, the editor. For a year I wrote about a subject in which I was manifestly less than expert.*

My first sexual feelings occurred at much the same time as my musical ones. The sense that parts of my body—well, a part—was able to give me pleasure coincided, though not literally, with my discovery that music could arouse my senses in ways that I couldn't name and didn't understand.

I was eleven, at a small prep school in Hampshire for the sons of naval officers, and I stood in a line of small boys for nightly prayers as the sun set and apricot light spread over the memorial panels on one side of the large Victorian hall. A prayer with a melancholy sense of foreboding—'Lighten our darkness, we beseech thee O Lord, and by thy great mercy defend us from all perils and dangers of this night…'—was followed by an equally contrite hymn:

Dear Lord and father of mankind
Forgive our foolish ways
Reclothe us in our rightful mind,
In purer lives Thy service find,
In deeper reverence, praise.

Perhaps the words touched me—'Reclothe us in our rightful mind' is quite lovely—but I think at that age I was as immune to poetry as to spinach. It was the music which awoke unfamiliar feelings and moved me to tears, which slipped down my cheeks like drops of olive oil. I smeared them away with the heel of my hand for fear of being dubbed a sissy. What was it in the hymn? Was it the cadences? The chords? The intervals? My loneliness?

My father had a small record collection which included a few LPs: *Noël Coward at Las Vegas*, *An Evening Wasted with Tom Lehrer*, *Ella Fitzgerald Sings Cole Porter*, *Blue Rose* (a Rosemary Clooney album), *Little Lemmy and Big Joe's Kwela Band* (acquired when his ship docked in Capetown) and several 78s of Spike Jones and His City Slickers as well as Offenbach's *Barcarolle*. The collection remained inchoate and random until he conceived a lust for Maria Callas—he called her 'the tigress'—who guided his record collection. Donizetti, Bellini and Rossini were joined by Verdi and Puccini, and then, having acquired a taste for the form, by Mozart's operas. I was not with him when he died, but saw his body a few hours later; *Così fan tutte* was still playing on a loop on his CD player.

At my prep school, music was as unacknowledged as masturbation—tolerated but not encouraged. An emancipated student teacher sat us down one day in front of an unused record player the size and shape of a cocktail bar and played part of Vaughan Williams, *Sinfonia Antarctica*. My grandfather had been on Scott's first Antarctic expedition so I was touched by a vicarious vision of the landscape as much as by the luminously painterly soundscape. The Vaughan Williams was followed, in the interests of diversity, with a record of Ted Heath's Band, the best British big band of the day. The teacher drew our attention to a drum solo which, as I was to learn later, followed the pattern of almost all drum solos: long, repetitive and ostentatious. But I was entranced and can remember the name of the drummer, Ronnie Verrell, to this day.

My awakened musical passion slumbered for a year or two until I was sent to Sherborne School in Dorset and joined the school choir as a treble. The school had the happy policy of leasing out its choir to combine with a local choral society and the church choir to perform a great choral work once a year in Sherborne Abbey—a glorious and grand sandstone church with the finest (and earliest) fan vaulting in England.

For two years I sang, twice every Sunday, a diet of hymns, psalms and liturgy. Once a year we joined forces with the town choir and sang a choral work with the Bournemouth Symphony Orchestra. So it was that I sang the Verdi *Requiem* conducted by Charles Groves, and was enraptured by being a molecule in a musical universe, awed and overwhelmed by Verdi's dark sounds, his tenderness and his bewitching rhythms. I was shaken by the *Dies Irae*, uplifted by the *Sanctus*, transformed by the *Agnus Dei*. It was an epiphany: a vision of God in man.

By the time it came to Haydn's *Creation* my voice had broken and so had my allegiance to sacred music, or indeed any music that wasn't in 4/4 time and sung by Elvis Presley.

————•————

I was introduced to Elvis's music by my best friend, whose father was based with the RAF near Frankfurt. He had access to the PX, a sort of shop (similar to the NAAFI) which operated on US military bases. In those days records—this was the day of the seven-inch, 45rpm single—would be released in the US a tantalising time ahead of the UK, but, via his father, my friend was able to get the latest US releases often months ahead of his schoolfriends, thus guaranteeing himself a magus-like status.

It's hard today, when popular music dribbles indiscriminately from mobile phones, to picture a time when public spaces were free of music, portable radios barely existed and Keith Fordyce's once-weekly programme *Rockin' to Dreamland* on Wednesday night and Alan Freed's Saturday show—both on Radio Luxembourg—were the latest authority on US and UK hits. We listened under the bedclothes through headphones to a faltering signal on a crystal set, the aerial attached to the iron bedframe.

We were hungry for intelligence from another planet. We would sit beside the Dansette record player with the earnest concentration of astrophysicists listening for signals from outer space, and the messages came through: 'Heartbreak Hotel', 'Don't Be Cruel', 'Hound Dog', 'One Night', 'Hard-Headed Woman'. And so on until the apostasy: 'It's Now or Never'. Elvis betrayed us by recording a nineteenth-century Neapolitan folk song ('O Sole Mio'), and worse was to follow. He released 'Are You Lonesome Tonight?', an irredeemably mawkish twenties ballad with a spoken verse which began 'All the world's a stage and everybody plays a part...' I felt vindicated when, years later in his self-mocking, drug-sodden, Las Vegas days, instead of singing 'Do you gaze at your doorstep and picture me there', Elvis sang 'Do you gaze at your bald head and wish you had hair?'

Elvis's betrayal scattered my loyalties into a prodigality of attachments: blues, folk, music, rhythm and blues, gospel and rock 'n' roll: Little Richard, Fats Domino, Ray Charles, the Platters, B.B. King, Sam Cooke. Little Richard said of Presley, 'He opened the door for black music.' He certainly did for me.

A year or two later, by the time the Rolling Stones came along, I had lost my heart to jazz, and with the arch snobbery of a middle-class student of English Literature I patronised the Rolling Stones for being white art students copying the music of their black betters. I joined the Cambridge Jazz Club and developed a friendship with a girl who worked in Miller's record shop, who occasionally slipped me Blue Note recordings and one day advised me actually to *buy* a record. 'You won't be disappointed,' she said. I wasn't: it was Miles Davis's *Kind of Blue*. I can still remember sitting breathlessly by the same

Dansette to the first wispy, haunting notes of Bill Evans's piano, Paul Chambers' searching bass, the repeated chords—*dee* dah *dee* dah—of Coltrane's sharp tenor and Cannonball Adderley's spicy alto and then the transcendent solo call of Miles's trumpet, weightless like great dancing.

I left Cambridge with a poor degree, having spent most of my three years acting, listening to jazz, and smoking dope. If I had learnt anything, it was to acknowledge my ignorance with something like shame. I started to read voraciously, not just the fiction and poetry that I had neglected during my degree course, but history and politics. And I started to listen to classical music, partly because I was weary of the ubiquity of blues in jazz, partly because of curiosity about what other people listened to, and partly because I had become impatient with pop music. I once met George Martin and asked him if he was doing any more pop records. He looked at me long-sufferingly. 'Pop,' he said, 'is for the very young.'

I started my musical self-education by working chronologically from Bach. Listening to the counterpoint and syncopation of jazz pianists had prepared me for Bach's keyboard music, and when I heard Casals' recording of the Cello Suites I knew I was home. They swing; it's music for dancing. I concentrated on one composer at a time. I've just emerged from a protracted Shostakovich session and today it's Messiaen. At this time of year the birds are playing his music all day long.

————•—————

Silence is music's twin: music occupies silence as sculpture does space. Silence is as elemental to music as pitch, tone and rhythm. A breath, a bar rest, a small gap between walls of music, can articulate moments of anxiety or expectation, provoke you, move you to joy, to sadness or to fear. The 'expectant waiting' of Quaker worship is intended to invoke self-examination; a recent study at Stanford University demonstrated that musical pauses within a piece of music cause a flurry of brain activity.

The first time I became aware of silence as a musical element was listening to the 5th Symphony of Sibelius. The second movement doesn't so much end as dissolve into silence, in preparation for the majestic final movement where the 'swan theme' of the first movement returns—first on the horns, then woodwinds, then in the tolling chords led by the trumpets which ascend to its apotheosis: six massive chords ruptured by silence, more shocking and surprising than the sounds that surround them. There's a monumental sense of awe, like staring down a vertical cliff face at the sea below.

Those massive, clamorous, tectonic silences remind me of the rows between my father and grandfather when I was a child. My grandfather cast a sepulchral silence over meals, punctuated by violent invective. The silences that followed these outbursts were epic, giant, immense, terrible, and terrifying. Only the scraping of the cutlery on the plates distracted from the dense absence of words and broke the thickness of the space between them. It was the rows that first alerted me to the possibilities of drama which, at least since Chekhov, tends to be about the spaces between the lines.

Debussy's famous dictum that 'music is the silence between the notes' is often taken to be saying the same thing, that music is surrounded by silence before, in the middle and after the note. He could, however, be saying something rather different: that music only exists when it is played and heard by an audience. Notes on a page are as two-dimensional as a sketch for a sculpture; only by being brought to life in three dimensions—in space and out of silence—do they become music. The rest is silence.

Everyone will have their own examples of musical silences. Here are some of my favourites: the unannounced and terrifying pause in *The Rite of Spring* at the end of *L'Adoration de la terre*; the moment in Mozart's *Fantasia in C Minor* when, after a few spare chords, the music is suspended in silence before crashing into the allegro movement with cascades of bass notes; the little caves of silence at the beginning of the second movement of Beethoven's *Piano Sonata No. 4* before the slow revelation of the melody; the almost unbearably moving pause at the end of *Le nozze di Figaro* when the Count asks forgiveness of the Countess and for a breathtaking moment she hesitates before responding.

Can silence be music in itself? John Cage's notorious *4'33"* rests entirely on the presumption that the audience is aware that noise is ever present in their lives, indeed, in the presence of their heartbeat. The piece starts when the piano lid is opened by the pianist, lasts for 4'33" (a period determined by consulting the *I Ching*) and ends with the closing of the piano lid. Cage believed that there was no such thing as silence—it was called 'silence' only because it didn't form part of a musical composition. He even examined silence by going into a room at Harvard University, where no external noise was audible even to the most sophisticated noise-detection devices. Cage, however, could hear two distinct noises at different frequencies: the first, at a very high frequency, was his nervous system, the second, at a low frequency, was the circulation of his blood.

The spaces between movements of a symphony or concerto or sonata are the most precious silences in the performance of music, and are the most ignored or abused. You are at a concert: a movement ends, the preceding music hangs in your head, you focus your mind and your ears on connecting with the music to come, then you are jolted from your concentration by the bitter, oaky, scraping noise of coughing and throat-clearing. I recently watched Simon Rattle with the Berlin Philharmonic in a Prom on TV at which Karita Mattila sang Strauss's *Four Last Songs*. The Albert Hall was occupied by several thousand people who were all familiar with the work. Or they could count to four and work out that there were to be three breaks between four songs. They could even console themselves with the promise that within twenty minutes their oh-so-necessary coughs could be combined with applause. But no, they hacked away between songs as if they had been paid to clear their nasal passages in public.

What stupidity, spite, what selfishness, what urge apart from an incurable tubercular condition obliged them to violate the silence at the end of each song? Why couldn't they participate in the event by restraining themselves, by honouring the silences that were as much part of the music as the notes? 'Coughing in the theatre is an act of violence,' said Harold Pinter. I'm beginning to agree with him.

———•———

There is no method that guarantees a good rehearsal. It's as hard to know why some highly articulate, learned and intelligent directors seem unable to animate a cast of actors, as it is to understand how the same orchestra can be inspired by some conductors, and seem commonplace in the hands of others.

I've recently had the opportunity of watching two conductors at work at first hand: Yannick Nézet-Séguin and Edward Gardner. They both conducted my production of *Carmen* at the Metropolitan Opera—Yannick at its premiere last December and Ed recently in a revival. It was the Met debut for both of these strikingly young (thirty-five) and strikingly good conductors, who were also strikingly good collaborators. Of course the music reigned supreme, but we sat side by side in the rehearsal room and shared views on performance, tempi, staging and motivation without demarcation. This artistic parity isn't inevitable in opera, where it's possible for the conductor (the 'maestro' as he—and it usually is a he—is unironically addressed) to imprison the entire rehearsal process.

Then it changed. The orchestra arrived, the conductor stepped onto the podium and, while it wasn't the end of the partnership, it was an end to discussion. I'm fascinated by the first encounter of an orchestra and conductor. There's rarely a word from the conductor—no 'I see this piece as X or Y or Z'—merely a greeting, a slightly nervous smile (not always reciprocated), the necessary instruction about where to start from in the score, a downbeat and then they're off. In this case they weren't on autopilot, though they'd played *Carmen* hundreds of times. They were playing expressively, they were following the conductor; they trusted him.

The means by which conductors achieve this is somewhere between thought transference and osmosis. Both were clear and vigorous with their batons. Ed occasionally made a gesture to one section like sprinkling salt into soup; Yannick sometimes turned his hand as if opening a door with a long doorknob. There were no theatrical gestures, no self-regard, no narcissism. They endorsed the musicians' skill, showed pleasure in their playing—glee from Yannick, joy from Ed—and, without verbal instruction or comment, within minutes of encountering the orchestra they had not only communicated their intentions but more importantly the orchestra had discerned that they *had* intentions and that they had the knowledge and technical capacity in their hands, eyes and body to communicate that knowledge. Conductors don't control an orchestra; they create the conditions in which it can function, in which the whole can become greater than the sum of the parts.

Shortly before the first dress rehearsal of *Carmen* a member of the (excellent) Met chorus said to me: 'We've enjoyed working with you.' I simpered gratefully. 'We give directors about two minutes to see if they know what they're doing.' Two minutes? I think orchestras give conductors about two measures.

———

I read this in an article about contemporary art recently: 'Putting on new plays feels about as astute as using a horse and cart for haulage, or having an operation without an anaesthetic.' It's a version of the modernist credo that has been proclaimed for most of the last century. Outdated art forms! Outdated buildings! Outdated humans! The perfectibility of man! The war to end wars! The final solution! The end of history! Over the age of isms—absolutism, fascism, socialism—modernism has spread over all the arts like a triumphal arch.

Modernism was (and is) an attempt to reflect and confront an increasingly confused and confusing world. Each age imagines that its revolutionary ways of seeing will endure perpetually. When Brunelleschi and Masaccio invented perspective in the early-fifteenth century they were as certain that an artistic limit had been reached as the passengers on the first railway trains were that their bodies would disintegrate if they went any faster than thirty miles an hour, or as Modernists were (are) that all 'old' art would become redundant.

How can a work of art become 'redundant' or 'wrong'? How can the representation of the human figure become 'irrelevant'? How can portraying the lives of human beings be seen as 'outdated humanism'? By that measure theatre will always seem outdated because it can never dissolve its reliance on the scale of the human figure, the sound of the human voice, and the disposition of mankind to tell each other stories. However hard you try to reinvent theatre that premise remains inextinguishable.

There's no such line in the sand in music. Tonality isn't an indispensable hierarchy of musical organisation; atonality flourishes; dissonance has been emancipated; the minimalism of Reich, Glass and Adams has become a common musical idiom, particularly in film scores. Stockhausen has been claimed as an influence by Frank Zappa, Pink Floyd and The Beatles. And yet 'modern music' still provokes extraordinary bitterness, demonstrations, protests at the Proms, as if some offence to the natural order was being committed, like laying waste to woodland or polluting a river.

Perhaps, like the hedonism of the free East Europe after the velvet revolutions, it's a delayed revenge for the absolutism of the past, which was a battle bitterly fought for many years, partly under the fierce evangelical leadership of Pierre Boulez. 'Praise be to amnesia,' he said when he set himself up against all traditional music in a manner worthy of Trotsky. 'Any musician who has not experienced—I do not say understood, but truly experienced—the necessity of dodecaphonic music is USELESS. For his whole work is irrelevant to the needs of his epoch.' He progressed beyond twelve-tone technique into what he described as 'total serialisation', his best known work being called, without irony, *The Hammer Without a Master*.

I have to admit that I find Boulez' music impenetrable. I can't understand twelve-tone music any more than I can understand the 'beautiful equations' which mathematicians speak of. Some 'beautiful' mathematical formulae provide a sort of gold standard for mathematical beauty which, if not immediately apparent to a student, demonstrate that the student will never become a proper mathematician. By that criterion I can never be a fit listener for some music; I can't get my ears—or my brain—round it. To me, marinated in conventional harmonies, it's an abstract conceit, I can't hear it as music. It's like the notion that you can make abstract theatre: an actor can't become abstract, he'll always be irreducibly himself.

I can't help wondering if, just as the art of theatre can't defy its law of gravity (that a human being is at the centre of the activity), so the human brain is inevitably programmed to hear things in a particular relationship to each other. But perhaps that merely reveals my innate conservatism. I think that any work of art should introduce something to the world that didn't exist before, but originality doesn't rely on rejecting the past in order to confront the present. To believe otherwise is, like creationist theology, to defy the obvious: that all art is in evolution not revolution.

The important thing is that music should be listened to with ears that are innocent of judgement or of the urge to categorise, which is partly an academic desire to pin down the wings of the butterfly and is partly a marketing expedient. Weaving through the aisles in record shops past subcategory after subcategory I have to resist the desire to cry out: IT DOESN'T MATTER WHAT YOU CALL IT! IS IT ANY GOOD? The essence of theatre, as Peter Brook described it, is this: 'A man walks across this empty space whilst someone else is watching him, and this is all that is needed for an act of theatre to be engaged.' The essence of music is noise, to which a musician brings order, but, try as I might (and I do), I still can't understand twelve-tone music.

210

Opera

I directed my first opera, La Traviata, at Covent Garden in 1994. The Financial Times asked me to write about the experience. The production, to my surprise and sometimes unease, is still in the repertoire twenty years later.

My late and much lamented near-namesake, Ronald Eyre, used to say that directing opera was like inflating a plastic elephant. A few weeks ago—before I started to direct my first opera—I thought I knew what he meant, and I thought I agreed with him.

I once did a show with Ken Campbell which did indeed require the inflation of a plastic elephant; it was tossed out into the auditorium at the end of the show, and bounced about by the audience above their heads. This compulsory audience participation did much to persuade those who doubted that they had had a good evening that at least they had done something. It was a brief gesture, which required a disproportionate amount of effort on the part of the elephant's minder, Mavis, to produce the desired effect. She started mid-morning repairing the small tears that had emerged on the skin from the previous night's exertions, and after a day with a bicycle repair outfit, she plugged the beast into a small air-compressor and waited patiently for the plastic pachyderm to achieve its majestic, fully inflated, form, only to see it deflate, devoid of dignity, in front of her eyes during its nightly appearance—a process, at least for Ron, remarkably similar to directing an opera.

I've always had powerful prejudices against opera, and although I used to enjoy listening to opera recordings and could recognise the obvious beauty of much of the operatic canon, I must confess, with some shame, that for many years I had an indifference to it bordering on distaste. Stuck for a conversational diversion, I once asked Princess Margaret—a noted (or notorious) balletomane—if she liked opera: 'Can't stand it. A lot of frightfully boring people standing still and yelling.' Blunt perhaps, but not a universe away from my own feelings at the time, or even from Rossini's opinion of the new breed of tenors that emerged in the 1830s, who flaunted their high notes like jewelled codpieces. When the tenor Enrico Tamberlik was astounding audiences with his famous high C-sharp he paid a call on Rossini. 'Have him come in,' said Rossini, 'but tell him to leave his C-sharp on the coat rack. He can pick it up on the way out.'

Being marinated in the art of theatre, and nourished by an aesthetic of 'truthfulness'—however relative, and however pretentious—I was unsympathetic until recently to a medium which transparently is not concerned with holding the mirror up to nature. Opera seemed to me to depend on the audience's acceptance of an elaborate conceit as remote to me as Freemasonry or the courtship rituals of Inuits are. The motor of 'music theatre' is music rather than theatre, and the making of music seemed to me to have little in common with the making of theatre.

Music doesn't have to have a point; that is its point. Music is. With good music, as Auden says, you have only to listen to it, and be grateful. Theatre, on the other hand, prospers, or labours, under the despotism of logic: it maintains a stubborn dependence on plot, which in many—or most—operas delights in its obscurity and revels in its resistance to common sense. And if its plots often appear absurd, its passions often seem either histrionic or bathetic.

I was uneasy about an entertainment which employed as many people as the population of a substantial village to achieve its effects, and could be as unwieldy as an aircraft carrier. I was uneasy too (and still remain so) about the cost, swollen not only by the numbers involved, but the need to submit to fees dictated by the international market, leading to seat prices that defy admission to anyone who isn't qualified to become a Lloyds 'name'. And to be honest, I have been put off opera much as people are put off hunting, not so much by the activity itself, as by the personality of some of its propagandists—the fans, the enthusiasts who criticise and catalogue every performance with the doggedly joyless pedantry of armchair cricketers poring over their Wisdens.

However, and not before time considering that I am ten days away from my first premiere, I've become a convert. It is still unlikely that you'll find me in future years in the Crush Bar extolling the virtues of Otto Schweppes' Leporello, castigating Helga Haagen Daas' Marschallin, and minutely examining the flaws in Guido Gamforalaf's *Ring*, but I have lost my heart to at least half a dozen works, not all of them by Mozart or Verdi.

I have come to accept that opera is a world like any other; like the theatre (which some people detest with a passion reserved by animal-rights activists for badger-baiters), opera has its own partiality, its own criteria, its own forms of truth and of excellence, no less exacting, and no less rare than in the theatre. I have recognised that I have earned Matisse's rebuke to the woman who complained that an arm in a painting of his was out of proportion to the body: 'It's not an arm, madam, it's a picture.' Opera is its own thing and it's as fruitless to blame it for not being like theatre as it is to blame theatre for not being film, or a melon for not being an orange.

My conversion has occurred through the sorcery of Sir Georg Solti, who, after a flirtation with me over *Falstaff* in Salzburg, lured me into directing *La Traviata* at Covent Garden: 'I have never conducted *Traviata*, you have never produced it: together we will make our first *Traviata*.' I have not regretted it, and I will never tire of watching him at work with the orchestra and singers—punching the air, moulding, sculpting, battering, caressing, on his toes in a half-crouch like a boxing trainer, singing and shouting like a muezzin. 'Play this forte,' he crows to the cellos. 'Break your wrists—and break my heart.' I enjoy as much our minutely detailed discussions about the meaning or value of a note, a word, a gesture; it's an obvious and extraordinary pleasure to work with a great conductor, but it's as rare and as important to work with a great collaborator.

'It's too early to jubilate about this enterprise,' Solti said to me the other day. But I can jubilate privately that my prejudices against opera have been cast off like a overcoat whose sleeves are too short, and my worst expectations have been defied: instead a soprano the size of a Wessex Saddleback I work with one who has a large and beautiful voice and a waist the size of a teapot, the tenor has a modest ego and a voice as unforced as a mountain stream, the chorus are cooperative and inventive, and rehearsals have been free of operatic (or theatrical) tantrums.

In one sense Ron was right: there is something of the elephant about opera—an awesomely large, sometimes cumbersome, and sometimes heart-stoppingly beautiful animal. But there's far too much poetry about it to be rendered in plastic, and directing it doesn't seem like pumping up an inflatable, however much huffing and puffing it involves. It's much more unpredictable than that: like getting an elephant to dance. On a tightrope. Oh yes, and sing too.

The Passion of the Christ

I had a fairly regular Guardian *column in the early 2000s. The following three pieces—all about bad art—were for this intermittent column. It's often said that it's easier to write scornful reviews than good ones. I don't know about that; I do know it's a lot more fun.*

'What was going on at the end?' said the Australian girl. 'It was Easter,' said her companion. 'Oh, yeah, see what you mean,' said the young Australian, not seeing, as we shuffled out of the cinema—the confused, the curious, the voyeuristic, the bored and even perhaps the faithful—at the end of *The Passion of the Christ* (note the meticulously messianic second 'the'). 'I couldn't follow the story,' continued the Australian girl. 'No, the book was better.' 'It was just one long crucifixion, wasn't it?' Yes, I thought, yes indeed.

The proposition of the film—directed by Mel Gibson—is remorselessly simple and relentlessly pursued: Christ died for our sins, by his wounds we are healed, see how great are his wounds, know how great are your sins. Christ is spat at, beaten with fists and sticks and chains, his head is pierced by a crown of thorns, his back scourged with lead-weighted flails, his hands and feet stabbed by nails, his body crushed by the weight of the cross then rent by the pain of cramp and asphyxia, after which he expires and his side is speared, while drops, gouts, even fountains of his blood are shed. I flinched occasionally, squirmed often as he soaked up his punishment, but remained wholly, bluntly unaffected. The story of the Son of God assuming human form in order to save the world lacked the one quality which could have made sense of it—humanity—and deprived the audience of the one element that might have justified this pageant of sado-masochism—empathy.

I know I'm supposed to believe that Christ died for our sake, was crucified under Pontius Pilate, suffered death, was buried, and on the third day rose again in accordance with the Scriptures, but does it all have to be so fatuously literal? Do I have to accept that when a giant stone rolls away on its own accord from the mouth of a sepulchre, a winding sheet is left behind like a clean white duvet, while the son of God, naked and unscarred, slips out of frame like David Ginola in an aftershave ad. And am I really expected to extract spiritual nourishment from seeing a young woman wipe Jesus's face as he staggers under the cross while her cloth becomes the Turin shroud? Or from watching Jesus restore a bloody ear in the garden of Gethsemane like a party conjuror pulling out a sixpence?

'We must love one another,' Jesus says at the Last Supper. Then we cut back to a huge nail being driven into his palm and another audience member defects. I stayed. I felt like Oscar Wilde when he was translating from the Bible (Greek not Aramaic) a few verses for his teacher about Judas selling Jesus for thirty pieces of silver. Teacher: 'That will do, Mr Wilde.' Wilde: 'Hushh… let us proceed and find out what happened to the unfortunate man.'

The unfortunate man turns heads with his holiness. 'Sanctus est,' says Pilate's wife. Why? Those without knowledge of the backstory—or what you might call the Christian myth—will be repeatedly baffled by this assertion for we learn nothing of Jesus's life prior to his arrest and crucifixion, save that he invented the dining table—possibly to replace those maddeningly low coffee tables so popular in Galilee. 'It'll never catch on,' says his mother in the film's only attempt at humour.

The Pharisees, of course, are preternaturally malignant or, as George Bush would say, bad guys, but no less bad than the Roman soldiers (itemised in the cast list as Scornful, Brutish and Whipping), who are fully professional sadists almost to a man. The good guys are there to illustrate that, if you believe in Christ, you are endowed with virtue and have joined the elect. Whether by accident or design, only Pontius Pilate is given the semblance of a living person and the casting of a good actor. He is allowed to display doubt, fear, guilt, weakness, cowardice and compassion—sometimes all at once. Jesus, however, as played by Jim Caviezel devoid of character or charisma, never deals with more than one emotion at a time. His soul is as inaccessible as the mind of God, and if the eyes are the window to the soul, it was surely a mistake to fit him out with rust-coloured contact lenses, which gave him the cast of a weary buzzard.

There were times during this film when I longed for the infantile verities of *The Greatest Story Ever Told*, which had John Wayne as the repentant centurion.

'Surely this man is the son of God,' he croaked with no less implausibility than Satan in Gibson's film—an epicene figure who pops up to ask Jesus if he really believes that one man can bear the full burden of sin—while the score pounds away in a risible pastiche of Verdi's *Requiem*, Barber's *Adagio for Strings* and the theme music for *Who Wants to Be a Millionaire?*

Much of the greatest Western painting and music of the last millennium is either inspired by the story of the Passion or is an act of worship in itself, offering hope, or consolation, or an exhortation to believe in a religion which embodies the remarkable injunction: love thy neighbour. Gibson's film, like the desolate kitsch icons of pure pain in Spanish country churches and Bavarian baroque chapels, is made for zealots by a zealot: it's propaganda.

I don't think there is much more cause for accusations of anti-Semitism against this film than against the New Testament, and it wasn't the depiction of the Jews that infuriated me, it was the depiction of the Christians. Are we really expected to be inspired by this reductive equation of suffering and redemption to forgive our enemies? Or are we being enlisted to punish those who fail to accept the truths of the Christian faith? And should we also forgive the centuries of Christian abuse of heretics, sceptics and unbelievers, the bullying and torture and mountainous piling-on of guilt, all done in the name of Jesus Christ?

The film is well staged, designed, photographed and edited, and it has been hugely commercially successful. It has revealed a niche audience rather bigger than that for most Hollywood films. For Gibson it has opened up the possibility of making other films for the same confederation of conservative religious extremists—Catholics, Protestants and even Jews. The efforts of Muslim filmmakers in the past—*Mohammad, Messenger of God* (Islam's answer to *Triumph of the Will*) and *Omar Mukhtar, Lion of the Desert*—seem positively benign in comparison.

The Passion of the Christ reflects an angry longing to return to a medieval world, uncomplicated by liberal ambiguity and scepticism. It's perfectly timed to coincide with the Manichean politics of the Bush administration. Like the Black Death, the plague of fundamentalism has remained dormant for centuries only to become virulent in the twenty-first century. Religion is being put back into religion. 'Zeal and sincerity can carry a new religion further than any other missionary except fire and sword,' said Mark Twain. The foul fumes of religious fervour are spreading sanctimoniousness and intolerance throughout the globe while those far-from-exclusively Christian virtues—love, mercy, pity, peace— are choked. There was a handwritten sign in the cinema: 'This film may not be suitable for those of a nervous disposition.' It should also have read: 'or for those repelled by the fraud of redemption through violence.'

The Da Vinci Code

Popular novels have taught me a lot. I'd know nothing of Moscow police procedure without *Gorky Park*; I'd be familiar with barely three, let alone fifty-five words, to describe snow without *Miss Smilla's Feeling for Snow*; and without *The Da Vinci Code* I'd be ignorant of the secret of the Mona Lisa's smile. These aren't insignificant additions to my knowledge of the world even if, like Donald Rumsfeld, I can only remember that these are things that I know that I know but can't quite recall. *The Da Vinci Code* has now reached the ultima thule of popularity—read on the Tube and the beach by those who don't read books, featured in broadsheet editorials, the object of a plagiarism suit and the subject, in this newspaper, of a piece castigating those who, like me, are snooty about its popularity. There's even a spin-off publishing industry—books describing the 'facts' behind the novel, exposing its 'hoax', expounding its 'truth'.

That the book is compulsively readable is indisputable but equally so is the fact that it is, from first sentence ('Renowned curator Jacques Saunière staggered through the vaulted archway of the Museum's Grand Gallery') to last ('For a moment, he thought he heard a woman's voice... the wisdom of the ages... whispering up from the chasms of the earth'), quite astonishingly badly written. It is, to borrow from *Blackadder*, as badly written as the most badly written bad book that you've ever thrown across a room in disgust. It's as bad as a bad novel by Jeffrey Archer. It's so bad then even Erich von Däniken would scorn its prose. It belongs, as Joe Queenan said, to 'that category of things that suck so bad even your kids know they suck'.

Given the popularity of the book, describing the plot is probably redundant. But for the disenfranchised: the body of the curator of the Louvre ('the most famous

217

art museum in the world'), splayed out in the shape of Da Vinci's sketch of a male nude enclosed by a circle, is discovered at the foot of the 'famous' *Mona Lisa*, with further clues written in blood by the dead man on the parquet floor. Sophie Neveu, the victim's granddaughter and a ('glamorous') French police cryptographer, and Robert Langdon ('Harrison Ford in Harris tweed'), a Harvard Professor of Religious Symbology, unravel these cryptic clues and initiate an investigation which develops into a treasure hunt for the 'fabled' Holy Grail. With 'a dogged determination bordering on the obstinate', the two protagonists follow the trail from the Louvre to a Swiss bank, a château in Versailles, the Temple Church, Westminster Abbey and the Rosslyn Chapel—all in the space of two days.

Labyrinthine conspiracies and religious relics are unearthed; truths of the ages are untangled. The 'mysterious' Catholic secret societies, Opus Dei and the Priory of Sion, provide obstacles to the truth, while spurious information about the nature of original sin, the 'obliteration of the sacred feminine', Vatican politics, Rosicrucianism, Range Rovers and Hawker 731 jets rains down mercilessly on the reader. The novel is not so much peopled as infested by an amoebic cast of characters—stocky detective, alluring cryptologist, dashing academic, sinister bishop, albino thug, camp aristocratic historian (English naturally)—who make Tarot cards look as vivid as Tolstoy. It doesn't even put the boot into the Vatican or Opus Dei: they're fine organisations plagued by the odd bad apple.

Nevertheless, in spite of the novel's clockwork plot and *Hello!* magazine prose, I was enslaved by it. Picture Angelina Jolie as Sophie Neveu—'her cryptological senses tingling as she studied the printout'—and you will understand that the scheme of the writing takes its model from *Tomb Raider*. It isn't a novel, it's a computer game. Each chapter is a new level of the game presenting new challenges to be overcome before the next level is achieved, and each challenge encourages in the reader the same solipsistic absorption. I'm familiar with this sensation: I once spent three days in self-enforced solitary confinement playing a computer game in which you had to found cities, irrigate grassland, send settlers to colonise your territory, diplomats to negotiate with other empires and armies to kill barbarians. With no irony but much prescience the game was called *Civilisation*.

That *The Da Vinci Code* should remind me of a computer game is not surprising; in Chapter 95 (of 107) the two protagonists enlist the Google search engine to aid their quest, and it becomes apparent that the co-author of the book is Google him/her/itself. A crude scaffolding of plot has been plastered with cryptic clues and decorated with otiose knowledge, name checks and local colour—'Langdon vaguely recalled the Chapter House as a huge octagonal hall where the original British Parliament convened in the days before the modern Parliament existed'—all plucked off Google's shelves. The age of the DIY novel has arrived.

Many people—appalled (or inspired) by the success of Jeffrey Archer novels—have thought it possible to manufacture popular fiction in this way, but they miss the one unfakeable ingredient: that it has to be done with utter sincerity allied to wilful self-belief. The readership will smell out the bogus. There is no clearer indication of this than the story of Jeffrey Archer lunching with an eminent publisher in the days before he was a novelist or a criminal. Archer gave him lunch and after some idle political gossip, said to the publisher: 'I'm thinking of writing a novel.' The publisher flinched. 'Do you think,' said Archer, 'do you think, that after writing several novels, that I might—' And here he paused, and there was an awkward silence as the publisher waited for the inevitable request not only to read the novel but to publish it. 'Do you think,' said Archer, 'that I might ever win the Nobel Prize for Literature?'

Michel Houellebecq

Encouraged by reviews—'English novels fell by the way in comparison' (Anita Brookner), 'centripetal concentration' (Jonathan Meades)—I have just read *Platform* by Michel Houellebecq. I know a disproportionate amount about its author: that he smokes heavily (in the Kenneth Tynan mode, cigarette held between index and third finger), drinks prodigiously (bourbon) and lives misanthropically on the outskirts of Dublin. 'Michel's not depressed, it's the world that's depressing,' says his wife. I know that he admires Françoise Hardy, Schubert, ginger rhum, Bret Easton Ellis and, particularly, wife-swapping. I know, too, that he had a loveless childhood (son of hippy parents who deserted him), has survived nervous breakdowns, alcoholism and morphine addiction, and I even know that his name is pronounced like the old telephone exchange: WELBECK.

The first-person narrator of *Platform* has something in common with his creator—he has the same name, is much the same age, and his only real enthusiasm is sex which, at the beginning of the novel, he achieves virtually ('pussy in motion') through peep shows, porn mags and videos. He is a miserable, friendless man who appears to differ from his author only in being an accountant at the Ministry of Culture and having a father who is murdered. Left money in the will, Michel is free to behave like 'all of the inhabitants of western Europe, I want to travel.' Which is just as well, because it gives the other Michel, his creator, the opportunity to ventilate his often blunt, sometimes droll and would-be provocative opinions on the travel industry, on Islam ('the most stupid of all religions'), on novels by Agatha Christie ('interesting'), John Grisham ('I ejaculated between two pages… it wasn't the kind of book you read twice') and on Frederick Forsyth ('halfwit'), on Thai prostitutes (he brings them to orgasm: 'Thai men, bad men… you, good man'), and on sex of all (well, heterosexual) varieties.

Fortunately for our hero he encounters Valérie, a sexual soulmate with 'superb breasts, round and high, so swollen and firm that they looked artificial' and, of course, a 'giving person'. All the women characters are given the perfunctory characterisation of pornography, essentially defined by the size, shape and quality of their breasts, bottom and vagina, but although Michel (novelist) is curiously discreet on the size, shape and quality of the organs of the male characters, they come off little better: 'Jean-Yves works because he likes working.'

Nevertheless, despite the etiolated characterisation, the statistics of the tourist industry and the insistent intrusive voice of the author, I am prepared willingly, as we say in the theatre, to suspend my disbelief. Moreover I am buoyed up by the occasional sharp observations of Michel the accountant—'the three of us were caught up in a social system like insects in a block of amber'—and by Michel the novelist's insistence that 'What I write is the truth'.

So I am prepared to accept as 'truth'—of a satiric, poetic, fictional kind—that a large Club Med-style resort business could mutate into a string of discreet brothels, that you can perform fellatio undisturbed in a Paris street in broad daylight and that you can be masturbated in a first-class compartment on a TGV train under the jacket of a suit ('I'll have to get this suit cleaned') and the gaze of a 'woman of about forty, very upper-middle-class but pretty stylish'.

I am even prepared to accept that this woman is staying in the same hotel as Michel and his soulmate and that the three of them merge in the Turkish bath in an inventive sexual trio… but STOP! Call the literary police! The actor's beard has slipped off, the scenery has fallen down, my willing suspension has wilted: I do not believe this scene. It is not the staggering good luck that Michel has with strangers on a train or the Kama-Sutran choreography in the steam room, it's more, much more, mundane: I am staying in the same hotel as the characters in the novel and I have to point out (if only to myself) with passion-extinguishing pedantry that there are no mixed-sex Turkish baths here. What is more, there are separate baths for men and women keenly invigilated on a twenty-four-hour basis by staff dressed in operating-theatre scrubs.

It is odd that fiction should provoke such irritation at minor solecisms—after all, isn't it the point of fiction that it is made up?—but it's also the point that you test your observation of the world against the author's and the two experiences oscillate together in harmony or discord. I have read *The English Patient* on a hillside in Tuscany and Olivia Manning's *Balkan Trilogy* in Bucharest but never felt the urge to show them the red card even if (or when) there were minor geographical errors. They do not, as Houellebecq does, appropriate the 'truth' and exhibit such transparent laziness about researching it. I feel the same kind of irritation and disappointment whenever I read a newspaper. It is a law as immutable as gravity: if you know anything about a story there will always be a small factual error which could have been corrected had the journalist taken a little more trouble. Your trust in every other item in the paper is destabilised: you think, if they can get that wrong, what am I to make of these 'truths' about Iraq, about Palestine, about…

The hotel of Houellebecq's novel is a smart modern spa hotel which looks out over a long beach leading to the unspoilt Breton town of Dinard. I was there for the Festival du Film Britannique, which cynics might suggest is like having a ceremony in Weymouth to honour Italian war heroes; to the Michels, dystopians both, it would 'reek of selfishness, masochism and death'. To my eyes the atmosphere was entirely benevolent, the audiences enthusiastic, the weather perfect and the only problem for a novelist would be how to make plausible a dinner at which a dozen young sommeliers stood on a stage tasting the sponsor's wines and describing them in French to a largely English-speaking audience.

But I had been training for this: the week earlier I was at another film festival—the Efebo d'Oro for films drawn from literary sources—in Agrigento, Sicily, the birthplace of Luigi Pirandello and home of several remarkable Greek temples. Their generous and amiably discursive ceremony was held in the Archaeological Museum under a giant (fifteen metre) stone statue from the Temple of Zeus. It was introduced by the Dixielanders of Sicily, who played Tiger Rag and seemed, if only briefly, to challenge the Houellebecqian universe: 'We live in a world in which there are no links. We're just particles.' I don't think so.

The Mousetrap

In 1997, six months before I left the National Theatre, I was asked by the then Controller of BBC2, Mark Thompson, if I would take part in a 'Millennium Project': writing and presenting a series of programmes about the history of twentieth-century theatre for BBC2. The series (and book of the series) was called Changing Stages. *For research I thought it was necessary to see the longest-running show in the history of British theatre.*

Agatha Christie's play has been playing in the West End for nearly fifty years, nearly 20,000 performances by the millennium. It opened in 1952—starring Richard Attenborough—and has played to more than ten million people by more than 340 actors and actresses.

Dazzling statistics, and surely enduring evidence of the lure of the live theatre—if it weren't for the show itself, which is like a minor shrine attended not by the faithful hoping for a miracle cure or sign of divine affirmation, but by tourists dutifully following an entry in the guidebook.

The play is set in an improbable guesthouse run by an improbable couple of indeterminate ages who occasionally peck each other on the cheek like budgerigars scouring for millet. Their baronial guesthouse would suggest a castle in Scotland, were it not for the fact that it evokes nothing more than the stage of the St Martin's Theatre. The plot (a murder the previous day in London) demands that the guesthouse is placed within an hour of the scene of crime, but has to be as isolated as an island in a hurricane. The solution: set the play in Berkshire, during a snowstorm, some time in the second Ice Age—although the furniture suggests s period sometime between late Marshall & Snelgrove and early Ikea, and the costumes mid-period C&A.

The characters are produced on stage, one by one, as if they were being announced for a formal dinner. Their entrance is heralded by a fanfare from a traditional wind machine (the *original*, we learn from the programme), which sounds like, well, a traditional wind machine, which sounds as much like wind as a comb covered with toilet paper sounds like a trumpet. It is turned with ferocious energy whenever the offstage front door is opened and another character is introduced to us, covered with snowflakes the size of feathers, looking as though they'd been rolling on the floor in a hen house.

The young men jump up from contact with furniture and other human beings as if their trousers were on fire, while the other characters boom in monotonous, uninflected sentences that dribble purposelessly off the stage like ping-pong balls falling on a wet carpet. The behaviour of the characters has no more resemblance to real life than the characters in a Kabuki play. Each character has a sexual abnormality and is therefore a murder suspect: a screaming queen (stripy coloured jumper), a young dyke (man's suit, white shirt and tie) who is also a Socialist— 'not red, pale pink'—an old dyke (sensible shoes, deep voice, big strides), a dubious Major (on loan from Rattigan's *Separate Tables*), and a camp foreigner dressed like Noël Coward, who wears make-up (rouge). Suspicions of cross-dressing can be banished; he is merely Italian.

The audience infers the homosexuality of the younger characters from their 'arty' and hysterical behaviour; the older ones—the mannish spinster and the foreigner—are less explicit. The Major (in spite of his seediness) and the married couple who run the guesthouse are not portrayed as sexually abnormal and are therefore not plausible suspects. In Patrick Hamilton's *Rope* (1929), the connection between homosexuality and criminal tendencies was made unambiguously: gay = murderer.

There are jokes—'Funny people, the English'—which cause a ripple among the audience who, given the evidence in front of them, can only agree. The highlight of the first act is the arrival of a skiing policeman outside the mullioned window. The highlight of the second act is the unmasking of the... The highlight of the curtain call is the request to 'lock the play's secret in your hearts'. During the first act the telephone lines are cut. A character picks up the handset, stares at it as if it were a dead rat, and says, 'This telephone's dead.' So is the play, but it has the innocence and familiarity of a fairytale. The audience watch it with good-humoured attention and curiosity, as if they were watching morris dancing or cheese rolling. Funny people, the English.

Changing Stages Diary

After I was asked to make Changing Stages, *a six-part documentary on twentieth-century theatre in 1997, I worked on two productions in New York as a freelance theatre director, for eight months on a film that collapsed, for five months* pro bono publico *on a report for the Government on the Royal Opera House, and—on the advice of Robert Hughes—wrote the book of the series (in collaboration with Nicholas Wright) before filming the series in 1999. The actual start had been over a year earlier, when I interviewed John Gielgud, 'in case I drop off the twig', as he put it. This is an account of the filming.*

13th September 1999. To the Aran Islands, to film a sequence about Synge, who went there in 1898 for four summers, out of which came three great plays. We arrive from Stansted at Knock Airport in Galway—a monument to the capital- ist instincts of the Catholic Church, developed by a priest keen for the advancement of the Shrine of Knock—and drive to an airstrip in Connemara, through Knock and Tuam and Galway City. The west of Ireland has an air of yesterday: no factory farming, not much speculative building, the shopfronts all gloss paint and Celtic lettering, none of the graphics and logos of the New Europe.

The airstrip for the islands is a small, thin tear of tarmac in a field. The plane seats six; we're weighed with our gear before we get on the plane, and placed according to weight. I get the long straw: sitting at the front with the pilot. We skim the sea and within minutes see the small island of Inishmaan before us, like a giant sleeping seal, scarred with hundreds of drystone walls containing pockets of scrubby grass, and houses dotted over the island like a ragged white-beaded necklace. We land on one of the few large unenclosed fields, next to a Gaelic football ground with, surrealistically, only one set of goalposts. We go out on a recce round the island and watch the sun go down through huge waves, standing on a cliff at the west tip of the island—nothing between us and America.

14th September 1999. Dawn. We film the sun rising over the hills of Co. Clare standing on a grey, sandy beach. It's very mild, a clear sky, butter-gold sun, a perfect morning. But for the colour of the sand we could be in Santa Monica. It doesn't seem to fit with what I've written about Synge coming to a bleak, weather-beaten place.

It's too sunny to film on the rocky outcrop where we stood last night, so we go off to another location: huge slabs of limestone pave the fields like abandoned car parks, and massive chunks stand up, sliced by the weather into great grey lumps with six-inch crevices. This is the spot for my first 'PTC'; I'm learning: PTC = Piece To Camera. I have to walk along the edge of a limestone cliff, stepping over the crevices, talking to the distant camera, following a route that I'm assured will look great on the screen but demands that I stop on the words 'edge of the world' at the edge of a fifty-foot drop. Ah yes, no trouble. It's hard enough to remember what I've written, but walk, talk, don't fall off *and* look at the camera? Now I really admire Anneka Rice.

The sun is hot. We move around the island to other locations. To someone used to filming drama accompanied by actors, extras, a crew of thirty-odd, and an army of vehicles, driving around in an old Land Rover (with grass growing on the windowsills) with a crew of three seems deeply enviable.

The weather changes: the cliff that we recced last night is thought to be suitably stormy. This time I have to walk towards the camera while stepping over large sharp rocks, skirting craggy pools, trying not to slip on seaweed, pointing to America, then to England, and talking to an unresponsive lens about the way that British drama has been dependent on the Irish for centuries. When I reach the camera without either messing up my words or slipping into the sea, there is huge jubilation from the crew. 'The waves behind you!' they shriek, 'We thought you were going to be dragged into the sea!' And me worrying about my lines.

15th September 1999. The cottage where Synge stayed: it's small, low and long. Perhaps a dozen people lived here in four small rooms, one of those being occupied by the paying guest. The cottage, dilapidated since her parents moved to a new cottage just below in 1978, has been restored by the great-granddaughter of Synge's hosts: it's a labour of love, she's raised the money herself. It has a new earth floor in the kitchen, floorboards next door in Synge's room, a new rye-thatched roof.

Synge was sent here by his producer, Yeats, who did something that producers often do, but it seldom works: he told Synge what to write about. 'Give up Paris,' he said. 'Go to the Aran Islands. Live as if you were one of the people themselves; express a life that has never found expression.' Yeats and Lady Gregory had been here; she was remembered for her snobbery, for refusing to give sweets to the kids, and for bribing neighbours to keep their dog quiet when she stayed in the cottage. Synge wrote listening to the comforting chatter of the women in the kitchen speaking Irish, which he learned from a Martin McDonagh—almost certainly a distant cousin of the prolific young author of *The Cripple of Inishmaan* (who himself lives at the Elephant and Castle). The islanders still speak Irish among themselves, many of them having only a few words of English. Synge's journals describe admiringly the women and their shortish red skirts. There's one in the house: heavy thick felt, a beautiful colour—rich rusty red. He writes of their sturdy bodies; no wonder, clad in a skirt as thick as an overcoat.

I walk through the house for a shot describing Synge's life here. I'm becoming an actor: hitting marks, modulating my voice, inventing a persona, feigning confidence. Every time I reach my line 'untouched by the modern world' I think of the mobile phones, outboard motors, scooters, telephones I've seen here. But life on the island is still hard and poor. There are photos of nineteenth-century evictions in the house: they had to pay a ground rent to an English landlord, only a few shillings, but imagine evicting people who had to make a living from this unforgiving soil.

In the evening we film in the bar; we've brought some musicians over from Galway. It starts to fill up around ten o'clock. Only one man complains of being 'exploited' by the BBC. He's an immigrant, a Dubliner, and he's told by an islander not to be so inhospitable. Mostly they seem indifferent to our filming—after all, they're used to film crews here: they had Flaherty doing *Man of Aran* in 1934. Rivers of Guinness flow; every table has black columns of creamy Guinness lined up like skittles. After we stop filming, people start to sing—unaccompanied, unselfconscious, Irish songs, the strange intervals made stranger by the loose relation with pitch, straying around the note like the wind through trees.

16th September 1999. We fly back to Connemara. At the tiny airport shop (which sells home-made scones) I buy a copy of Synge's journal *The Aran Islands*. 'He was through here today, you know,' said the man behind the counter. 'You could have got him to sign your book.'

22nd September 1999. At the Old Vic I'm being filmed musing about its past: it's a house of spirits, haunted by the ghosts of actors and audiences. Every time I come here I wonder at the wisdom of exchanging this theatre for the Kabah on the South Bank. I say this to Ian McKellen (who I'm interviewing) as we wander round backstage. As I utter this heresy, there's a huge thunderclap and torrential rain. Water starts spewing over the stage from the flies and gushing out of an imperfect downpipe near huge electrical junction boxes, and Ian ruefully says: 'Well, I suppose that's your answer.' But at the National we used to have a bucket to catch the rain that leaked into the foyer from the terrace.

30th September 1999. I'm going to Barnes to interview designer Margaret Harris, who with her sister, Sophie, and Elizabeth Montgomery—as Motley—dominated British theatre design for many years. Margaret Harris (universally known as Percy) is a very sprightly ninety-five and, like all lively old people, is very moving. She spoke, among other things, about Gielgud's generosity, about cutting away the 'fuss' from the stage, and about the abstract being incompatible with theatre—you're always stuck on stage with the irreducibility of human beings.

To the National Theatre to interview Tom Stoppard. I feel very dislocated, doing something unfamiliar in a wholly familiar place. But, as a professional necessity, theatre doesn't condone nostalgia: when a show is over, it's over, and a new show makes its demands on your attention and your affections. Tom and I talk, among other things, about whether buildings outlast the expansionist impulse to create them, looking around at the cathedral of the NT, a monument to the 1960s. We wander into the bookshop. They don't have my book on display, but do have a shelf of Tom's work. You've written more than Proust, I say to Tom. More jokes too, he says. We walk through the rain for the film. I'm holding an umbrella which turns inside out. The director chastises me for stopping rather than keeping going. It pours, and there are buckets in the foyer.

7th October 1999. Drive to Stratford-upon-Avon. It feels like an island resort: Shakespeare-on-Sea. The theatre always has the air of an end-of-the-pier show, and cutting-edge Shakespeare production sits uneasily beside the heritage relics and the national trustery. It's pouring with rain. I meet the cast of *Othello*, who we're going to film in a backstage sequence in Newcastle. I explain to the actors what we're up to, and say that among other things I'm interested in Shakespeare's take on the world—the POV of an actor and producer, sceptical of authority. Shakespeare writes brilliantly about soldiers (which is the profession of most of his protagonists), and the actors sit there—as actors often do—patient as soldiers being briefed about a possibly suicidal strategy.

I watch the matinee of *Othello*. The play more often than not fails to work its magic, but this is a clear production with a moving performance from Ray Fearon as Othello; this is rare, Othello is usually trampled underfoot by Iago. I've been thinking a lot recently about Shakespeare's originality: above all it's in his characterisation, which is universally detailed without a hierarchy of detail. 'That William Shakespeare, he certainly knew how to write,' said the cockney comic actor Arthur Mullard when he was offered a part in *Twelfth Night*. In the circle and balcony the audience are young and attentive; in the stalls I'm the youngest by a few years. In the bar of my hotel I listen to a conversation by an aged couple about whether they'll go to a friend's funeral, discussed in the tones of deciding whether to go to the theatre or not.

8th October 1999. I do a piece to camera on a motorboat, passing under a bridge as I refer to 'entering a time warp'. By take five we've achieved the desired combination of position and timing of boat, presenter, Shakespeare Memorial Theatre, swans, ducks and dialogue. This is acting, trying to appear spontaneous and facing the actor's perennial paradox: how to tread the line between being conscious of your self, and being self-conscious. The rest of the day I wander pensively for the camera and sit on a tour bus which takes me round the various Shakespeare shrines. I learn nothing except the meaning of pin-money and a 'Roker' (a form of cow), and how rich Shakespeare became. That's one of the dark secrets of the theatre: successful playwrights do very-nicely-thank-you.

12th October 1999. 'Success smells of Brighton,' said Laurence Olivier, which is why I'm going there on a train. As I settle in my seat, a woman asks me if she can have the job supplement of my *Guardian*. 'You don't look as if you need it,' she says. Mmmm... For me Brighton always smells of sauciness rather than success. In the mid-sixties my sister's best friend asked me if I would help her with her divorce: I had to be photographed by a private detective semi-naked engaging in simulated sex in a Brighton hotel room to provide evidence for her husband to cite me as co-respondent. I can't think why I refused. But here I am being photographed fully clothed talking about Olivier, saying that Brighton has the characteristics of his acting: raffish, cocky, sexy, and a bit flash. Ray, the keeper of the whelk stall that we've commandeered, seems to think it's true—of Brighton, at least.

We've been told that Olivier had a beach hut, so we find ourselves outside a row of concrete boxes—No. 1, Madeira Drive—as unglamorous as lock-up garages in a council estate, deserted but for the occupant of No. 2, who tells us 'It's a very thespian town—Laurence Olivier, Max Miller, Terence Rattigan and Dora What's-her-name.' We end the day on the Palace Pier, which is celebrating its centenary. Perhaps we should be doing a programme about a hundred years of British piers. There's another BBC film crew there, for a children's programme; their presenters, all three of them, are young enough to be my grandchildren. I do a piece to camera about the decline of heroic acting as nature provides a perfect picture-postcard Technicolor sunset. 'Larry would have loved it,' says Robin, the researcher.

14th October 1999. National Theatre. Spend the day feeling like a returned exile, hugging, greeting, explaining what I'm doing and increasingly feeling that I've abandoned my profession. I'm like a seeded Wimbledon player who's unaccountably become an umpire. I interview Trevor Nunn today in his office (my old office). He's touchingly nervous. He's thought hard about my questions and is very cogent. When I'm interviewing people some remarks appear highlighted—the ones I know that we can use in the film flash like Day-Glo colours. We talk about the difficulty of large theatres. He tells me that he's just had a letter from Denys Lasdun, the architect of the National, congratulating him on using the Olivier 'properly' for his production of *Summerfolk*. Trevor says he should write back saying: 'Thank you. I had to raise the stage by three feet, move it downstage by seventeen feet, and cover most of the walls of the auditorium with black drapes. Apart from that, everything was as you designed it.' Roger, the director, remarks on how similar the NT is to the BBC—i.e. a maze of departments and not much apparent contact between them.

18th October 1999. The Globe Theatre to interview Mark Rylance, Actor-Manager-Director, who is dressed piratically in a bandana under a pork-pie hat, large gold earring, tartan jacket and bow tie. I'm not sure about the synthetic Elizabethanism of the Globe, but Mark makes a passionate defence of it. His evangelical zeal has carried many sceptics away by the sheer pressure of his enthusiasm and his own protean gifts as an actor. To be among an audience who are unquestionably moved by the sight and, above all, the *sound* of a Shakespeare play in broad daylight is to be obliged to recognise that it's folly to be proscriptive about the experience of theatre. And his theatre is full; he made a small surplus this year without any subsidy.

19th October 1999. Interview with eighty-nine-year-old Luise Rainer, in an airy flat in Eaton Square—in a house, as the blue plaque tells me, where Vivien Leigh once lived. Luise Rainer became an actress in defiance of her parents' wishes when she was sixteen, acted in Reinhardt's company in Vienna, went to Hollywood, won an Oscar twice in a row, married Clifford Odets, withdrew from movies (having crossed Louis B. Mayer), and barely acted again—the odd play, and a happy life with a new (publisher) husband in New York and London. Yes, she has regrets, but she gives no sign of bitterness—'Never look back,' she advises me. She's extraordinarily lively—birdlike, bright, funny, a Pierrot face, with the large deep eyes of a marmoset. And still beautiful, wonderful cheekbones, and when she turns away from the camera as she speaks, the light perfectly sculpts a shape unchanged since her Hollywood days.

Our conversation could be entitled 'Meetings with Remarkable Men'. She still talks about Clifford Odets with great love, even though he was clearly consumed by self-obsession. She talks about The Group Theater, who were clearly protective of their star playwright and jealous of his wife; of the Actors Studio and Lee Strasberg: 'They were nuts. NUTS!' And of Brecht: 'A horrible man, hoorrrible,' rolling her 'r's' with her still-strong Viennese accent. 'He was like a spider—red hair. I think it was red. I don't like red hair.' Brecht offered to write a play for her; she suggested a version of a play she'd seen as a child: *The Caucasian Chalk Circle*. She procured money for him from a New York producer, went off to serve in the war (in Egypt), returned to find he'd written one and a half pages: 'Double spaced!' Before I leave she shows me a photograph of a man with frizzy grey hair and a large moustache, white beach trousers rolled up to the knees, and a smile of pure contentment on his face. Close beside him, also in white, is the heart-stoppingly beautiful twenty-six-year-old Luise Rainer. 'Albert Einstein,' she says, 'was a very nice man.'

20th October 1999. Interview with Judi Dench. She's recently had appendicitis, so of course we're doing the interview four floors up at the Haymarket Theatre. It's about the one theatre in London she's never played in. She seems astonishingly fit, and, being Judi—ever stoical and generous—makes no complaint about the stairs. Within minutes of meeting her the crew have become passionate Denchophiles. We talk about Shakespeare, and she gives an effortless demonstration of verse-speaking: rhythm, sense and sound in perfect synch:

> His face was as the heavens, and therein stuck
> A sun and moon which kept their course and lighted
> The little O, the earth.

It's glorious to be sitting a foot or two away from her as she speaks Cleopatra's lines to me. Then we film her take off make-up as if at the end of a performance, leaving her bare, beautiful and humane face. It's to illustrate something Artaud said: 'The human face carries a kind of perpetual death on it. It's up to art to banish death by giving life to its features.'

After lunch it's Julie Taymor, who's just opened *The Lion King* and recently finished a film of *Titus Andronicus* with Tony Hopkins. She's hugely relieved because Tony's just left a message on her machine saying he's seen the film and likes it.

231

As we sit under the heads of the hyenas, Julie talks immensely coherently about the poetic nature of theatre, about spectacle, masks and magic.

Then on to the Rose Theatre, where Shakespeare got his break as a playwright. The last time I was here it was for a Save the Rose Theatre demonstration in 1989. I suppose it wasn't entirely in vain: there's an office block over our heads but the developers have preserved the ruins in the basement. I walk in wellington boots through a deceptively deep puddle of water that covers the outline of the foundations, marked out by an X-ray green pattern of light. 'Shakespeare,' I say, 'is our theatrical DNA.'

21st October 1999. The Freud Museum. Surely the place which housed one of the men who shaped our century should be a national monument, but in Britain it's easier to get a grant for a museum of tanks or pop music. The museum gets a lot of visitors, many foreign. According to Erica, the curator, Brazilian visitors always say it's very *'emotivamente'*. It is for me, but I find that after half an hour I've become entirely at home in his congenial study—unchanged since his death—stuffed with exquisite Greek, Chinese and Egyptian objects, and floored with opulently coloured Afghan carpets. I sit on one of the most celebrated pieces of furniture in the world: the couch where a thousand dreams have been unravelled. It's comfortable and plain, but covered with a thick, rich, red and blue Persian rug. The room houses a large library of books, many of them beautifully bound, and as I talk to the camera—about Freud being used by actors to help them play Shakespeare—I leaf through Freud's 1891 edition of *King Lear.* It's a nice irony that he was inspired by Shakespeare, whose plays he's said to have read (in translation) when he was eight. When I express doubt about this, Robin, the researcher, tells me to remember he was a genius. Sitting in his room, I think: yes and a very benign one. As we leave the house, Paul, the sound recordist, pretends to slip on the wet path. 'See that,' he says, 'Freudian slip.'

I'm becoming like the sort of actor who infuriates you when you're directing. As we get in the van I ask when we plan to wrap: it's the actor's equivalent of 'Are we nearly there, Dad?' On to interview Vanessa Redgrave at the Gielgud Theatre. She's just been in Sarajevo with her mum, who's eighty-nine and is now playing in a Coward play, *A Song at Twilight*. She's very eloquent about Coward. When she was very young in an N.C. Hunter play he came to see her, and gave her a wonderful compliment. I practically have to pull her fingernails to get her to tell me. He said that she was incapable of being untruthful on stage. 'Not true,' says Vanessa. But she says he valued truth very highly, and we talk about the paradox of his plays being about concealment, repression and never quite fulfilling his own ambitions for his writing. We also talk about Shakespeare and for the second time in two days I'm sitting within touching distance of a great actress who is speaking Shakespeare. Vanessa's—or, to be more accurate, Ros-

232

alind's—epilogue from *As You Like It* moves me to tears. Her performance in a TV version of Michael Elliott's production in 1962 was the first Shakespeare performance that took my heart completely, and it made me want to work in the theatre: 'It is not the fashion to see the Lady the Epilogue: but it is no more unhandsome than to see the Lord the Prologue...'

26th October 1999. Interview with Peter Hall at the Old Vic. It's an unintended unkindness to have arranged to interview Peter here. He was very happy here three years ago with his repertory company and, robbed of that by the Arts Council's unwillingness to underwrite him for another season, he's tinged with melancholy and anxiety for what the future holds. But he talks with great energy and lucidity of founding the RSC—which he says, not altogether jokingly, he wants on his gravestone—of directing, of acting, of working with Peggy Ashcroft and Olivier and Gielgud and Richardson; of standing at the back of the theatre in Stratford with Jean Renoir while the seventy-year-old Renoir fell in love (as I did too) with Vanessa Redgrave's Rosalind, of verse-speaking being like playing jazz, and of the need to fragment the two behemoths—the RSC and the National—into eight or nine companies. He talks movingly of his early years as a director: the script of *Waiting for Godot* arriving on his desk at the Arts Theatre, and his production of that most ascetic play being the springboard of his career, leading to Stratford, to Tennessee Williams, to Leslie Caron... He talks with such warm enthusiasm for his early years that I can't help feeling that nothing could or did match the frenzied thrill of helping to reinvent the British theatre in the early sixties. I tell Peter that by the time I finish this series I won't have directed anything new for nearly two years. He looks really concerned. 'I'd go mad,' he says.

In the afternoon we drive to Gloucestershire to interview the designer John Bury, who designed *The Wars of the Roses* for Peter in 1962, establishing the RSC as a major international theatre company. John tells the story of his start in the theatre just after the war; he was drawn to Joan Littlewood's Theatre Workshop company like a small boy to the circus. He joined (after spending three years in the Fleet Air Arm) when it was a small agitprop touring company, and he stayed for about twenty years, becoming actor/electrician, then lighting designer, then ('I couldn't light scenery on the stage that I hadn't designed') designer. Completely untaught and independent, he arrived at an aesthetic that was as radical as Caspar Neher's (Brecht's designer) or as Jocelyn Herbert's at the Royal Court, and gave a visual syntax to much of British theatre for a generation. I ask him what he thinks is the essence of theatre, he says: 'When I first started I was playing the narrator at the side of the stage and also operating the dimmer board, which had to be onstage. And as I stood there saying, "And then came spring..." I changed the lighting from cold to warm, and that was the sort of madness we went in for. But that first drew me to theatre.'

27th October 1999. Yesterday driving to Gloucestershire, today to Provincetown in Massachusetts, after flying to Boston. 'Massachusetts is a glory in the Fall,' says John Proctor in *The Crucible*. And it is—gold, red, pink, bronze, brown, and yellow. I'm always pleasantly surprised by rural America; it's so unlike the urban clatter of New York, Los Angeles and Miami that passes for our TV-induced view of the country. There are so many Stars and Stripes—huge ones flapping like sheets, small ones waving like Tibetan prayer pennants. In our country the Union flag (apart from its official use) is only ever displayed ironically or as a sort of defiant assertion of Imperial status. Here the flags are like the shrines that spatter the Italian roadside, homely advertisements of faith. When we reach Provincetown there are as many rainbow coalition flags as Stars and Stripes, declaring a different sort of faith—a belief in sexual tolerance. Which is possibly why writers and painters were drawn here since the 1890s to escape the summer heat of New York. One of the writers was Eugene O'Neill: it was here that he first had a play of his produced.

28th October 1999. The day is a clear, bright autumn day, sky of Della Robbia blue. I've written something about O'Neill's story being an American folktale—unperformed playwright to Nobel Prize-winner—and Chris, the director for the American episode, has translated this into film imagery: I'm on a horse posed like a frontiersman on a ridge of sand dunes talking about the small shacks where O'Neill and his pals stayed to write and paint. O'Neill lived here, off and on, for nine years—a stay punctuated by wild drinking bouts, and capering on the beach half-naked in a fright wig, like Edgar in *Lear*. My horse is a handsome chestnut named Buddy; he has a Western-style saddle which, after riding an English saddle, feels like a comfortable office chair. Buddy proves himself to be eponymously named, and galloping along the edge of the incoming tide, long having ceased to care whether this sequence is in any way gratuitous, I'm having about as much fun as one can have legally. Fred, the French cameraman, kneels by the seashore and asks me to gallop as close as I can to him; the hooves pass inches from the lens. Afterwards he confesses that he closed his eyes as I passed.

29th October 1999. Early morning in Provincetown finds us under a pier squelching through the wet sand to the accompaniment of the chanting of seagulls. O'Neill's first play was staged in a converted shed on an old pier, which stunk of fish and smoke from a recent fire. I doubt if any play had such a launching: there was a storm during the performance which rocked the pier and drove the sea up through the gaps in the floor, wetting the feet of the audience and actors. Afterwards we walk through the main street of the town, and feel like we've been inserted into *The Truman Show*. The town has the same genial, hospitable air of the movie—the same colonial-style clapboard houses, the same universal goodwill. But the extras have been reprogrammed: instead of conventional couples with 2.5 children, the shops and the pavements are peopled with gay and lesbian couples, and instead of groceries and hardware stores, there are gay clubs, art galleries and leather shops. Tennessee Williams spent a summer here—'a sort of crash course in growing up'. I'll bet. He returned a few years later to finish writing *The Glass Menagerie*. It's an engaging paradox that the town's most famous resident now is the archbishop of macho: Norman Mailer.

In the afternoon, we're onboard a schooner called *The Hindu*, and I'm talking to camera about the initiators of the American Dream, the Pilgrim Fathers (who landed at Provincetown), and their no-less-idealistic successors who gave birth to the New Drama of the New World. It's a perfectly beautiful day, calm sea, almost silent but for the slap of waves and the flap of the sails. We dock in the golden glow of the setting sun.

30th October 1999. Dawn. Hoping for a dour sea mist to match O'Neill's dolefulness, we have a lavender dawn by Caspar David Friedrich. Then on the road to New York. As we drive out of town we pass what at first I take to be evidence of a lynching. It might be a sexual bigot, but it's a dummy with a skull for a head, hanging from a tree for Hallowe'en. O'Neill said Provincetown was 'hard to get to and hard to get out of'. The latter proves to be uncomfortably true: it takes us eight hours to drive to New York, after getting lost in New Rochelle, landing up in New Jersey, and wondering whether there is something in the Constitution that forbids the provision of comprehensible road signs.

31st October 1999. Interview with Arthur Miller. Arthur is, incredibly, eighty-four, but he is very energetic, physically and mentally unbowed. A new production of *The Price* is about to open on Broadway, so he'll have two of his plays running—a total rehabilitation after years of being patronised by the New York critics, but being much performed and respected in Britain.

For two hours in his apartment we film Arthur talking about the past, present and future of American theatre. He tells stories about the first performance of *Salesman*, of appearing before the House Un-American Activities Committee, of being in London with Marilyn, of copying out speeches of Shakespeare to see how he wrote—all told as if he was recalling them for the first time. After the interview we go to Brooklyn, which is where he used to live (in Brooklyn Heights) and work (in the US Navy yard). We walk down to the riverfront to be filmed in the shadow of the pillars of the Brooklyn Bridge looking out over the East River. 'These are our cathedrals,' says Arthur, looking up at the bridge. 'I thought those were,' I say, pointing across the river to the Business District and the twin towers of the World Trade Center. 'Oh sure. "The business of

America is business", that's what Calvin Coolidge used to say. He was the first President I can remember.' Then he stares at the buildings. 'None of them were here when I lived here. Not one. And in all those windows there'll be somebody counting figures. Piling up money.' Then he smiles ruefully. 'And snorting cocaine, I guess.'

1st November 1999. Sunday. It's very sunny and I'm sitting in my room in New York all day writing Episode Five: Brecht and Beckett. 'This is somehow not the right country for me. The people are too strange,' said Beckett, the only time that he visited New York. I know what he meant: I got into the hotel lift this morning with four not-so-young women: 'I love your jacket,' said one. 'I love your hair,' said another. 'I love your eyebrows,' said a third. 'I love you,' said the fourth.

2nd November 1999. Interview with Celeste Holm about *Oklahoma!* She was in the original cast, stopping the show nightly with 'I'm Just a Girl Who Can't Say No.' She's told her stories many times before, and if I interrupt her flow she has to reset herself to recover the sequence. But the stories are good, and I particularly like the tale of changing the title of the show in New Haven from *Away We Go!* to *Oklahoma!* Posters were printed by the time they reached their next date, only for a further change to be made, which compelled a small army to patrol round Boston in a freezing March pasting posters with exclamation marks.

Then we drive for an hour or so through a landscape quilted with autumn colours to Tony Kushner's house, a beautiful bottle-green clapboard house on the banks of the Hudson River in New York State, a hundred yards from where Washington put a chain across the river to stop the British from getting to New York—something now achieved by American Equity. Tony talks with marvellous lucidity and grace about Williams and O'Neill and Miller. His mother, a talented amateur actress, played Linda in *Death of a Salesman* when Tony was four. He says the play had a powerful effect on him then, so perhaps I should be less sceptical of Freud's love of Shakespeare at the age of eight. 'With Shakespeare's plays,' says Tony, 'you don't feel trapped while the parade moves in front of you. The parade is there and you're moving around in it and you have room to turn around and that's a great thing to strive for in the sense that a whole world is contained in a play.'

If you run a theatre you hope for the sort of luck that Peter Hall had when *Waiting for Godot* dropped on his desk at the Arts Theatre, or Brendan Behan's *The Quare Fellow* on Joan Littlewood's; for me it was Tony's play *Angels in America*, which seemed Shakespearean in its ambition. It still seems a fearful indictment of New York producers that his play wasn't produced there until after its National Theatre opening.

4th November 1999. Back beneath Brooklyn Bridge. There are gaffer-tape marks on the ground, evidence of another film crew. This is a common hazard in New York, film crews leave their spoor all over this film-friendly town. On the way back uptown, we pass two feature-film crews, swaggering like occupying armies, filming in the Village. In the evening we're filming a piece about Broadway in the middle of Times Square, vying with yet another feature-film crew, as well as a rival documentary team, countless Japanese photographers, and a group of silver-haired women from out-of-town—perhaps from New Haven—staring up at the neon signs as if expecting the arrival of extra-terrestrials. Walking in a circle followed by the camera, dodging taxis and tourists, while speaking about Ziegfeld's discovery of the showbusiness Theory of Relativity (sex + elegance + money = success) above the noise of police sirens, car horns, and street musicians, I feel that I may have come of age as a presenter.

In the afternoon I interview the playwright Arthur Laurents, who's an astoundingly—even by the standards of Arthur Miller—sprightly eighty-two-year-old. Arthur wrote the book for *West Side Story* and *Gypsy*. He's indiscreet, caustic— '*Oklahoma*? Tap-dancing cowboys. I'm just a girl who can't say no? No!'—and political: 'You couldn't live through those times,' he says, 'and not be political.' He's still fascinated and disturbed by the friends of his who informed for the McCarthy hearings—'Why did they do it? They didn't *have* to? If they didn't work in Hollywood it wouldn't have made a blind bit of difference to their careers.' I ask him about the fact that most of the people who made the American musical are Jewish. 'Or dead,' says Arthur.

5th November 1999. I interview Arthur's long-time friend and colleague, Stephen Sondheim—emphatically not dead. He's tired—he has a show in workshop, so he's writing at night and rehearsing by day—but he's concise and precise about the history and the making of musicals, about Brecht and Joan Littlewood, about the execrable taste of the contemporary poperettas, and about the satisfaction of 'true rhymes'—'It's not that you'd get a gold star for using perfect rhymes, but if you rhyme "phone" and "home", "home" doesn't land the way "phone" and "moan" land. And that's a tiny little paradigm of what I think happens in all arts. I mean you know, that's why you can't just look at a Rothko and say "Oh I can do that." No you can't.'

Then on to the Public Theater to interview George Wolfe, who's its director. He had to follow Joe Papp—a producer with a gargantuan enthusiasm for not-for-profit theatre and a matching ego: he substituted his own face for Shakespeare's on the posters for Shakespeare in the Park. Joe enfranchised many talents—playwrights, directors, actors—and most of them grateful but eager to preserve their souls, fled from Joe's bear-like embrace. George, in spite of having had a kidney transplant and running the Public Theater, has limitless energy and talks without stopping about social responsibility, the Group Theater, Odets, Miller, the Federal Theater Project and—he's black—racism, the fault line in American society. We talk about 'cultural strip-mining': 'I think that there are very few things that happen in this country that I don't see as some kind of minstrel show,' says George.

6th November 1999. Interview with Kim Hunter, the original Stella in the play and movie of *Streetcar*. She has perfect recall, apart from (understandably) not being able to remember the name of the actor (John Garfield) who was cast first and backed out when he realised it wasn't Stanley's play. Not that the part did Marlon Brando much harm. Kim talks of him with great affection as a thoughtful, responsible, hard-working and thoroughly engaged actor. When we asked him if he'd be interviewed for this series he said that the last thing in the world he wanted to talk about was acting; he'd only talk about the plight of the American Indian. Reasonable enough, but Stan, our van driver, says of him: 'His elevator doesn't go to the top.'

Once again Broadway by night: a piece to camera about what the American theatre has given to the British. With the words 'The New World gave life to the Old', I get into a taxi, which then drives off into the night. To me this feels a bit cute, but Chris, the director, assures me it's fine, so I happily negotiate the crowded pavement and the inscrutability of the taxi driver, who asks me if we're making a documentary about taxis; it seems simpler to say yes. When we finish filming, three small girls ask for my autograph. I tell them that my signature is worthless, but they meekly persist: the presence of the camera has convinced them that I'm a catch, so strong is the national religion of celebrity. So I write: 'To Kira, with best wishes', wishing that I could make her day by adding the words 'Clint' and 'Eastwood'.

7th November 1999. Irene Worth interview, then off to New Orleans. Irene talks (and does impersonations) of Noël Coward, T.S. Eliot ('I only dared to call him Tom after years. He always seemed old'), and John Gielgud, off whom she says she had the best piece of advice on acting, which he'd learned painfully: 'Acting is half shame, half glory. Shame when you're aware of yourself, and glory when you can forget yourself.'

It's a two-and-a-half-hour journey (and a different time zone) to New Orleans. We arrive after dark, happy to be wrapped in humid, semi-tropical night. We're staying in the French Quarter—elegant two- or three-storey houses, a louche and lively street life, live oaks dripping with tearful Spanish moss in the square, small courtyards with fountains and greenery, and balconies with lacy ironwork. We have dinner sitting on one of them, directly opposite the room where Tennessee Williams lived—the justification for our visit.

8th November 1999. Driving out of town to rendezvous with a steamboat (as in *Showboat*, the first real Broadway musical). I grew up in Hardy country in Dorset, so I'm used to people decoding landscape familiar to them from literature. For me, Louisiana is familiar from *Huckleberry Finn*, the plays of Tennessee Williams, the novels of James Lee Burke, and the life of Huey Long, the demagogue Governor, assassinated in 1935, chronicled brilliantly in Robert Penn Warren's *All the King's Men*, and played by Broderick Crawford in the movie. I tell Warren, our New Orleans van driver, about my interest in Huey Long. 'He was a big BS-er,' he says. We pass over the Mississippi on a bridge named after him, and look down on large freighters, which seem tiny as toys in a bath.

The steamboat—*The American Queen*—is moored on the Mississippi beside a levee, the steep man-made flood barriers that line the river. The scale of the boat matches the river: it's like a white-gothic aircraft carrier with a huge, red paddle wheel at its stern, a floating hotel. Opposite the levee is a beautiful white-columned 'Greek revival' house, situated at the end of an arcade of 250-year-old live oaks, surrounded—at a distance—by sugar fields and small thin-roofed clapboard houses. It doesn't take much imagination to picture the slave plantation, and we're reminded that the Old South isn't dead when our camera assistant, Andy, who is part-Malaysian, asks a tourist if he minds waiting till we've finished the shot. 'MOVE, BOY!' shouts the no-neck. Later I spot *Little Black Sambo* for sale in the tourist shop. Is racism alive? 'It's a Roger,' as our van driver would have said.

9th November 1999. Late start as we're night-shooting, so I wander round the French Quarter in the morning. Swarming with tourists, the objects of veneration being the ubiquitous T-shirt, tabasco, souvenirs and Cajun-music CDs. In contrast, the Louisiana Museum is almost empty; it's next to the St Louis Cathedral, whose bells Blanche Dubois refers to as the only pure thing in New Orleans. Just to see the chronicle of slavery, the forced migration, the auctions, the division of families, the systematised brutality, is to feel that here is a crime as great as the Holocaust, and possibly less well digested by its perpetrators and its victims.

The Museum has its go at reminding the unhappy present of its past, and there are plaques all over the French Quarter describing the dates of the houses and their ownership. There is nothing, however, to record the residence of Tennessee Williams, who put New Orleans on the map as much as Louis Armstrong and Sidney Bechet did. At night we film on the balcony where we had dinner two nights ago, opposite the house where Williams worked on a play set in Chicago called *The Poker Night*, as the streetcars rattled below his third-floor window. They came from a district called Cemetery and ended in Desire: the setting of his play became New Orleans—a street called Elysian Fields (it exists

239

but it's not in the French Quarter)—and the streetcar became celebrated in its title. Later we film on a streetcar (well, a bus) heading for Desire. It seems a cruel irony for its inhabitants that Desire is all embers rather than all promise. It's the end of the line: shacks, tenements, urban wasteland, the expense of spirit in a waste of shame. We spend two hours filming on the bus—Desire twice consummated—and feel that segregation, at least by poverty, still persists: we're the only white people who travel on the bus.

15th November 1999. Back in London at the Hackney Empire, built in the 1880s, a beautiful theatre (designed, like many of our best theatres, by Frank Matcham), an ex-music hall, now home to pantomime, alternative comedy and Shakespeare, and struggling to raise money for restoration. It has perfect proportions and excellent acoustics—every architect who is asked to design a new auditorium should be taken here and asked to examine why this theatre feels—and is—right. We're doing a piece about the inclination of Edwardian actor-managers towards the thuddingly literal in their Shakespeare productions, not stopping short at live animals on the stage. I walk over a grassy mound, through a bevy—well, four—of grey rabbits, who are so undeterred by my presence and by being on television that they happily shag away like teenagers at an Ibiza disco. And it's then that I am reminded of the occasionally unbridgeable gulf between director and actor. 'Do you think I should put my hands in my pocket, or one hand, or none?' I ask Roger, the director, and realise he is thinking, as I would be: does he really think that in the context of the camera crane, the lighting, the rabbits, the leaves and the moving scenery, that it matters *where* his hand is? Acting seems more than half shame today.

18th November 1999. Newcastle. The RSC is on tour at the Theatre Royal—another wonderful Matcham design (where were you when we needed you?). We're filming *Othello* from the wings, and occasionally filming me watching the production. I'm like a bird on a battlefield, hopping from hotspot to hotspot, avoiding the combatants, untouched by the outcome. I can turn from the intense onstage concentration, viewed through the frame of narrowly packed black flats, to the (to me) equally alluring backstage action—actors preparing like athletes to sprint on the stage, running for quick changes, picking up props, chatting in whispers, flirting, even dozing, while stage managers and stage staff pick their way between them like stretcher-bearers.

23rd November 1999. Berlin. We're on to a new episode, with a new director and crew: Brecht and Beckett, and their influence. I haven't been in Berlin since just after the Wall came down. 'Berlin is a pile of rubble next to Potsdam,' was how

Brecht found it when he returned to live in the Eastern Sector in 1947. To see the reunified Berlin is a shock: the monotonous doughy bleakness of the East has been replaced by a show of capitalism as propagandist as anything that Communism ever perpetrated: at the corner of Unter den Linden and Freidrichstrasse, at the heart of the Eastern part, there is now a car showroom which displays the latest Bentley with as much swagger as ever a statue of Lenin was displayed.

24th November 1999. Berlin is a building site, and we film on a terrace of the Reichstag: it's surrounded by industrial cranes—twenty or thirty, a herd of them, like long-necked, long-headed dinosaurs. The building has been beautifully converted by Norman Foster, and at its core is the metaphor made literal—it's possible to look down from the upturned sugar bowl of the cupola at the parliament: transparent government. The most moving part of the conversion is the preservation of the graffiti left by Russian soldiers when they occupied the building at the end of the war: triumphalist messages in Cyrillic script, burnt with candle flame onto the stonework.

Berlin is 'forever in the process of becoming, and never in the state of being', said a nineteenth-century art critic, who was buried in the same cemetery as Brecht, along with Schinkel, the architect responsible for much of the process of becoming, not to mention Hegel, Heinrich Mann, Brecht's wife Helene Weigel, and many of his collaborators. Brecht's own gravestone has no date, but the grave is scattered with votive offerings: fresh wreaths, potatoes with a topping of snow, a rose in a shell-case, a cigar butt.

Brecht lived beside the graveyard. We film his house: from the front you might think it's a small block of working-class flats, from the back it's a bourgeois villa. 'It reflects his character,' says our translator, Angelika, tartly. His rooms are pleasant and peaceful. I put my overcoat on a chair. 'Don't put it there please,' says the curator, 'it's an old piece of furniture.' And nice too: simple and elegant, a desk where he could stand to write, a table for typing—his typewriter, a Royal Quiet Deluxe. Chinese wall-hangings, Chinese theatre masks, a life mask of himself; no paintings, but a few photos: Lenin, Marx and an unrecognisably young Engels.

The bookshelves contain a huge and eclectic selection ranging from leather-bound Shakespeare and Schiller, philosophy, science, novels, to paperback thrillers (in English), such as *Stone Cold Blonde: the Case of the Nude Beauty's Corpse* and Somerset Maughan's *Liza of Lambeth.* There are several feet of shelves of the Complete Lenin, Marx, Engels and Hegel, which he took with him in exile to Denmark and Los Angeles. We look at his manuscript of *Galileo,* scrawled over by Charles Laughton and by Brecht. A correction of tense from conditional to subjunctive convinces me that his English was much better than he let on. I look at his copy (in German) of *Waiting for Godot*. Like the irrepressible *auteur* he was, he's made large cuts and inserted suggested rewrites. He planned to do a production in which scenes of world revolution would have been projected behind the characters on a cyclorama.

For all the asceticism of his work and the austerity of his ideology, the copious photographs of him show a man who loved to be photographed, in clothes that prefigure Maoist chic—good leather, good tweed—who allegedly shaved through muslin to cultivate designer stubble. By the time of his death at the age of fifty-eight he was rotting from within, corrupted by bad faith and political compromise; he'd had a heart attack, and was depressed by a recent statement from Stalin about how all art had to be social realism. But also, as the curator says, 'he had too much smoking, and did not give time for sporting activities.' We film in the cell-like bedroom where he died: a small truckle bed, more thrillers, Arthur Waley's Chinese poems, Henry Miller's *Tropic of Cancer*, and a copy of the *New York Herald Tribune* by the bedside. He died an Austrian citizen with a Swiss bank account.

We go downstairs to a surprisingly pleasant restaurant (menu including dishes from Helene Weigel's recipe book), papered with wonderful photos of Brecht and his women, and several exquisite model boxes of sets designed by Caspar Neher. Brecht's lasting gift to the theatre was in his staging: clarity, simplicity, realism. They look as if they've been designed yesterday.

24th November 1999. We drive to Dresden—two-and-a-half hours (extended to four by a characteristically horrendous accident) to film a Caspar David Friedrich painting. Dresden has been miraculously restored, but it still bears the half-healed scars of the firebombing, sandstone scorched the colour of pitch. It also bears the marks of a new assault from the West: McDonald's, Toys R Us, Holiday Inn. The Friedrich painting is called *Two Men Observing the Moon*, and shows two men standing by the trunk of a curved bare tree, looking at a golden misty moon. It's one of the few clues that Beckett ever gave away to his work—he said it had inspired *Waiting for Godot*: each act of *Godot* ends with two men and a rising moon.

25th November 1999. We film the exterior of Brecht's theatre, home of the Berliner Ensemble. It's an enviably beautiful baroque theatre—theatrical revolutions always prosper when there's a tension between the innovation on stage and the decor of the auditorium: the Royal Court, the Old Vic, the Aldwych, the Bouffes du Nord... Seeing the theatre, I'm a little less confident of condemning Brecht for having endorsed the Stalinist regime and been rewarded with his own theatre: a ghastly kitschy statue of Brecht outside is his perpetual punishment. Like every other building in Berlin, the theatre's having a refit, in preparation for a new season under a new director, who is, daringly, not opening with a play by Brecht: just one about him. We drive an hour out of Berlin to Wannsee: deserted oak woods surround a glassy lake, a ferry crosses, a solitary canoeist paddles into the distance. Silence. Sunset. Clouds rake across a sky the colour of a dying bruise. In a large, handsome house beside this lake the Final Solution was planned.

30th November 1999. Paris, in search of Beckett. He went from Trinity College, Dublin, to study at the École normale supérieur, the polishing ground for the cream of France's intelligentsia. We film outside the gates as students stream out, all of them looking as if they would comfortably fit into an Éric Rohmer film. But come to that, I would too: a man in a black overcoat hanging around young girls.

Beckett's flat from the sixties until his death was in a post-war, art deco-ish block on a wide boulevard bisected by the above-ground Metro, next to a Christian Science Church on one side, a supermarket on the other. I don't know what I'd expected—a thin, austere, nineteenth-century garret, I suppose. We film the bar he used to favour, just off the Boulevard Montparnasse. It's a pub which advertises Guinness and Kilkenny Ales and about 300 Belgian beers, where a homesick football fan might end up. But there aren't any, they're all native beer and whisky lovers. There's no relic or memorabilia of Beckett, but there is an Orson Welles Room—is it because he played Falstaff or because he drank there?

For the playwright whose subject is despair and inertia, Beckett seems to have had remarkably active life—he played first-class cricket, had numerous love affairs, was stabbed, joined the Resistance during the war, evaded the Gestapo, and was convivial company. All the people I know, and there are many, who 'had a drink with Sam', speak of him with great warmth. Nothing is as one expects from the gaunt, reclusive, melancholic persona that we infer from the plays, but why should it be? It's only celebrity interviewers who expect the work to be like the man. We film in the street where he was stabbed by a pimp, who just missed his heart. There is a black cat in the street; we ask his owner, an old woman, if we can use the cat to add a *Third Man* touch to the sequence. 'You must ask him,' she says.

3rd December 1999. Today interviews: the first with the director Bill Gaskill. I start unthinkingly: 'When you were growing up, did you feel that you were caught between two absolutes, the Bomb and the Holocaust?' Bill looks bewildered by this lumbering question. After several years, he answers: 'No.' He goes on to give a fascinating interview, particularly about the Royal Court, which he ran for several years. I love Bill's precision: 'There are certain groupings on the stage which mean one thing and one thing only. If you put a chair in the middle of the stage it means one thing, and if you move it to the side it means another. There is a kind of something to be worked towards which is precise and defined.'

And then to interview David Hare, who anatomised the bad faith of the nineties with a succession of wonderful plays about life in our times. His workplace in Hampstead, which was once the studio of painter Mark Gertler, who painted his most celebrated picture here, *Merry-Go-Round*, and wrestled with Carrington but she didn't yield to him. I'd always thought that Gertler had hanged himself from one of the iron beams above us, but apparently not—another iron beam in another studio—but if his ghost is still in residence here, it's a very benign one. David's a practised master of the role of interviewee: fluent sentences with beginnings, middles, and ends, Christian names always attached to surnames, and passion attached to ideas. He ends optimistically: 'The instinct for theatre's never going to go away—it may take an amateur form in the twenty-first century, it may not survive in these lavishly subsidised concrete palaces, but the urge to enact our destinies in person is never going to go away.' We hope.

7th December 1999. Dublin: it's swaggering with Euro enterprise, barely fewer cranes on the skyline than in Berlin, and a feeling that this is no longer a dependency: they've shaken off the British. We film by the canal where Beckett paced and looked up at the window of the nursing home where his mother was dying. Our driver tells me he's a cousin of a cousin of Beckett, who had a wooden leg, which she used to take off for swimming. He says that Beckett was once so hard up and desperate for a cigarette in Paris in the middle of the night that he went out and sold the sheets off his bed.

Off to the Wicklow Hills, where Beckett walked with his father—a continent of heather and peat and little mountain peaks in the background, wild and desolate. Standing here in the biting wind facing a camera talking about the theatre of Brecht and Beckett seems more than usually absurd. And no less so, walking mournfully on the long pier at Dun Laoghaire past a public lavatory that appears to be a popular cottaging spot. The pier features in *Krapp's Last Tape*; the lavatory doesn't.

8th December 1999. Interviews with Alan Ayckbourn and Harold Pinter. Alan has written more plays than Shakespeare, and a few years ago a poll revealed that his plays were second in the *world* to Shakespeare's in popularity (next to Brecht's). Like Shakespeare, Alan has a company (in Scarborough) and has to provide a play for them every year. He speaks admiringly of Beckett, but confesses to going to sleep during Lucky's speech while on stage playing one of the tramps. He describes Shakespeare as a big, sandy beach—every new generation comes down and scrawls furiously on it with a piece of stick, and then the tide comes in and the whole thing's as it was.

Harold talks openly, vividly and amusingly for about an hour and a half: about his own work, about Coward, and Wilde, and Brecht (who he admires greatly), and Beckett, who, he says, loved gossip: 'What's the latest?' he'd say to Harold— the 'immeasurable tenderness' of the man set against the despair. And we talk about politics. Our generation, ostentatiously cocky in the seventies, used to think that Harold came late to politics, but he points out that he was a conscientious objector against National Service in 1948, and was prepared to go to prison—taking his toothbrush along to the trial—which is a rather more thorough act of political engagement than I or any of my contemporaries made. He recommends me a poem of his—'it's pretty good, actually'—called 'Requiem for 1945', about the death of post-war hope.

Like Alan, Harold was (and still is) an actor, and talks about the tension between actor and audience that 'has to be addressed': 'You can't let them win.' He deplores the way that nowadays the audience is part of the action, and the actors part of the audience: 'I remember once when I went to see a production of *Nicholas Nickleby* at the Aldwych, and an actor I had actually directed was prancing around before the show, pretending to sell hot coconuts or something, and he came up to me, and waved a hot coconut in my face, and I said, "Bugger off." And he went away and then just as the curtain—the whole thing was about to start, he—danced down the aisle, and thrust a hot coconut in my lap...'

16th December 1999. There was the traditional fuck-up by the BBC transport department, so the taxi is waiting up the street at the wrong number. 'If BBC transport had invented sex, we'd all be virgins,' says the driver when I finally find him. We're filming in a studio off the Marylebone Road. The sequence is a piece of electronic conjuring: I stand in front of a blue screen talking about Brecht's design aesthetic, while the set of *Mother Courage* (which we filmed in a model box in Berlin) is superimposed. It seems to defy logic, but it helps if I remind myself that both I and the image of the set are in only two dimensions—which is what I feel like most of the time that I'm masquerading as a TV presenter.

Then I interview Steven Berkoff, and feel it's a shame that he can't appear in three dimensions. As if to argue his case for the body as his instrument, he uses his hands with sculptural expressiveness. He has a reputation (not entirely earned) for being a theatrical Rottweiler, but he's genial, eloquent, even witty, about the theatre he admires and has tried to create. After we've finished, the studio technicians talk about theatre. 'It's dead, isn't it?' says one genially. I slink away, not for the first time wondering who this series will be addressing.

21st December 1999. I interview Alan Bennett in my kitchen. I should have used Alan's adage as a reply to that studio technician: 'I don't think people should be made to go to the theatre if they don't want to. It makes it such hard work for the actors.' There's no playwright in the country who's better known or better liked by the public; he's one of the—quintessentially English—family, a familiar face, a national institution, even adjectival: 'very Alan Bennett', people say. Alan isn't at his happiest when talking about his own work: he reveals a 'self' in his plays and his diaries, but when he's sitting in my kitchen facing an interrogation, the 'self' is undeniably himself. But he rallies generously and answers my questions with a practised ease, aware, from his countless TV appearances, of the virtues of pithiness and brevity. Of *The Importance of Being Earnest* he says, 'Most plays are nearly completed circles and the production completes the circle; *The Importance of Being Earnest* is completed there on the page. It was a perfect play, and I think Wilde knew it. If all that business hadn't happened, he wouldn't have gone on writing plays.'

In the afternoon Deborah Warner and Simon McBurney talk about new spaces, new audiences, and, I suppose, new dawns—the need to reinvent ritual and performance. Deborah says: 'If the National Theatre suddenly had an asbestos scare and was closed down it would be the most desirable place in town to put on a show.' When I ask him if the spoken word is dead, Simon ends his interview with a marvellous paradox: 'All this fascination with the spoken word is actually an interest in the nakedness of the human body. What could indicate a greater fascination with the human body than to concentrate only on the mouth in Beckett's *Not I*? People who say there's a division between the text and the body are actually talking out their arse.'

5th January 2000. New York. I interview Liam Neeson about Irish theatre. Liam is a veteran of a thousand promotional interviews for films, so it's a comparative novelty for him to do an interview where he doesn't know the questions and has to consider the answers. He speaks feelingly and fluently of Irish theatre and being a voluntary exile and wishing he's been in Dublin for the first performances of O'Casey's plays, and of Wilde's *folie d'amour*, and his elocution lessons and his out-Englishing the English. 'I remember when I decided to come over and live in England I was very, very, very conscious of being Irish. I was aware especially when the Queen's cavalry were blown up in Hyde Park. If I was in a shop or something like that I'd put on this faux-English accent.'

Then to the Village—to Wooster Street—to interview actor Willem Dafoe about his involvement with The Wooster Group. Acting in movies underwrites his work with this avant-garde group, and he lives the enviable life of a man unencumbered by ambition, liberated from the market, pursuing his passion. He's very charming and engaging about working with the group, creating theatre like collages. I ask him what are the special properties of theatre? 'Well,' he says, 'where else can you get spat on by an actor?'

August Wilson is the best-known black playwright in the US, and getting on for the best, regardless of label. He talks about writing plays in a different way, of an African-American tradition, partly from Africa, then helped on during slavery, when it was a crime to teach a black person how to read or write. 'We simply have a different aesthetic that we've made. It's very similar to jazz: jazz is created using European marching-band instruments, and the availability of the instruments came about because of the Civil War and the marching bands and suddenly the instruments were available. Blacks took those instruments and because of their sensibility they created entirely different music out of the European instruments, you see. So I think, I see theatres the same way, if you have the tools.' And the money for the 'tools'—the theatres, and the training—has to be found. And he's optimistic that it will: 'I think that the government can be supportive, but I don't want to rely on government. I think the artists have a responsibility themselves to go out and make their art, and make it happen, on their own.'

7th January 2000. Los Angeles in pursuit of Brecht, who lived for five years in the perpetual summer of Santa Monica, in a street that could comfortably pass for Weybridge in Surrey. We drive through smoggy downtown LA to get a view over the city from Mulholland Drive, from where, as they say, you could see the sea if you could see the sea. There's a sign which tells us that the city was founded without any natural resources, like a harbour or fresh water, which gave Mr (or Colonel, as he was) Mulholland the chance to collar water-rights and make a fortune. On to Sunset Boulevard, where we stop outside a pet shop called Hound Heaven, opposite the Hollywood gothic Chateau Marmont, to do a piece to camera beneath a giant Marlboro Man. 'SMOKING CAUSES IMPOTENCE' reads the legend beneath the cut-out. Marlboro Man's cigarette displays a glorious irony: his cigarette has brewer's droop.

We film at the house where I'm staying, which belongs to my friend Gordon Davidson, the director of the Mark Taper Forum—a thriving LA theatre. The house used to belong to Viennese-born actress and writer Salka Viertel, and is haunted by Garbo (Viertel's lover), Heinrich and Thomas Mann, Schoenberg, Eisler, Brecht and Christopher Isherwood—in whose old room, in the converted garage, I'm staying, as Christopher Hampton did many years ago when he wrote

Tales from Hollywood. LA had such allure for exiles from Europe—a place with no past, where you don't have to start over by acquiring another culture—you carry it with you.

Brecht worked in this house on a screenplay with Salka Viertel. They agreed to play by Hollywood rules: no art, all compromise. The story involved a woman collaborator in the French Resistance, whose head was shaved when her treachery was revealed. The film remained unmade: Viertel failed to convince Brecht that no movie star would agree to appear with a shaven head throughout the film. These days they'd have been trampled in the rush.

I meet actor and producer, Norman Lloyd, who co-produced and acted in Brecht's *Galileo* with Charles Laughton after many had rejected it (including Elia Kazan). Brecht asked Norman to persuade Charles Laughton to stop absentmindedly playing with himself under his robes; Helene Weigel solved the problem by sewing his pockets up. Brecht also asked Norman to help him sell his house: he wanted $11,000—which is what he told Norman he had paid for it—and sold it for $13,000. Then Norman discovered he had actually bought it for $4,000. But for everything bad that can be said about Brecht, there is an opposite.

11th January 2000. Back in London outside the Theatre Royal, Drury Lane, talking about the way that playhouses expanded and spectacle replaced dialogue. The theatre that preceded the present one was owned by Sheridan and it burned down. He watched the fire from a nearby pub and wryly observed that 'a man may surely take a glass of wine by his own fireside.' This drollery has been taken to heart by a pair of cider and meths drinkers, who shelter in an alcove in the side of the theatre. I have to do several takes; each time I pass them by, they mutter feelingly: 'Prick...' Which is the word that I apply to myself as I stand on the revolve of *Les Misérables* talking about the mega-musicals later that day. I interview Cameron Mackintosh, who gives a good refutation of hierarchy of taste: 'Whatever the art is, as long it is absolutely of the best and true to what it's trying to do, then it is a marvellous piece of work, and to me there is absolutely no difference.' Popular entertainment can't be faked: it has to be in good faith.

I round off the day with another piece to camera in the subway leading from the new Imax cinema to the National Theatre. It has displaced Cardboard City, and now houses only one young man, made doubly homeless, who half-heartedly tries to extract a toll from passers-by. When I give him some money, he thanks me and says I must have been homeless once. 'No,' I say, 'just lucky', thinking of Lear's discovery of 'houseless poverty'. The subway glitters with a Milky Way of small sparkling blue lights; commuters brush by the film unit, entirely uninterested, and my memory keeps failing like a stuttering carburettor.

12th January 2000. Today we're all frayed, thin-end-of-wedge-ish, as it becomes clear that we have to achieve a great deal more in an ever-diminishing time. I stand on the Garrick stage under the rain on the set of *An Inspector Calls* with a leaking umbrella, and then interview Stephen Daldry, conscious that I'm willing him to be pithy because I know that we have to be off the stage in time for the matinée. Stephen is more thoughtful than provocative today. He says that in our disenfranchised, fractured society people want stories in the theatre—and film. As we leave the theatre an audience of schoolchildren is gathering outside the foyer. 'They won't buy anything,' says the genial Australian girl setting up the bar, 'but who'd pay £2 for a Coke?' The Coke has cost the management 12p—which goes some of the way to explaining why the young are reluctant to go to the theatre. Our day is complete when we discover that the van has been clamped.

14th January 2000. I'm in Paris to talk to Peter Brook at the Bouffes du Nord. It's the most congenial theatre I know: perfect acoustics, a sense of the past, like worn stone steps in a church, layer on layer of human presence, a touch of oriental in the tracery above the proscenium, beautifully distressed walls, plasterwork like medieval frescos. Peter has stimulated British theatre for fifty years—the last twenty-five of them from outside the country. He disclaims any desire to escape from the insularity of British theatre, but his self-exile appears to have inoculated him against the infection of self-doubt, the vagaries of fashion, the attrition of parochial sniping, the weariness of careerism, and the midlife crisis that affects most theatre directors (not always in midlife), and which comes from repetition, from constant barter and compromise. But, he stresses, nothing is achieved in the theatre that doesn't come from the practical rather than the theoretical. He's wearing a tangerine sweater with an indigo shirt, and sitting in the circle of his theatre against the terracotta walls, he glows with well-being and undiminished enthusiasm. All Peter's sentences have a shape; he speaks with no hesitations—no 'ums', 'ers' or 'wells'—by turns grave, impish and passionate.

He's still planning a huge project based on a West African novel, like all of his work a philosophical parable, but blocked at the moment by the executor's unwillingness to release the rights. He says he's liberated, undistracted by no longer being offered projects as a freelance or lured away by having to work outside the Bouffes in order to support it. Peter asks me whether I miss the NT. Well yes, I say, I do, even though I was longing for freedom. Peter talks about Prospero at the end of *The Tempest*. What would he do, he asks, without his island? You have to get a theatre, he says, and, feeling as if I'm never going to direct again—wrapped in the endless ribbon of this project—I say Yes. I say, Yes I do.

17th January 2000. 'Snow is its own country,' says the poet Douglas Dunn, which goes some of the way to explaining the foreignness of the city of Quebec—closer to New York than Toronto, but looking and feeling like a French provincial city. We're here to film Robert Lepage and his theatre. I find it hard to be pessimistic about the theatre when it harbours such a singular talent as Robert. He was born here, where his father was a bilingual taxi driver, from whom he unquestionably inherited his passion and facility for storytelling. It is bitingly cold, more than 40° below even with sun out. My grandfather was a Polar explorer so I ought to be genetically conditioned to take this in my stride. He remarked laconically in his journals: 'Minus seventy, pretty cold, I'd say.' He would have scorned my feebleness: I feel as if I've been locked in a meat freezer, throat dry with cold, lungs catching on frozen breath. We film on the ferry that crosses the St Lawrence River. The viscous glass-green water eddies violently as we cut through the ice floes, skirting huge crystal slabs like giant mouthfuls of broken teeth, garlanded with wispy freezing vapour floating over the river like ectoplasm.

Robert, not untypically, has just arrived from London. Or actually from Barcelona via London, and had to wait overnight in the airport lounge at Toronto. But he looks unusually tanned after a few days holiday in the Dominican Republic, and his energy seems undiminished as he talks about his many projects and about his new one-man show, *The Dark Side of the Moon*, which is about the Russian space project, the moon's phases, and his own childhood. All his shows make connections between subjects and cultures and people and different media. Here in his own theatrical laboratory—a converted fire station—balanced between insularity and internationalism, he devises his shows with his collaborators. Like Peter Brook, he seems to have as utopian a theatre as can be devised. And his optimism about the future of theatre is unswerving: 'I think that the theatre will, still, continue to be the mother art, and it will have, with time, been enriched by so many aesthetic, technical, ideological, revolutions that it will be even richer and even more alive and even more ephemeral.' In his hands I believe it.

18th January 2000. I've written a piece for the beginning of the series about the ephemeral nature of theatre: Michelangelo's greatest sculpture was said to have been done in snow and, like a theatre performance, it melted away, living on only in the memory. So here I am in a white wasteland, trudging, sometimes up to my knees and over, through a desert of snow, trying to illustrate the metaphor, and fearing that the sledgehammer of literalism is being applied to the nut of metaphor. I start as a black dot on the horizon and when I reach the camera, several years later, out of breath, my face feels as if it has been gnawed by a pack of wolves. I pant out my piece as if I'm pleading for freedom.

After lunch in a local café, where we discover that 'Pâté chinois' is Québécois for Shepherd's pie made with Smash, corned beef, carrots and sweetcorn, we have a treat: dog-sledging. The dogs—wolves in dogs' bodies—live in a gulag, chained to trees in a barbed-wire compound. My grandfather said that in the Antarctic the baying of the dogs 'touches the lowest depths of sadness in this vast desolation.' These huskies bay at us as if crying for a return to their wolf state, but bark happily at the thought of dragging a man on a sledge. When I get the chance to drive the dog team through the woods, they are silent; the only sound is the hush of the runners and the pad of the paws on the ice.

19th January 2000. New York again, and they're complaining of the cold. I scorn it. 8°? You don't know you've lived. Today it's Jason Robards and Peter Shaffer. Robards is a sharp seventy-eight. He talks intensely about O'Neill, almost a doppelganger: like O'Neill he had a father in the theatre, grew up in theatres, had a disturbed mother and a fractured married life, was a sailor and an alcoholic. Unlike O'Neill, he's beaten the demons: 'On the road for about four years until the parents settled down in New York again, and being at sea for so long, and being a drunk—I drank like a crazy man—all these things, and I guess I got it almost out of my system by acting in his plays.' He's probably acted in more O'Neill plays than any actor in the US, and like a campaign veteran he speaks of the music of *Long Day's Journey* in the tones of a man who loves the smell of napalm in the morning: 'Sure there are repetitions, but each time it's different, it's a symphony—each time something's repeated it's under different emotional circumstances.' I get him to speak the last speech of the play: 'That was in the winter of the senior year. Then in the spring something happened to me. Yes, I remember. I fell in love with James Tyrone and was happy for a time.'—the saddest lines of the saddest play ever written.

Peter Shaffer talks vividly about Gielgud and Brecht and Joan Littlewood and Oscar Wilde and the celebrated West End impresario Binkie Beaumont: 'I gave him the manuscript of *The Royal Hunt of the Sun*, and I'd written a line that became slightly notorious, a stage direction about the Spanish army. The line was: "They now climb the Andes." I was staying the weekend at Binkie's and John Perry was there, the partner, and they had referred not at all to the manuscript, but I overheard John Perry describing it to Binkie: "Well dear, they climb up the Andes, do they? And what do they do then? They climb down them, dear. Fancy." And I thought, I don't think this is quite the management for this play.' He talks about the endurance of the power of theatre, of the reticent Chichester audience in 1964 leaning forward, with their hands palms upwards willing Robert Stephens as Atahualpa to rise from the dead.

21st January 2000. Coulsdon mental hospital for a piece about Antonin Artaud, the French actor, director, visionary—and madman. The hospital has been disused for two years; it must have housed hundreds of patients, now beneficiaries of the 'care in the community' policy, which gave the mentally ill the franchise of the open streets. Mind you, if you weren't mad when you came here… This is a sick building, soaked in misery. Its infinitely long, tiled corridors have been made even more depressing by the addition of brown paint for a TV series called *Psychos*. Roger, the director, is anxious about using the word 'magus' in my piece about Artaud. I fight for it on the grounds of dumbing up, but he's probably right on the grounds of pretentiousness. In Berlin I had the same argument over the word 'dialectic'.

Then we drive though the galactic sprawl of South London—Coulsdon, Purley, Croydon, Streatham, Brixton, Vauxhall, Southwark, towards Patrick Marber's flat in the City. Patrick says that I made him into a playwright. It's not true: he would have become a playwright regardless. Like all producers, I'm an opportunist, I was just lucky enough to be in the road when Patrick rode by.

24th January 2000. It's the Irish episode: we're in the foyer of The Savoy Hotel, it's 6.30 in the morning and I'm talking about Oscar Wilde, who ran up a large bill here—feasting with panthers in the bedrooms, and dining with Bosie in the Grill Room. The hotel staff are wholly helpful, but we have to be out before 8.30 as they have a delegation from the MoD arriving for a meeting with a Slovenian Military delegation. Or the other way round. On to Blacks club in Dean Street, then Lobb's the bootmaker. In Lobb's the clock has stopped in 1951, redecorated by the previous Mr Lobb for the Festival of Britain. It smells of age and leather and money, but is agreeably immune from marketing, management, advertising, display, and post-modernism. The present Mr Lobb shows me round: the shop is flanked on one side by display cases including two tiny pairs of shoes—one belonging to Queen Victoria, the other to Haile Selassie. On the other side, blue-aproned shoemakers rasp away at wooden lasts for new customers. A book displays the outlines of feet from many kings, maharajahs, film stars, thriller writers, and, infamously, Horatio Bottomley and Guy Burgess. No doubt Jeffrey Archer has his shoes made here, but the ever-courteous and ever-discreet Mr Lobb merely smiles gnomically when I suggest it. He takes me below stairs, where thousands of lasts are stacked on shelves like scrolls in a catacomb. In corners of the basement sit more shoemakers working away with welt beaters, heel irons, waist irons, burnishing irons, lasting pincers, skiving knives, breasting knives, prick stichers, scrapers, fudge wheels, crow wheels, channel openers, bones, and last hooks, which draw the last from the finished shoe—they normally take about a year to make and cost £2,000. Next door is Lock's the hatter, equally revered, even if a little more prone to merchandising and modernising than Lobb's. They have an unpaid bill for Mr Wilde: he had to leave the country in a hurry. I end the day being filmed walking down Old Compton Street—not quite Wilde territory, this, but you get the idea.

25th January 2000. 'I didn't know huskies wrote plays,' says my daughter, when I tell her about my Canadian exploits. I didn't know Oscar Wilde smoked cigars. He didn't, but I find myself in a cigar shop in St James's, a little sceptical of the relevance to his life and work, but almost persuaded that there's a connection by Mary, this episode's director, and by the manager of Davidoff's, a charming and passionate evangelist for his product, which he describes as one of the last few legal pleasures. The room in which the cigars live is a huge walk-in humidor, warm and moist and smelling of wet hay. The manager offers me a small Cohiba, after rolling a few between his fingers to test their freshness and consistency. Hesitating for at least a third of a second on the grounds of propriety, I take it. This is Castro's favourite make of cigar. He smokes the nine-inch 'Esplendidos'—£32 a piece to us capitalists.

Then off to interview director Peter Gill about Lawrence's plays, which Peter directed definitively at the Royal Court in the late sixties. Peter is a Welsh working-class Catholic; he's like a highly intelligent, worldly and charming Jesuit priest. He talks in a maze of subclauses, which spiral round the subject, sparking observations about the romanticism of British theatre, the shapelessness of great plays, and the ineradicable presence of class in our culture.

Night. As the audience emerges from the National Theatre, I'm talking to the camera about the history of the campaign to establish it. A familiar face appears, accompanied by a week-old baby in a carry-cot: it's John Caird, director of *Candide,* which has just had its last night. John says he wondered who it was talking so knowledgeably about theatre history. I wish. I'm intrigued by a couple who stand looking at a leaflet for the Christmas show, *Honk! The Ugly Duckling.* 'Look, Sheryl,' says the man. 'It's got frogs in it. We must come to that.'

26th January 2000. Manchester, to do a piece about Miss Horniman, who was an Edwardian heiress to a tea fortune—a handsome woman with an artistic bent, who smoked in public, rode a bicycle in trousers, and offered a large sum of money to an actress and fellow member of her occult group, Florence Farr, for the purpose of putting on plays. Farr commissioned Yeats—also a member of the occult group—which is how Miss Horniman ended up as the money behind the Abbey Theatre in Dublin. Florence Farr, incidentally, believed in daily sex as a health tonic. Shaw was a beneficiary of this regime, as was Yeats, after years of petitioning. Miss Horniman supported the Abbey for many years, but her enthusiasm was dampened by Yeats's scorn for her artistic ambitions and her disapproval of Home Rule. She didn't like the Irish and they didn't like her, so she withdrew her money and initiated the English Repertory Movement by buying the Manchester Gaiety Theatre and endowing a group of playwrights, who wrote for the North about the North. They were called the 'Manchester School', and included Harold Brighouse (*Hobson's Choice*) and Stanley Houghton (*Hindle Wakes*).

I'm 150 feet up on a cast-iron fire escape on the side of a factory in Ancoats that is as old in years as it's high. It's very cold, I have mild vertigo—a faint desire to plummet towards the ground—and have ample time to reflect on film-making. I've directed a dozen films for television and invariably found the process wildly invigorating: every minute of the day is crammed with interest—strategy, decisions, the picture, the sound, the logistics. Every day spent making a film produces a finished piece of the puzzle, a complete element, whereas rehearsals in the theatre stretch out for ever like a snake of molecules. But acting for film is like being in the army: hours of waiting followed by a few minutes of action. And often feeling like a glove puppet. When you're directing film, the enemy is time; when you're acting, it's boredom. Later I do a piece to camera under a railway bridge, arching above me in a film-noir-ish sweep. A spectator stops for a moment, fascinated by the film camera and lights. I start my piece with the words 'George Bernard Shaw…'—at which point the spectator scarpers as if his trousers were on fire.

27th January 2000. I have a similar experience walking up a steep terraced street in Eastwood in Nottinghamshire. 'What yer filming?' says a passing woman. 'D.H. Lawrence.' 'Oh, 'im,' she says with a vinegary face. Eastwood has been comprehensively heritaged: follow the blue line on the pavements and it will take you to all the principal sites of veneration. The afternoon brings me to one of my stations of the cross—the auditorium of Nottingham Playhouse, where I was Director from 1973–1978. To remember a time in the seventies when a regional theatre did mostly new plays, as we did, with a permanent company in a changing repertoire, seems like recalling the Roaring Twenties.

1st February 2000. En route to the west of Ireland. Aer Lingus have grasped the literary opportunity: handwritten texts in the fabric of the seat covers. All I can decipher are the words: '…what has posterity done for you?…' and '…the wailing of the rain…' On the former, precious little, judging by knowing articles in the *Guardian* and *The Times* about the shortcomings of the BBC Governors, of which I am one. A few hours later, standing on the wild coast of Co. Clare, battered by the wailing rain and the lashing wind, the words of all media correspondents seem like thin spittle.

2nd February 2000. 'I will arise and go now, and go to Innisfree,' wrote Yeats, and we've risen early to follow in his footsteps to Lough Gill in Co. Sligo. The sun is rising, invisible behind the lacy mist. As the mist lifts, the landscape beyond the lake reveals itself: the hills known as the Sleeping Warrior are skirted by browny-purple, grey-green trees, heather, walled fields, and brambles shot through with iridescent slashes of red dogwood. The Isle of Innisfree itself is a disappointment. Yeats writes longingly of returning there to plant 'Nine rows of beans', and of living alone in 'the bee-loud glade'. Poetic licence, of course: Innisfree doesn't amount to a hill of beans; it's a small pimple of an island, a third of an acre, barely large enough for a single beehive. According to George, the boatman, who takes tourists round the lake in summer, the island that Yeats's 'Innisfree' celebrates was a larger island—populated at the time by a single woman whose father came from the family who lived in the nearby great house, and whose mother was a housemaid, exiled to the island when she became pregnant by him. For the tourists, George reads the poem and lards his commentary with observations on the landscape and the Nobel Prize, but today he recites 'The Lake Isle of Innisfree' for me alone (plus the ever-present cameraman and director) as he rows me to the island. We talk of Yeats having had an overwhelming moment of recollected childhood, standing in the Strand staring into a shop window at a small wooden ball balanced on a fountain, advertising mineral water. He rushed back to Chiswick with 'Innisfree' forming in his head, an anthem to homesickness.

A two-hour drive to Coole Park, often losing our way owing to the intriguing Irish sport of reversing road signs. We arrive in time for twilight, and a flight of wild swans overhead—'those brilliant creatures,' said Yeats. I do a piece to camera about Yeats and Lady Gregory, and we're treated to a sunset which smears the sky and water, bisected by the black silhouette of the wooded far shore, with magenta, lilac, topaz and lavender, distilling to the colours of fruit—peach, water melon, tangerine and blood orange—before giving way to night. The forester arrives to check up on us. I tell him that tomorrow we'll be filming on the Cliffs of Moher. 'Why's that?' he says. 'Well, it's the edge of Ireland,' I say. 'Oh, yes,' says he, 'America is the next parish.'

3rd February 2000. If the globe were not curved, if I had perfect eyesight, and if there were not a thick sea mist, I could see the next parish now. I'm standing on the titanic Cliffs of Moher, hundreds of feet above the sea, which slams their slate base with uncontained fury. It's a civil war in nature, far from the 'murmuring surge/That on th'unnumbered idle pebble chafes' that Edgar speaks of in *King Lear.* He says that fishermen appear like 'mice upon the beach'. If there were a beach here, they'd appear like earwigs. The cliffs are—what?—sheer, precipitous, vertical, immense and vertiginous. Each time I look down, my heart races. Even the gulls look scared. They settle on ledges up the cliffs, like the occupants of high-rise tenements in Hong Kong. A helicopter circles me—lone figure on the edge of Ireland looking towards the New World—but each time it passes over the cliff to the sea, the updraught thrusts it upwards, like a ping-pong ball on a column of air. After an hour or two passing through the seven stages of hypothermia, I fall greedily on a banquet of Mars bars, crisps and sausage rolls, before going to stand near the edge of another part of the cliff to perform a piece to camera. The wind is whirling in circular eddies about me, and every time I start to speak I'm blinded by hair in my eyes. Sellotape is the solution. So, with the back of my head trussed like an ill-tied parcel, I straddle the rails on which the camera is tracking, turn my body at 30° to the lens, fight to overcome a spasm of vertigo, walk towards a mark as if unaware of its presence, while trying to remember to say the words I have written in the right order, with passion, purpose and meaning. There must be easier ways of earning a living.

4th February 2000. Dublin. The old Abbey Theatre—Yeats's theatre—burnt down in the fifties. It was replaced by a building which would have looked at home in Lodz in Poland or Cluj in Romania any time in the 1960s. In Dublin, ringed by Georgian splendour, it looks preposterously ill at ease. The old theatre witnessed riots at the first performance of Synge's *Playboy*, and by the third the police had to be called. Yeats was in Aberdeen on the first night, and was woken by a telegram from Lady Gregory: 'AUDIENCE BROKE UP IN DISORDER AT THE WORD SHIFT.' Is there anything that can cause a riot in the theatre now? I suppose people fighting to get tickets to catch a sight of Nicole Kidman's coyly half-revealed buttocks is about as near as we get. Sarah Kane's magnificently provocative *Blasted* ignited a lot of hot air from theatre critics, ever eager to find a *cause maudite* to get a story placed on the front pages. Later we film in the heartland of Georgian Dublin—Trinity College—where we watch part of a literary tour of Dublin performed by two actors: Derek, who compères the show, and Ethne, his partner. They do excerpts from *Waiting for Godot* (playing Vladimir and Estragon as man and woman brings out (a) the tenderness of the relationship, and (b) their mutual dependency: the tramps have a good marriage). They perform the handbag scene from *The Importance* and anecdotes about Wilde, Shaw, and Yeats, interspersed with droll quips. 'We're standing under a bell-tower built over the spot where the first part of the college was built by Queen Elizabeth—not single-handedly you understand. Legend has it that the bell rings when a virgin passes underneath. It's been silent for years.' When we ask Derek for more anecdotes to film the reaction of his audience, he obliges us with some splendid Behan reflections on Irishmen and their relationship to drink and women (endorsed by Ethne in muttered asides) and a joke about a priest, some nuns, and a donkey's dick. Sadly not for this episode.

5th February 2000. Interview with Stephen Rea in Ryan's Pub, an ideal set for Act Two of *The Plough and the Stars*—no concessions to the fickleness of pub fashion, even down to the brass cash register. Stephen and I have been friends for nearly thirty years, and he still looks more or less the same. I look closely at him to see how he does it. Facelift? Hair dye? But, exasperatingly, no, he's just as nature intended. Stephen is anxious about the interview, but is eloquent about O'Casey and Synge and Behan and Beckett. 'We were rehearsing *Endgame* and Clov has to say to Ham, I leave you. I pointed out one occasion when he says it, and I asked Beckett, I said, when he says he is leaving here, does this mean he is going to the kitchen or he is leaving for good? "Either. Both," said Beckett. "It's always ambiguous." '

7th February 2000. London. We're filming two pieces to camera about looking back on the post-war period from the perspective of the new millennium; which, as we're on the London Eye, is roughly the perspective of the average seagull. From here people look not so much like mice or even earwigs, but ants walking on their hind legs. It's exhilarating. On a clear day you can see forever, but today it's murky and monochromatic and perfect for a pastiche of the Ferris-wheel scene in *The Third Man*. My speech is not about 500 hundred years of peace producing the cuckoo clock, but six years of war producing Brecht and Beckett. I had no problem earlier in the day remembering lines while travelling on the up-escalator under the elegant vaulting of Norman Foster's Canary Wharf station, but when it comes to doing it several hundred feet above the Thames in a glass pod under the gaze of a British Airways press officer, it's a different matter altogether. From the ground the wheel appears to turn imperceptibly; from inside, conscious that at only at a particular segment of the arc of revolution is the light, the pod, and the view in perfect synchronicity, it appears to move all too quickly, and I find astonishing and humiliating difficulty in remembering how to connect my brain and my mouth. The PR girl is very comforting: 'I only did A-level English,' she says, 'and it makes sense to me.' Back on the ground Jamie Muir, the director of the day, draws my attention to another Harold Shipman lookalike, our fifth of the day. Then to the Almeida Theatre to interview Edna O'Brien, who, as ever, skirts on the edge of Irish mysticism while talking with an intense lucidity, knowledge and sharp wit about Irish literary history.

9th February 2000. To Windsor Great Park to interview Lieutenant-Colonel Johnny Johnston, last Comptroller to the Lord Chamberlain, or, not to put too fine a point on it, the last State Censor. He's a very affable and engaging man, who explained how he had retired from the Grenadier Guards to work for the office responsible for administering royal weddings, funerals, palaces, parties and paintings, only to discover that he was also expected to adjudicate on indecency, bad language, offence to foreign dignitaries, living people, the Monarch and the Deity. The Lord Chamberlain had made several efforts to throw the job back at the politicians, but they were having none of it, so it remained an anomaly, along with responsibility for the royal swans. It was always notoriously difficult to second-guess the Lord Chamberlain's office. Who could have anticipated that 'firk' would be permissible, but 'fuck' beyond the pale? Col. Johnston clearly regarded the whole thing as a faintly exasperating farce. It's hard to escape the conclusion that much of the censorship was, implicitly, on the grounds of class— the middle and upper classes being protected from the realities of working-class life and vice versa ('Would you allow your wife or servants to read this book?' asked the Prosecution in the Chatterley Trial), and the upper classes protecting themselves from too-close scrutiny by the lower orders. When Noël Coward's *The Vortex* was submitted in 1924, the then Lord Chamberlain said that 'This picture of a frivolous and degenerate set of people gives a wholly false impression of society life and to my mind the time has come to put a stop to the harmful influence of such pictures on stage.' Which is much the same as many commentators said about Sarah Kane's play only four years ago.

Until the 1970s the only British theatre company that made an attempt to seek out an audience of people who didn't, wouldn't, or couldn't go to the theatre was Joan Littlewood's Theatre Workshop company. For years they toured the country, playing one-night stands in small halls and small theatres without a penny of support, before coming to rest at the Theatre Royal, Stratford East, where with *The Quare Fellow*, *The Hostage*, *A Taste of Honey*, *Fings Ain't What They Used T'Be*, and *Oh! What a Lovely War*, the company established a legend at least as enduring and significant as that created by the Royal Court over the same period. When *Oh! What a Lovely War* was submitted to the Lord Chamberlain he demanded that the word 'rollocks' was omitted from the song 'I don't want to be a soldier' and the word 'buttocks' was substituted. Was it for this the clay grew tall? We've travelled to Bath to interview Howard Goorney, who was an actor in Joan Littlewood's Theatre Workshop from 1938 to the sixties. What three adjectives, I ask him, would you apply to Joan Littlewood? He thinks a moment, his gaunt face crinkled like an El Greco, and then replies: 'Energetic. Knowledgeable. Loving.'

10th February 2000. At 11.30 in the morning it's too early for a drink, but I'm in The Colony Club, where I feel undressed without a glass in my hand. The small room, decorated in hangover green and eternally sparkling fairy lights dulled by centuries of nicotine, looks like the morning after a fancy-dress party. It was the genial haunt of Francis Bacon and pals, and now of the new BritArt clan. George Melly, I think, provides the continuity. It's as good a place—well, rather better than good—to do a piece about Rodney Ackland and his great play, *The Pink Room*, which was murdered by the *Sunday Times* critic, Harold Hobson. It was he—a sanctimonious Christian Scientist—who was memorably celebrated by Penelope Gilliat: 'One of the most characteristic sounds of the English Sunday is the sound of Harold Hobson barking up the wrong tree.' He barked viciously at Ackland, chewed his play to pieces and pissed all over the corpse for good measure. 'The audience at Hammersmith had the impression of being present, if not at the death of a talent, at least of its very serious illness...' he said. When Ackland rewrote the play as *Absolute Hell*, the most unsympathetic character in the play was a theatre critic, a vain, self-aggrandising, bullying bull-dyke, humiliated by having her wig pulled off.

In the afternoon we discover that pointing a camera at a public building—St James's Palace—is far from a simple matter for a UK citizen. But then, of course, we are not citizens but subjects, and as such we have to have permission from the Queen's Press Office, the Lord Chamberlain's office, the Parks Police and the Metropolitan Police (West End Central Division), before we may stand a camera on a public pavement to film the royal residence. Two musical-comedy guardsmen do a routine every minute and a half, slapping their rifles with their palms, and stamping the cobbles as if Her Majesty's enemies lay beneath them. A helpful policeman points out that we have failed to spot Princess Anne and Camilla Parker-Bowles, who have—separately—driven past us. A very large, maroon Daimler with a royal crest above the windscreen draws up outside the gates. A large, well-lunched man, who none of us can identify, gets out of the car and enters the Palace. In a gloriously comic gesture, the driver takes a black prophylactic out of his glove compartment and places it over the royal crest before he drives off. We return to The Colony Club for a shot of me approaching the club from Dean Street. One of the regulars is emerging. 'Are you going in?' he asks. 'I haven't had a drink there for twenty years,' I say. 'You should join,' he says, 'Only they wouldn't have an arsehole like you.'

11th February 2000. Brighton to interview Victor Spinetti about Joan Littlewood. He's a great anecdotalist and conjures up Joan in her prime with great vividness. While we talk, as in a séance, I can see the figure of a woman over Victor's shoulder emerging on a balcony beyond the window at the end of the room in which were sitting: it's Joan, haunting us. She's staying with Victor, as she often does, but has refused to be interviewed. 'Nothing against you, love,' says Victor, 'but she says that talking about the past would be like a dog returning to its vomit.' It's a melancholy, even tragic, way to describe a career that, at least to me, seems as important as any in the post-war British theatre. She doesn't feel that she's been remembered as she deserves, and I think she's right. The Royal Court, the 'writers' theatre', has been amply chronicled and memorialised, but then history favours those who write things down. Littlewood's productions have defied the historians: their legend lay in their spontaneity. From Victor's house we go to the West Pier, which is fighting its own battle with the past. In its heyday it housed the sort of Pierrot show on which *Oh! What a Lovely War* was based and, indeed, it featured in the bafflingly literal-minded film of the show. The pier is now derelict, but work to restore it to its full glory will start in the autumn. Until then it's home to a constellation of starlings, whose droppings decorate the elegant Edwardian ironwork like the crustaceans on a Gaudí cathedral.

14th February 2000. Dawn finds us on the M3 heading towards Southampton, the sun rising over a dusting of icing-sugar frost. By the time we've reached our destination, the apricot sunshine filtered through thin mist has been replaced by a grey drizzle. We're on an old RAF base at Calshot—a narrow spit of land, which projects into Southampton Sound. It used to be the home of 'flying boats'—planes with floats instead of wheels—which even up to the late fifties operated from here. During the last war it was used for RAF training and Terence Rattigan trained here, which explains our presence. Rattigan was once confronted with an unusual dilemma for a playwright: his plane was attacked over the Mediterranean, and he had to jettison all his possessions in order to save fuel. His new play *Flare Path* was in his kitbag, so he tore the pages out of his heavy, hard-backed exercise book and stuffed them into his flying jacket, before throwing everything else into the sea. One of Rattigan's later plays was *Ross*, which was about one of his Calshot predecessors, Aircraftsman Shaw, whose other alias, of course, was Lawrence of Arabia.

'Actors are always shy people,' says Alan Bates, when I interview him later about *Look Back in Anger*—Alan was in the first cast. It's difficult to recall the details of our feelings forty years after the event but Alan does well. What was John Osborne like? I ask. He was like a rather charming actor, says Alan. 'Luvvies? Simon Gray says we should be called toughies.'

We end the day filming in Stratford East, transformed from Joan Littlewood's day by a glamorous new-wave Tube station, a shopping centre, an independent cinema, and her theatre undergoing restoration. George Devine thought of his theatre as a church; Littlewood wanted hers to be more like a pub. Her friend, the French director Jean Vilar, said a theatre should be a place where you can embrace your neighbour, eat and drink and piss on the floor. The only time, incidentally, I have seen someone piss on the floor of a pub was in the pub next to the Royal Court in the seventies: a middle-aged woman, drunk, weary and perhaps just a bit eccentric, cleared a space like a crop circle among the crowd of actors, Grenadier Guardsmen and Sloane Square shoppers. Tonight I'm walking and talking along a pavement between a church and a pub enduring the poultice effect of a film camera. Tossers are waving and shouting through the pub window: 'Fucking luvvy!; other tossers jump in front of the lens shouting ecstatically: 'I'm on telly!!' It's not that exciting, it really isn't.

15th February 2000. In the newly restored Royal Court, the history of the build-ing is artfully acknowledged without encrusting it with self-regarding historical baggage. The restoration recognises that theatres are marinated in audiences, they soak up layers of tone like musical instruments—even the apparently impermeable concrete-walled Lyttelton and Olivier theatres (although Albert Finney once said to me: 'Who'd make a violin out of fucking concrete?'). In the Royal Court now, as in a Rogers building, the innards are outwards: brick, plas-ter, wood, metal girders and rivets have been exposed. At the heart of the theatre—the auditorium—everything is right: the slope of the stalls, the rake of the stage, the elevation of the circle, the width and height of the proscenium; actors can be seen and heard, the audience feel comfortable with them, the atten-tion is focused, everyone shares more or less the same viewpoint of the action. The architect, Stephen Tompkins, tells me that Jocelyn Herbert and Bill Gaskill, who are the closest living protagonists of George Devine's regime, have given the restoration their blessing. They had an informal ceremony to recommission the building, standing on the stage in silence for a minute with the lights out. The architect told me that Jocelyn gripped his arm and thanked him. He said that the least enthusiastic body to have done the tour of the theatre was the Lon-don arts editors, who only wanted to know how much it had cost.

It's not Devine that I'm celebrating today for the series: it's Harley Granville-Barker—actor, playwright, director, father-figure (at least to me)—who ran the Royal Court (with manager John Vedrenne) for three years from 1904. He antic-ipated George Devine's regime with seasons of new British plays (including many by Shaw) and European ones (including Ibsen and Maeterlinck). They set criteria of vision and adventure for the whole century—and happily the theatre building acknowledges this.

16th February 2000. I interview Fiona Shaw about Shaw, Wilde and Yeats in my house. With a film crew squeezed round the sofa where I'm used to sitting watching TV with my family, I feel as if we're playing an ambitious children's game. Fiona is nervous and self-deprecating, but when the interview begins she pours out an almost seamless stream of dense argument, anecdote and epigram-matic wit. Dublin, she says, was 'the jumping-off ground, the Ellis Island of culture', Irish wit 'the self-destructive ability to score in the short term whilst losing the war'; the tragedy of the famine was 'that the country just bred its nation for export'; drink was always an Irish curse: 'Caesar wrote about going to Hibernia, and he said that they just talked and drank all the time, so I suppose it isn't connected to recent modern history'; Wilde on Shaw: 'GBS is no truer in reality than a pantomime ostrich'; and the future of theatre: 'the theatre is a fan-tastic whore and could be anything, if a thousand atom bombs drop somebody will stand up in the ashes and tell a story.'

Many actors (most good ones) are highly intelligent; few are highly articulate. Fiona's fluency never leads her into waffle, but as an actor she often has to struggle to conceal her intellectual brilliance, like a great beauty concealing her glamour.

17th February 2000. It's five o'clock in the morning, and I'm watching The Savoy wake up. Like a slow-motion natural-history film, the hotel unfurls before me: the smart, dark-suited staff move unostentatiously about their business like undertakers, newspapers are slotted into paper bags for delivery to individual rooms, brass fittings and ashtrays are polished, telephones tinkle briefly and rooms are booked from different time zones, bin bags of bread rolls and pallets of loaves arrive, Japanese guests depart, all of this accompanied by the melancholy obbligato of a vacuum cleaner.

From the backstage at The Savoy Hotel to backstage at the Theatre Royal, Drury Lane. The theatre is dark, and I stand on the vast stage with my interviewee, Nick Hytner, looking out at an auditorium which seats 2,500 but seems comparatively intimate, and wondering, not for the first time, why contemporary architects are so hopeless at theatre design. The front of the circle features a roll of honour: Sheridan, Garrick, Irving, Kean... The sign-writers are probably getting to work on 'Cameron Mackintosh', whose musical *Miss Saigon* was directed here by Nick. Chariot races have been run here with real horses in *Ben-Hur*, a full steam train has mauled a passenger in *The Streets of London*, and in *Miss Saigon* a helicopter lifted Vietnamese refugees to safety. Nick felt that he could have done the helicopter with a couple of revolving lights, but he was outvoted by his colleagues who said the audience wanted to see a helicopter, just as they had wanted to see horses and a steam engine. What they want, of course, is to have their heart touched, as they did with grand opera, but now the music is all bathos and the feeling all pathos, and classical music and popular music are divided by an unbridgeable chasm.

I end the day on the roof of the Gielgud Theatre at sunset. The Gielgud used to be The Globe, and was the headquarters in the forties and fifties of the theatrical empire of Binkie Beaumont. Actors, directors and writers were subject to his absolute control over star-studded, middlebrow, West End theatre. He ruled with an iron whim from an eyrie at the top of the theatre, which was reached by a lift which became known as 'The Smallest Lift in the World'. Legend has it that the matronly Dame Marie Tempest, having shared the lift with a young actor, turned to him at the top and said: 'After all that young man, we will just have to get married!' Other actors found themselves sharing the lift with Binkie himself after meetings in his office. A bit of a squeeze.

18th February 2000. We're back at The Savoy Hotel to do another piece about Noël Coward, this time about *Private Lives*, which involves a divorced couple, each just married to a new partner, meeting on adjoining balconies of their honeymoon suites… The play—title and all—came to Coward in a sleepless night, which is why I'm talking about it to a camera while it tracks past an unmade bed and follows me to the window, where I stare down at the Thames at dusk wondering what 'The Master', as he was preposterously known, would have made of the London Eye. It would have been the subject of one of those droll remarks like the one he made at the Coronation in answer to the question: 'Who is that man sitting next to the Queen of Tonga?' 'Her lunch.' All Coward's witticisms— like Wilde's (of whom Coward said: 'One of the silliest, most conceited and unattractive characters that ever existed')—have to be spoken in the 'voice', in Coward's case an arch, contrived, synthetic sing-song voice, designed, according to Nick Wright (with whom I'm writing the book of the series), to put the public off the scent of his sexuality. It was supposed to be the antithesis of camp: 'definite, harsh, rugged', according to Cecil Beaton. I don't think the plan quite came off.

His best work—*The Vortex*, *Private Lives* (written, like *Look Back in Anger*, in three days) and *Design for Living*—brilliantly combine high comedy, social satire and ambiguous sexual identity. *Blithe Spirit* and *Hay Fever* are very funny comedies, but even so I've always found them oppressively insular, straitjacketed in remorseless silliness. As a child I knew only his songs. One of my father's few records was *Noël Coward at Las Vegas*, whose iconic cover featured Coward standing in the desert in a white tuxedo holding a teacup and saucer, face tanned like a handbag. The photograph—even at the age of eight—always struck me as infinitely sad.

Saturday 1st April. I'm wandering in Abney Park Cemetery, Stoke Newington, among tombstones which mark the graves of those who have been 'called to rest', or 'passed', 'departed this life', or 'fallen asleep'. 'The WORLD'S greatest MUM' is buried here, and a straying apostrophe has created an Irishism: 'ETERNAL REST GRANT UNTO HIM O'LORD'. A little further on a tombstone reads 'THEATRE: RIP'. This artfully death-like, lichen-covered stone has been placed here by our designer so that I can do a piece to camera about the death of theatre. I'm wary of offering a hostage to fortune; I delivered a lecture ten days ago, a passionate defence of the theatre and an exhortation to the Government and the Arts Council to revive the ailing regional theatre, and my reward was to be celebrated in every 'Quotes of the Week' column with this excerpt: 'Theatre is often regarded in Britain as the cricket of the performing arts—meaning archaic, quaint, thinly attended, and not done as well as it used to be.' This quote will dog me for years, being invoked to mock the medium which I cherish.

A cemetery official tells us that Maurice Chevalier is buried here. He interprets our disbelief as ignorance, and does an excerpt from *Gigi* (with dance) in order to remind us who Chevalier was. He points vaguely towards a clump of ivy-covered tombstones and leaves. Only later do I realise that it is April 1st.

A wet afternoon in Dean Street finds us at Soho Theatre to do a piece to end the series. I stand on the stage with my back to the auditorium; the camera is then locked off as the audience, including me, are filmed in a series of time lapses as they take their places. I sit in the front row and for a long time I am the oldest person there by possibly twenty years, most of the audience being fans of Adam Garcia, star of the *Saturday Night Fever* stage show and this afternoon's play. The teenage girls leave a cordon sanitaire around me as if grey hair is catching. Finally I am joined by someone as old as me who, says Spike the cameraman, looks like Teresa Gorman's mother. The auditorium is full: at least in the first theatre to be opened in the new millennium at 2.30 on a Saturday afternoon, it is triumphantly obvious that the death of theatre has been greatly exaggerated.

Playing Mad

I was asked to give a lecture to the South London branch of the British Psychoanalytical Society in 2009.

———•·•———

I'm not fluent in the language of psychiatric discourse, or at least I'm fluent only in the fashion of a dilettante who can pretend to any expertise under the guise of fiction. I play at it. I pretend. That's my craft, a professional pretender or, as novelists often say about their craft, a professional liar.

Like all people who work in the theatre I'm drawn to madness. Not because my mother went mad—or at least lost her mind with Alzheimer's disease, if that's the same thing—or because, as they say on notices in local government offices 'YOU DON'T HAVE TO BE CRAZY TO WORK HERE BUT IT HELPS', but because it's the raw material of much of drama, and because as a director I'm obliged to take the view of the psychotherapist: that the last thing that can be said of a mad person is that his actions are without cause. Or as G.K. Chesterton said: 'The last thing that can be said of a lunatic is that his actions are causeless… for the madman (like the determinist) generally sees too much cause in everything.'

Drama is our way of seeing into people's lives, and, because the stuff of most of our daily lives is much the same as our neighbour's, drama concerns itself with the extremities—families falling apart, a mother killing her children, a son killing his father, a brother killing a brother, hating, fighting, dying, and—occasionally—loving.

The two best—and best-known—plays in the English language—*Hamlet* and *King Lear*—concern themselves with madness and fear of madness, and at the other end of the spectrum—what we might call the EastEnder part—schizophrenia, personality disorder, psychosis, manic depression are common plot devices that offer the scriptwriter the possibility of apparently motiveless action, random character development, violence, suffering, pain, and panic. In short, a jolly good episode.

We've become vicarious observers of madness through our media. We're offered deranged people as part of the currency of so-called 'normal' entertainment, and as part of the daily diet of news reporting. The serial murderer obliges us with an episodic narrative structure to his crime—a beginning, an extended middle and an end. A Frederick West offers us a banquet of indignation, sickened horror, moral outrage, and the fascination with something that we find hard to give a name if we can't call it 'evil'.

I found the trial of Rosemary West extraordinarily disturbing. This was a trial whose evidence was so unsettling that even the tabloids felt unable to publish the details. That wasn't an uncharacteristic fit of propriety on their part. It was this: that it was impossible to reconcile the literally unthinkable cruelty with the palpable humanity of the woman. An observer wrote at the time: 'Her testimony so stilled the court that journalists hesitated to turn the pages of their notebooks. When her daughter looked at Rose, said one of them, it was with such gentle yearning that it capsized all who saw it.'

By any definition of behaviour, the Wests' actions were insane—'mad'—and yet within their family there existed a sort of 'normal' family life. Said one of the daughters of her father: 'It was the only kind of love I knew from him, and I never complained.' No amount of reportage or analysis will enable me to understand these relationships. Only by making a huge imaginative leap, by putting oneself in the position of the child—or the father—only through empathy, through the agency of art—through drama or through fiction—is it possible to begin to grasp the all-too-human paradoxes of the banality of evil.

Within drama itself there is a similar problem: the actors and directors have to see each character not from the perspective of the protagonist, but as the epicentre of their own universe. In any production of *King Lear*, it's vital that the production makes us see Lear through the eyes of his daughters, that they are not presented as motivelessly malignant monsters. And any production of *Hamlet* has to make us feel that the love between the frankly awful Polonius and his son Laertes and his daughter Ophelia is so strong that his death can engender wild rage from him and madness in her. As the West daughter said: 'It was the only kind of love I knew from him, and I never complained.'

Shortly after I had become a director, or at least called myself a director, and had found someone to support my calling, I wrote a play, an adaptation of a novel about schizophrenia. The novel was written by Jennifer Dawson, and it was called *The Ha-Ha*. It was light, frightening, and witty.

Researching for the production of the play, I visited a mental hospital in Lincoln. I spoke at length to a doctor, who, unlike the other doctors, wore a white coat and had a stethoscope tumbling out of his pocket. There was little he didn't know about the pathology of schizophrenia, and little that I could do to stop him telling me. After twenty minutes I was anxious to leave to talk to some patients, and as I turned away he said: 'You know why I'm here, don't you?' 'Mmmmm, no, I don't think I do.' 'The Prime Minister is trying to kill me,' he said, and only then did I realise that the doctor was a patient.

The Ha-Ha had an epigraph. A poem by Blake, called 'The Fly':

Little fly,
Thy summer's play
My thoughtless hand
Has brushed away.

Am not I
A fly like thee?
Or art not thou
A man like me?

Am I not a fly like thee? The question is this: whose perspective is given authority? It is the job of the artist—and the psychiatrist—to be impartial, to be innocent of judgement. As Chesterton said: 'If a man says he is Jesus Christ, it is no answer to tell him that the world denies his divinity; for the world denies Christ's.'

I suppose the proposition of my play—and it was a proposition that was at the time, in 1968, being propagated evangelically by R.D. Laing—the proposition was that in some sense schizophrenia was a strategy for dealing with a world from which you had become alienated. Thus playing mad is paradoxically living on your wits.

Laing was of the school of psychiatry that called itself 'anti-psychiatry', whose practitioners saw madness as a blessed event, an apotheosis on the trip to discovering one's self. But, as the writer Jenny Diski wrote recently: 'I'm inclined to doubt now that the mad really wanted their doctors to be as mad as they were.'

But it's sometimes hard not to be persuaded of the legitimacy of madness when you read something like this entry in the journal of Henry James's sister, who fought for Irish liberation and in her head fought for her own liberty and her own sanity:

As I used to sit immovable reading in the library with waves of violent inclination suddenly invading my muscles, taking some one of their myriad forms such as throwing myself out of the window or knocking off the head of my father as he sat with his silver locks, writing at the table, it used to seem to me that the only difference between me and the insane was that I had not only all the horrors and suffering of insanity but the duties of doctor, nurse and straitjacket upon me too.

Like many young men I was influenced by *Hamlet*, and I suppose I often flirted with the notion that to play mad is a plausible tactic, even a choice, a way of negotiating a difficult family, a means of gaining authority and attention, but I was disabused of this satisfying metaphor when a friend of mine—a schizophrenic—walked barefoot into a line of oncoming traffic. It's an alluring construct that madness offers a critique of society, or the family, but it's self-serving to believe it.

I'm not convinced that the Laingian fallacy has disappeared. In many books, populist and scientific, we are offered speculation about the boundaries and connections between sanity and madness with the sometimes explicit assertion that the perceptions of the mad—even if they are in acute pain—are somehow superior to those of the sane. I think this is a pernicious romanticism no less disturbing for being propagated by a nineteenth-century poet than a twentieth-century drug visionary or a clinical psychiatrist.

In *Touched with Fire*, Kay Jamison makes an good case for the link between manic depression and creativity, citing Byron, Coleridge, Van Gogh, Robert Lowell, John Berryman, Sylvia Plath, Virginia Woolf and many others as examples. Her argument is not reductive: she doesn't insist that madness is the sine qua non of creativity, but that the manic-depressive and artistic temperaments have a great deal in common. However, it's hard not to infer from her book that artistic genius is sanctified, as it were, by a touch of madness. For the manic-depressive plumber or electrician this is bad news; they have to suffer without the solace of literary success. But a bipolar state is not, I think, a career choice.

Shakespeare anticipates most of our debates about madness in *Hamlet*, the story of a highly neurotic, grief-stricken young man who chooses to play mad both because it offers him protection, but also because it's the role for which he is temperamentally suited, and for which, in a sense, he's rehearsed. When he says, towards the end of the play, that he was punished with a sore distraction, it is hard to deny his own assessment—his extreme grief, his seeing the ghost of his father, his reported encounter with Ophelia and his actual encounter with her and with his mother, his killing of Polonius, his self-doubt and his self-contempt all add up to irrefutable evidence of 'sore distraction'. He's labouring under an overwhelming fault, that of incipient insanity, even if, in a Laingian sense, his madness, feigned or real, is an objective response to a world that's mad, whose politics—the usurpation of the kingdom, the repression, the spying, the fear—have destroyed all natural feeling and affection. To play mad is sometimes the only sane option.

The poet Robert Bridges described it brilliantly when he spoke of

> the artful balance whereby
> Shakespeare so gingerly put his sanity in doubt
> Without the while confounding his reason.

When Laurence Olivier came to play Hamlet in the 1930s he wanted to make his performance 'real'. For Olivier, 'realism' meant psychological realism, which meant sexual subtext, which of course meant Freud. Olivier visited Ernest Jones, Britain's leading Freudian, who fed him the Oedipal readings of *Hamlet*, which Olivier swallowed hook, line and sinker. Olivier's Hamlet was a man of action driven to impotence by the subconscious realisation of his love for his mother. By 1947, when he came to make a movie of *Hamlet*, Olivier was so convinced of Freud's theory that the finished film is a vivid testament to Freud, complete with phallic towers containing swirling staircases which lead endlessly upwards, and a vividly erotic relationship between mother and son, accentuated by the actors' evident similarity in age.

The irony about Olivier turning to Freud to play Shakespeare is that Freud had turned to Shakespeare for understanding and inspiration. He'd read Shakespeare from the age of eight and was convinced that art often revealed more about the mind and emotions than psychology.

Hamlet is a poem of death. It charts the great human rite of passage: from immaturity to accommodation with death. Hamlet grows up, in effect, to grow dead. Until he leaves for England—'From this time forth/My thoughts be bloody or be nothing worth'—he's on a reckless helter-skelter swerving between reason and chaos. When he returns from England he is changed, aged, matured, reconciled somehow to his end. We see Hamlet in a graveyard obsessed with the physical consequences of death, and then, in a scene with Horatio prior to the duel, he talks to him about his premonition of death:

> thou wouldst not think how ill all's here about my heart. But it is no
> matter... it is but foolery... We defy augury. There is a special
> providence in the fall of a sparrow. If it be now, it is not to come; if it be
> not to come, it will be now; if it be not now, yet it will come. The
> readiness is all. Since no man of aught he leaves knows aught, what is't
> to leave betimes? Let be.

It's an astonishing resolution which comes shortly before his death. It is as if out of the vortex of his own suffering, his extended bout with his own sanity, he has emerged to find some sort of peace, some sort of balance to which perhaps we might put the name 'sanity'.

I directed the play first in 1980 at the Royal Court Theatre with Jonathan Pryce. His father had just died, and it was the immediacy and intensity of his own grief which gave birth to the notion of doing away with the ghost of his father—Old Hamlet—and presenting, to an audience sceptical of paranormal phenomena, the father speaking through his son. Jonathan made the phenomenon of 'belly speaking' terrifying and, at the same time, touching. His whole performance walked a knife edge between danger and an almost childlike vulnerability. Madness never seemed far away.

Although my production of *Hamlet* made a feature of possession, the phenomenon is at the heart of the process for all actors of assuming a character, of 'playing a part'. It's the most mysterious, even mystical, element in acting. Like the 'belly speaking' of Jonathan's Hamlet, it has the characteristics of demoniacal possession—the phenomenon in which the devil besets the soul inside the body, when Satan is said to 'inhabit' the victim. Virtuous people were supposed to be immune from it, and perhaps the facility of actors to be possessed not by demons but by the characters they are playing has made some contribution to the fiction that they are in some way less virtuous than the normal run of society.

The phenomenon of possession is often apparent in flashes during rehearsals when an actor suddenly develops a particular rhythm, an inner ear for the character, and the voice and movements of his body no long seem his own. It is as if, rather than the actor occupying the character, the character has occupied the actor. During an early runthrough of a play, the actors are always charged with a febrile nervous energy, and at this point the 'spirit' of the character often seems to drive the actor's imagination and invention, and things that have never happened in rehearsals occur spontaneously and effortlessly. It is almost unnerving to see the actor's own personality, which may be quiet, unforceful and inarticulate, be wrenched, thrown about, transformed, and, literally, possessed by another persona. At the end of the runthrough, when this has occurred, the actor is left exhausted, etiolated, as if the 'spirit' has departed and left him to learn how to summon the demon again, and how to harbour and accommodate it. In effect, the actor's problem is how to repeat the experience without the wasteful energy; an actor can't live the experience every time, he has to learn to simulate it. This is the true test of the professional—they must experience possession, endure passion and yet, like firewalkers, remain untouched by the experience.

For all its sensational associations, it's a remarkably unsensational event to witness. To some degree it's an essential part of all rehearsals and, if not entirely taken for granted by actors, is no more celebrated than the rising of a soufflé would be by a chef. Audiences take it for granted and recognise the phenomenon only when it's inescapable—when Edna Everage, for instance, strikes them over the head with a gladiola despite being a rather studious, thoughtful, mild-mannered man.

Acting is a mystery. It is, in the medieval sense, a craft, and yet is also something that is obscure, enigmatic, beyond comprehension. The actor is a person who imitates other people—that's how we learn as children, mimicking the language and the gestures of our elders. As adults, all of us, consciously or not, are actors—we simulate feelings we don't feel, we lie, we pretend to be what we aren't. It is this latent though practised skill that lures so many people to believe that they can become actors: if everyone does the actor's job in life, then anyone can do it on a stage. Couple this with a desire, among shy people, to assert an alter ego, and you go some of the way to explaining why the acting profession is so overcrowded with hopeful aspirants. It's a tantalising paradox that what seems so familiar and attainable to us should be so exasperatingly difficult to do; without talent, will and character, it's impossible.

Good acting embraces a number of paradoxes: actors must be conscious of themselves, but not be self-conscious; they must know themselves, but they must also, on stage, forget themselves; they must be self-less, but will undeniably be selfish; and they must find the balance, while acting, between the heart and the head, instinct and reason.

It's difficult to achieve this equilibrium in life, which is probably why we give such extravagant praise to those who achieve it in art. To act properly, in life as in art, implies a moral dimension that makes us want actors to be exemplary beings. It's an impossible prescription—to seek attention for oneself but not be narcissistic, to perform but not to show off, to communicate, but in someone else's voice—is it any wonder that actors often seem as ill at ease offstage as politicians outside the House of Commons?

The best actors have much in common. They know how to use a space and invariably make the space they occupy onstage or in the frame of a film seem expressive. The bad ones just stand there. Nureyev said: 'A great dancer is not one who makes a difficult step look easy, but one who makes an easy step look interesting.' It's the same with actors, the ability to transform the commonplace—to make gods of men, and men of gods. The best actors need to communicate with each other and with an audience; the bad ones never make contact, never make themselves heard. Courage is essential to the good actor; in the bad it is mere folly.

In life, acting breeds bitterness—pretending to feel what we don't feel, feigning interest when we're bored, being polite when we feel resentful, delighted when we're disappointed, sane when we feel insane. But acting for a living breeds resilience and fortitude, a kind of stoicism. Once I saw a performance of Ralph Richardson, and afterwards I told friend of mine who was in the production how remarkable I thought he'd been. 'Yes, it's amazing,' she said. 'I saw him looking very melancholy before the show, and I said "Are you alright, Ralph, you look very sad?" "Oh, you know," he said, "I've had a bit of bad news," he said, "My brother's been killed. In a fire." "Oh Ralph," she said, "How awful." "Yes," he said. "Still, there's one consolation—it can't happen again."'

Which might be said of King Lear's return to sanity—unless you believe, as I don't, that Lear suffers from senile dementia. Lear's madness is not senile dementia, even if it has characteristics of it—incoherent rage, obsession with sex, and telling the truth about politics to the blind Gloucester:

> A man may see how this world goes with no eyes. Look with thine ears… Get thee glass eyes, and like a scurvy politician seem to see the things thou dost not.

As I understand it senile dementia is irreversible. The only known case of reversal was the businessman, Ernest Saunders, who was sent to prison for financial fraud. He appealed and in his appeal a doctor said he had diagnosed him as a sufferer from pre-senile dementia. After his appeal was allowed, astonishingly, he recovered.

Lear too recovers. He is a lonely eighty-two-year-old who wants to know if he's loved for himself. He's a domestic tyrant. And aren't we all at times if we catch ourselves shouting at our children, and exercising arbitrary justice, and exploiting our natural but unearned authority? Lear wants to be young again with no cares and no responsibility. He just wants to hunt, eat, drink, and knock around with the lads. He sees everything in terms of price, of number, of capital. He tries to measure his daughter's love for him in terms of their worth, and gradually he's forced to construe his relationships in terms of feelings.

> O, let me not be mad, not mad, sweet heaven!
> Keep me in temper; I would not be mad.

But Lear *does* go mad through an overload of remorse and pain and anger. His madness is a purging of his mind. When he is recovered and reconciled with his daughter Cordelia, he speaks with calm wisdom. These lines are almost my favourite from Shakespeare:

> Come, let's away to prison.
> We two alone will sing like birds i'th'cage.
> When thou dost ask me blessing, I'll kneel down
> And ask of thee forgiveness; so we'll live,
> And pray, and sing, and tell old tales, and laugh
> At gilded butterflies, and hear poor rogues
> Talk of court news, and we'll talk with them too,
> Who loses and who wins, who's in, who's out,
> And take upon's the mystery of things
> As if we were God's spies.

When I was at the National Theatre we took a production of *King Lear* to Broadmoor Hospital. The patients sat close to the action, which was played on the floor in a large room in daylight. They concentrated with a rapt intensity and were absolutely motionless until Lear's line:

Is there any cause in nature that makes these hard hearts?

And a young patient slowly and sadly shook her head.

There are countless thousand meretricious fictional representations of the disturbed mind which seek to reveal the meaning of the mad to a public ever eager to observe, be curious, and, above all, be entertained. In this respect are we that far from the eighteenth century, when people used to go to Bedlam, pay a fee—it was free on Tuesdays—peer into the cells of the patients and laugh at their antics? Visitors were allowed to bring long sticks with which to poke and enrage the inmates.

In the case of bad art we're involved in the same sort of voyeurism, vicariously poking the victims through the bars. We're tourists of human behaviour, being asked to observe some at best half-truths about human behaviour marinated in a sentimental soup. Good art, however, invites empathy: good art enables an audience to see within a character, to witness the extent to which we are all human, but at the same time all different. We all have some hint of madness in our selves, some flash of anger, some uncontrollable passion. The point of acting, of drama, is to inhabit other people's brains, to create characters with whom one can empathise, understand, feel compassion, or—if they're evil—acknowledge as fellow humans.

The philosopher Simone Weil wrote this:

> The love of our neighbour means being able to say to him: 'What are you going through?' It is a recognition that the sufferer exists, not as a specimen from a social category labelled 'unfortunate' but as a man exactly as we are. To forget oneself briefly, to identify with a stranger to the point of fully recognising him or her, is to defy necessity.

Drama—indeed all art—is a way of 'defying necessity', drawing us into a heightened awareness of other people's feelings and other people's lives. It enables us to put ourselves in the minds, eyes, ears and hearts of other human beings.

Fiction and drama also act as a sort of template against which we can measure our own lives, perhaps to confirm our own sanity, or to comfort ourselves that 'There but for the grace of God, go I'. Nor *do* I go there—to madness, I mean—except in the rather limited sense of being prone to what I'd describe as 'occupational depression'. Or as Byron said, 'We of the craft'—he meant poets—'are all crazy, some are affected by gaiety, others by melancholy, but all are more or less touched.'

Directors are subject to the occupational hazard of obsession and exhilaration leading up to a first night or the end of a film, being followed by the withdrawal of adrenalin and consequent depression. Ingmar Bergman said he'd been depressed most of his life, and he'd always thought that it was just his nature. Then he stopped running the Royal Dramatic Theatre and his depression lifted.

Depression should have a blacker name: 'melancholia' is better, a shrinking of the spirit. William Styron in his wonderful book *Darkness Visible* talks of its indescribability and of 'despair beyond despair'. This is the sort of thing—from Virginia Woolf's diary:

> I'm screwed up into a ball; can't get into step; can't make things dance; feel awfully detached; see youth; feel old; no, that's not quite it: wonder how a year or two is to be endured. Think, yet people do live; can't imagine what goes on behind faces. All is surface hard; myself only an organ that takes blows, one after another... the inane pointlessness of all this existence; hatred of my own brainlessness, and indecision; the old treadmill feeling of going on and on and on, for no reason.... worst of all is this dejected bitterness. And my eyes hurt; and my hand trembles.

Or, less eloquently, here's my own version from my diary: 'I feel as if my brain has a number of compartments, like dog traps, out of which wild things emerge—insects, spiders, frogs, snakes, and wolves, surrounded by a gnawing cold damp wind that permeates everything. I'm like water, everything moves me.' Depression is treatable—work cures everything. Until it doesn't.

I don't think it was an idle whim of Freud to look to drama for an understanding of the mentally ill—and the limits of dealing with that understanding. This is from Macbeth's conversation with his wife's doctor:

> Canst thou not minister to a mind diseased,
> Pluck from the memory a rooted sorrow,
> Raze out the written troubles of the brain
> And with some sweet oblivious antidote
> Cleanse the stuff'd bosom of that perilous stuff
> Which weighs upon the heart?

To which the doctor replies:

> Therein the patient
> Must minister to himself.

Epilogue

Gardening

These two final pieces were largely inspired by my mother. The first was written for the Daily Telegraph *in 2007, the second for the* Daily Mail *to be published on Mother's Day in 2011.*

My mother loved flowers, mostly geraniums, pelargoniums, gladioli and dahlias. She nurtured cuttings and grew seedlings in her greenhouse, lavishing an attention on her plants which I resented for not being directed towards me. Out of self-interest I was less disdainful of her raspberries, strawberries, gooseberries, redcurrants, onions, runner beans, peas and artichokes—she was a wonderful cook—but I never gave her the credit for being knowledgeable and passionate about something that I thought, with the careless cruelty of an arrogant teenager, was a contemptible activity.

In spite of my mother's enthusiasm and my sister becoming a successful landscape architect, the suggestion that one might be nearer to God in a garden seemed as implausible to me as being nearer to God in a dodgem car. I would skitter—as you may be doing now—over lines as beautiful as these (by Shelley): 'And the Spring arose on the garden fair,/Like the spirit of love felt everywhere./And each flower and herb on the earth's dark breast,/Rise from the dreams of its wintry rest.' When people started talking about their gardens—and there are allegedly twenty-seven million self-confessed gardeners in the country—I would recoil as if avoiding tubercular infection, and if I had any feelings at all about gardening, it was to want to dynamite every village fête and flower show. Frankly I would have been more interested in coracle-making than

277

gardening. My position was pretty close to the Michael Gambon character in David Hare's *Skylight*: 'Fucking gardening! If I could make it illegal, I would!'

Then I changed. But by that time my mother was lost to Alzheimer's disease and was beyond gardening, cooking or even speech. With a wry poetic justice, I became a gardener because of my mother's death. When she died my sister and I sold the house in Dorset that we had grown up in. With the money from the sale my wife Suze and I bought a house in Gloucestershire: three small cottages joined together and strung out in a ragged terrace on the side of a sheer valley, with a striking view of a beech wood and a steeply tilted field sprinkled with hawthorn bushes, barely another house visible. The couple occupying the house had separated: wife and children in the old part of the house—soon-to-be ex-husband in the other. He had marked out his territory by planting a row of leylandii, a fortification that marked the boundary between spouses.

The garden, about three-quarters of an acre, had not been cherished—a few half-hearted beds, a tufted lawn that sloped steeply away from the house, and below that a wilderness as impenetrable as an enchanted forest: brambles, hawsers of old man's beard tangled in thickets of hazel and willow, old sheds, paint tins, wardrobes. However, the ground was well-drained, sheltered and south-facing, with a fertile if limey soil. My first step was to savage the leylandii with a chainsaw, an action which characterised my early period as a gardener when the garden was an extension of the toolbox, boy's stuff with saw and shredder, mower and strimmer. With generous friends we started to discipline the wilderness, hacking through the brambles with an axe, filling countless skips with rubble and corrugated iron. With the vicar's second-hand rotavator, I cleared the roots. Meanwhile, Colin, the drystone waller, built retaining walls and imported tons of soil for the lawn and terracing. Sue started to plant—tentatively at first—the few beds and borders.

She planted a wild patch—meadow grass, scabious, cornflowers, daisies, clover, poppies—and encouraged forget-me-nots and aquilegia to grow in the grouting between the York stones, while I worried about the male things: neatening up the hedges, turfing the lawn, marking out paths, creating rose beds. In our first year we would come down from London on Friday night or Saturday or even Sunday for the day—I was running the National Theatre then—and work in the garden from dawn of day to blink of night until we were mud- and sweat-stained and numbed with fatigue.

Within eighteen months, Colin—with his friend Brian—had turfed the lawn and carved out and walled terraced beds. We had planted them with a reckless lack of strategy in spite of studying a growing library of gardening books. Only one long sliver of a bed had a theme: the iris bed, my favourite flower. We gave no thought of how large or how fast shrubs would grow, how compatible they would be as neighbours or in what season they would flourish; we were naive pioneers, migrants from the city, but for all our flagrant innocence by the end of our second year we had become gardeners. When our daughter, Lucy, came back from a round-the-world trip in her gap year, we picked her up from Heathrow and drove to the cottage late at night. The next day she came into our bedroom to find me sitting up in bed reading *Gardeners' World* while my wife read *The Reader's Digest Gardening Year*. She was as horrified as if she had discovered us sharing a pipe of crack cocaine. 'Oh God,' she said, 'you've turned into Felicity Kendal and Richard Briers!'

Is it possible that the interest in gardening grows as age increases because the loss of fertility is compensated by a desire to encourage it in nature? Or is it simply that until you have a garden you can't imagine it being interesting to you, just as babies seem obscurely dull creatures until you have one of your own? Like child-rearing, gardening can only be learnt by doing it. 'Only a garden can teach gardening,' says the poet Douglas Dunn.

What my garden has taught me is to take delight in the simple but vastly complicated mystery of how things grow and whether things grow and why some things refuse to grow. I marvel at the sight of a wisteria growing from a slim tendril to cover the side of the house, its branching stems the size of a well-muscled forearm, while a rose bought at Woolworth's weaves itself along its branches. A passion-flower which started life in a tiny beaker bloomed in inexhaustible profusion; a choisya cutting became a bush the size of an Indian elephant; an epidemic of saxifrage has spread from a little clump to fringe paths and clad steps.

There have been failures: we took three tries to find a place for a crab apple, two for a Canadian maple; shrubs swelled beyond their planned dimensions and a rampant bamboo had to be moved in an operation as ambitious as moving bluestones to Stonehenge; the wild meadow stuttered after its first season and became a triangle of lawn; some euphorbias wilted; some fuchsias became listless; a plum tree expired; an oak tree fighting for dominance with a neighbour beech fell in a storm but saved us from making a judgement of Solomon. Not exactly a litany of catastrophe and nothing to the pain and damage caused by the annual invasion of the badgers, as unwelcome in my garden as the Waffen-SS and at least as brutal. They come for the crane-fly larvae—'leather jackets'—and leave deep scars on the lawn like a face ravaged by a lion's paw. Appropriately, only trickling lions' urine round the perimeter of a garden is said to deter them.

On the whole we've been blessed. Things grow with a casual ease in our microclimate, some of them—bluebells, wild orchids, aquilegia, daisies, primroses and Japanese anemones—emerge serendipitously, uninvited but gloriously welcome. And many of our plants—the saxifrage, the passion-flower, the cranesbill, the Wedding Day roses—are the next best thing: grown on the same side of the hill in the same sort of soil and bought at the village plant sale. They're hard-won though. It's not an event for the faint-hearted: when the doors of the village hall open, the plant-buyers (mostly women) fight for the front of the queue as if they were seeking shelter in the Blitz, their sharp elbows used like knives on a chariot wheel. Suze always emerges with trays piled eye-high of cuttings and seedlings, while I stand in the middle of the room, inert with amazement and inadequacy.

We should have stuck to buying our plants annually for 10p a pot because if we were surprised by our discovery of the joy of gardening, we were dumbfounded by the cost of it. It's the last thing that addicts consider: and our passion, at first an infection, had become an addiction. It's not just our occasional bouts of culpable extravagance, like buying semi-mature trees, it's the recurrent attritional flood of serious expenditure on small shrubs, bulbs, bedding plants and pots and pots and pots—so seriously and obsessively profligate that I still can barely admit to myself, let alone a stranger, the sums of money that we have poured into our local garden centre. Enough to say that had it been spent on drink or drugs we would both be long dead.

Notwithstanding its cost, I have begun to understand the medium of gardening: a living form whose variables are size, texture, colour, shape and time. Every day there is a change and the space surrounding a plant is defined in a different way. I might be tempted to say that gardening is kinetic sculpture if it didn't belong to the same category of pretentiousness as talking about a garden as an 'outdoor room' (a phrase which lowers my mood as quickly as 'easy listening') or plants as architecture or gardens as tapestry. Part of the delight of a garden is that it's the thing itself, unlike anything but itself, a world entire: a garden is a garden is a garden. Metaphors are made out of gardens, not the other way round.

Art should open our eyes to nature; for me it's been the reverse. I've started to appreciate what so much of art seeks to do: to celebrate the nature of nature. And I now know what Constable meant when he said that 'The art of seeing nature is a thing almost as much to be acquired as the art of reading Egyptian hieroglyphs.'

We've got it bad, garden sickness. I was in New York a week ago and I found myself thinking about my irises and I felt a lover's pain of longing. A year or two ago our daughter caught Sue talking to the lilac. 'You're out!' she said. 'Mum, I think it knows,' said Lucy with a weary bemusement. On his deathbed the novelist John Steinbeck was asked by his wife when he had been happiest. Write it down, he said. Both wrote down the same thing: 'Somerset contentment 1959'. If Sue and I did the same thing we might write: 'Gloucestershire garden 1994'. There is a large (about twelve foot tall) bay tree which stands in a herb garden outside our kitchen; it was a small, neat shrub when it was given to us for our wedding (nearly forty years ago) by an ex-girlfriend of mine. 'A bay tree tells you the state of your marriage: if it flourishes so will you,' she said.

I grew up in the country in a (then) unspoilt part of England, indifferent to the coming of spring and the miraculous greenness of green. Now, in my early sixties, I understand what Dennis Potter felt when Melvyn Bragg asked him in a TV interview a few weeks before his death what he would miss most. 'I won't see another spring,' he said. And I'm affected by the intensity of Ranyevskaya's rhapsodies to the spring blossom in *The Cherry Orchard*, written by a man who knew all too well that his time was running out: eighteen months to go, one more spring. Your garden is a laboratory for studying how your life is spent, counted out in the coming of the changing of the seasons. Shelley again:

> Fresh spring, and summer, and winter hoar,
> Move my faint heart with grief, but with delight
> No more—oh never more!

I wish I could share my garden with my mother. I'm still not won over by the flowers that she loved, but I wish that I could tell her that now I understand her desire to put her signature on a little patch of earth. In her marvellous history of the British garden, Jenny Uglow writes that the Saxon word for a garden is 'a lovely place'. So it is, and so I must go: *Il faut cultiver mon jardin*.

Mother's Day

Here's a test. When you forget something, your house keys perhaps, do you say, 'Oh, ha ha, I must be getting Alzheimer's'? Or when you've heard that someone has got Alzheimer's do you do a little snort and titter, 'Well, he'll never have to watch reruns on television'? Do you find it harder to laugh at the news of cancer? Unless, of course, you've heard that someone has cancer *and* Alzheimer's in which case do you say—ha ha—that they were lucky: they'd forget that they'd got cancer.

No, probably not. But it's curious that we find it so easy to empathise with cancer—with physical pain and decay—and so hard to empathise with mental pain or to imagine the decay of imagination itself. We've all experienced physical pain from infancy: we know that if we cut ourselves, it hurts. We're familiar with knocks and bruises, even, as we age, with a withering of the muscles and a stiffening of the joints. We can alleviate physical pain, but mental pain—grief, despair, depression, dementia—is less accessible to treatment. It's connected to who we are—our personality, our character, our soul, if you like. 'Physical pain however great,' said Alice James (the sister of Henry, the novelist), 'ends in itself and falls away like dry husks from the mind, while moral discords and nervous horrors sear the soul.'

Alzheimer's disease is a 'nervous horror', a form of dementia—a word that means 'without mind'. If there's a physical disease it resembles it's leprosy, which eats away the body as Alzheimer's does the brain. The first signs are a loss of short-term memory, but forgetfulness, non sequiturs and vagueness give way to loss of bodily control, as if the brain can no longer remember what to tell the body. Then the disease is spun out with a malicious cruelty: the personality recedes and, as if in mockery, leaves only the body to breathe and be fed.

Alzheimer's disease is always in the news. So it should be. There are estimated to be 750,000 dementia sufferers in Britain. That's a city the size of Glasgow. There's recently been a proposal that, just as there is now routine screening for breast cancer, the NHS should screen all over-seventy-five-year-olds for signs of dementia. There are those who argue that the tests are inadequate and that a positive diagnosis needlessly blights the remaining years of lucidity. I disagree. Firstly, it has to be better for carers and for sufferers to prepare themselves for what is to come. And, secondly, there are some signs that drugs can be effective in arresting the condition even though research is desperately underfunded: a mere 2.5% of the government's medical research budget in is spent investigating dementia.

I'd be happy to take the test myself now—even though I have a few (seven) years to go before I'm seventy-five. I don't want to tumble over a precipice without knowing it's there. If the test were negative then there's much to celebrate. But if positive, as Hamlet says, 'The readiness is all.' He's talking about death, of course, but that's what Alzheimer's disease leads to: a slow waning of life. Better to know yourself, and better still for those who will have to care for you. Meanwhile, at best, carers are given training in empathising with sufferers from dementia by wearing goggles that distort vision, gloves that reduce the sense of touch, and white noise to induce frustration, confusion and loss of control. At worst, they are given no training and dementia patients lie neglected and rotting, like human garbage.

Over a decade or go I was asked to direct a film called *Iris*, which starred Judi Dench as the novelist Iris Murdoch, and Jim Broadbent as her husband, John Bayley. The story was a sort of love story, but also an account of her illness and death. 'Why did you ask me?' I asked the producer. 'You know about these things,' he replied. The 'things' to which he referred were not so much making films or directing actors in difficult roles, but a 'thing' I'd rather have been entirely ignorant of: Alzheimer's disease. Iris Murdoch was diagnosed with the disease in 1997. My mother also had it and died in 1992. Iris Murdoch's decline was over a period of two years, my mother's was over twenty.

John Bayley wrote a marvellous and moving account of his wife's illness on which my film was based. At the time it was published many people criticised him for appearing to capitalise on his wife's decline. Those people have not lived with an Alzheimer's sufferer. They have not known the weariness of dressing and undressing, bathing and feeding, or the despair and exasperation engendered by broken nights, incomprehensible sounds, unpredictable moods and inexpressible needs. And all the while watching, watching the loved one simply fade away.

When she was fifty-two my mother fell downstairs on her head carrying my sister's daughter. The baby, who was two at the time, was unharmed, but my mother fractured her skull. The fracture healed and at first it seemed as if the only further damage was to my mother's nervous system. She was a wonderful self-taught cook, by any standards touched with genius; the secret of the perfect meringue died with her. So it was distressing to her, and a painful loss to her family, when she began to lose her sense of smell and her sense of taste and, naturally enough, her skill and enthusiasm for cooking.

But then, little by little, other things dropped away, and it became apparent that the concussion and the brain fracture, indeed the fall downstairs, was not the cause but more likely the effect of her condition. She was diagnosed as a sufferer of what was then called 'pre-senile dementia'. It was the same thing by any name: she was old before her time.

Alzheimer's disease respects the person's individuality, as each person responds differently to the illness, which often magnifies the characteristics of their temperament. In her illness, Iris Murdoch responded, as she had in health, to humour and to goodness—a quality that she examined in most of her novels. In my mother's case her temperament had been modified by the long attritional drizzle of a not-very-happy marriage. So when she started to lose her mind it was the woman she had become whose characteristics were being amplified: disappointment, anxiety, anger and loneliness. Perhaps it's self-protection, but if I think of her now it's not as she was when she was diminished by Alzheimer's disease or even in the few years before that; it's as she was when I was a child, when there was everything to look forward to.

She was a dedicated, knowledgeable and enthusiastic gardener who spoke of plants by their Latin names with the confident certainty of an expert, and she was an organiser with an idiosyncratic but systematic method of reducing chaos to order: list followed list as she marshalled her resources with the flair of a natural general. It wasn't unusual to be asked at supper what you wanted for breakfast, lunch and dinner the next day, or to find her planning her Christmas shopping in June.

So it was alarming to stagger through conversations in which she would forget her previous sentence while halfway through the new one and to see her stare speculatively at her knife and fork as if unsure of their use. With Alzheimer's disease, short-term memory dissolves, while the long-term continues to be active for a time.

My mother started to watch television a lot, sitting mostly silent and immobile until one of her ex-partners appeared on the box. She had been a debutante ('the merriest girl of the year'), so she had opportunity enough to recognise retired cabinet ministers, senior businessmen, even a 'society' serial murderer when they appeared in documentaries or on the news. In the case of the then US President, she even remembered his name: 'Ronald Reagan,' she said. 'Dull man, but frightfully good dancer.'

Later, as the illness took hold with a glacial slowness, she would start to cry in frustration when she forgot how to write the 'M' in her Christian name, Minna. Then, unable to write her lists, she started to forget what she had to do, or even where she was, and when she took my daughter, aged four, to the village shop, a journey of a few hundred yards, my wife thought it safer to follow them as the two set off hand in hand, chatting simultaneously, uncertain who was leading whom. For a while I tried to convince myself that her illness was reversible, but when one day I opened a door for her and she stared at the door, then at the doorway, and asked me with undisguised terror: 'Which side do I go?', I knew she was losing her mind, and that there was no way she would ever recover it.

For a while she was living at home but, with her bouts of terrifying rage, followed by incoherence, followed by blankness, followed by clear breaks of sanity that were more frightening to her than anything that had preceded them, it became impossible for my father to look after her properly. My sister and I helped from time to time—not enough in my case—but we were mostly far away in London, which is where my mother longed to be as if her life, or her sanity, depended on it:

> Please, please, please, please, please, please… take me home… take me back to my mother… my friends… take me to London… let me go in a train… please, please, please, please…

Then there was a silence, an absence of words and a despair so deep that it almost seemed as if her breath were speech, then a sigh:

> I think I am dying.

But she lived on for years, lying on the floor in a foetal position on a beanbag in the local hospital in Dorset. For years she was losing her mind, and for years death seemed ashamed to approach her. But little by little she was slipping away, and we never knew when to say goodbye.

My mother's face became impassive as her mind receded—the so called 'lion face' of Alzheimer's sufferers—but Iris Murdoch retained her ability to smile, albeit only intermittently, until the end. As John Bayley said: 'Only a joke survives, the last thing that finds its way into consciousness when the brain is atrophied.' The joke didn't survive with my mother, but in some way, in spite of becoming less and less the person I knew in looks or speech or manner, she was not exactly absent: she retained her soul until her death.

I used to sit with my hand on my mother's forehead. She seemed unbearably lonely, but she'd seemed like that to me even before she lost her mind. My sadness at her illness became muted over the years, but I never lost the distress of the things I had left unsaid. There are those who leave us without our detaining them; we have said all there is to say. It wasn't so with her; there was a continent of regret and guilt.

Her face and her body wasted away. No sight, no hearing, no sense at all. She breathed and ate and wasted away. I can still see her hand, bony like a claw, plucking at her face, as if she was surprised that it was still there. When she died her body was like a child's.

Acknowledgements

The author and publisher gratefully acknowledge permission to quote extracts from the following:

'September 1, 1939' © 1940 W.H. Auden, renewed, reprinted by permission of Curtis Brown, Ltd. *7½ Cents* by Richard Bissell, published by Little, Brown & Company, an imprint of Hachette Book Group. 'The Friends' originally published in German in 1964 as 'Die Freunde', translated by Michael Hamburger © 1976, 1964 by Bertolt-Brecht-Erben/Suhrkamp Verlag, from *Bertolt Brecht Poems 1913–1956* by Bertolt Brecht, edited by John Willet and Ralph Mannheim, reproduced by permission of Liveright Publishing Corporation. *The People's War* by Angus Calder, published by Jonathan Cape, reprinted by permission of The Random House Group Ltd. *The Voysey Inheritance* © Harley Granville-Barker, reproduced by permission of The Society of Authors as the Literary Representative of the Harley Granville-Barker Estate. *The Smoking Diaries*, *The Year of the Jouncer* and *The Last Cigarette* © 2008 Simon Gray, reproduced by permission of Granta Books. *Amy's View*, *Acting Up*, *Murmuring Judges*, *Plenty*, *Racing Demon* and *Skylight* © David Hare, all reproduced by permission of Faber and Faber Ltd. *Sons and Lovers* by D.H. Lawrence, published by Vintage Classics, reprinted with an introduction by Richard Eyre in 2011. *Sage-ing While Age-ing* by Shirley MacLaine, published by Simon & Schuster UK. *Closer* © Patrick Marber, 1997, 2007 and *Dealer's Choice* © Patrick Marber, 1995, 1997, both reproduced by permission of Bloomsbury Methuen Drama, an imprint of Bloomsbury Publishing Plc. *Cat on a Hot Tin Roof* by Tennessee Williams, published by Penguin Books © 1954, 1955 The University of the South, renewed 1982, 1983 by The University of the South, reproduced by permission of Sheil Land Associates Ltd. *The Night of the Iguana* by Tennessee Williams © 1986 by John Allman, reprinted by permission of New Directions Publishing Corp. *The Rose Tattoo* from *The Rose Tattoo and Other Plays* by Tennessee Williams, published by Penguin Books © 1950 Tennessee Williams, reproduced by permission of Sheil Land Associates Ltd.

Every effort has been made to trace copyright holders and to obtain their permission for the use of copyright material. The publisher apologises for any errors or omissions, and would be grateful if notified of any corrections that should be incorporated in future reprints or editions of this book.